MAKING CONTACT

What two people communicate during their first four minutes of contact is so crucial that it will determine whether strangers will remain strangers or become acquaintances, friends, lovers, or lifetime mates.

How those first few minutes turn out hinge on how each person evaluates themselves and how they evaluate the other person; on the assumptions and preconceptions each person brings to the first minutes of contact; and on the circumstances under which the people meet—environment, timing, and emotions.

The first four minutes are not only the key to dealing with strangers, but are also the critical link everytime we renew our "contact" with family, friends, and business partners. For everytime we say "hello" we are opening the door to success, happiness, and harmony in our lives.

CONTACT:
The First Four Minutes

Leonard Zunin, M. D.
with
Natalie Zunin

BALLANTINE BOOKS • NEW YORK

With Love to Our Children:
  IRA
  CINDY
  LAINA

My sincere thanks to Lou Jacobs, Jr.,
who diligently collaborated in the writing of this book
based on the original material
of my work and experience in the field of
interpersonal communication.

ACKNOWLEDGMENTS

We want to thank the following people who read the manuscript and offered many helpful suggestions and words of encouragement: Norma Marcus Barr, Norman Barr, M.D., Phyliss Cyr, Margaret Donovan, M.S.W., William Glasser, M.D., Ina Zunin Gross, R.N., M.S., Walter Gross, R.Ph., Barbara Jacobs, David Krause, Vincent Numbling, Barry Rumbles, M.S.W., Owen Williams, D.D.S., Don Woolf, Betty Zunin and Louis Zunin.

We wish to extend our appreciation to the following individuals who shared experiences and ideas with us which are incorporated into this book: Kathleen Olsen, Cosmetics Executive, Saks Fifth Ave., Los Angeles, James E. Rota, D.D.S., Brian Sharpe, M.S.W.

Sincere thanks to my secretary, Aileen Grossman and to our typist, Beverly Rumbles.

Our thanks to Alice Le Bel, Coordinator of Special Programs, Daytime Extension, University of California at Los Angeles, for her enthusiastic support and interest in initiating the first Contact workshops at UCLA.

We owe a debt of gratitude to our publisher, Ed Nash, his wife Diana and the stimulating, energetic staff at Nash Publishing Corporation.

A special thanks to our editor, Jim Miller, for his invaluable assistance and the pleasure of working with him.

Finally, a word of appreciation to the many individuals who expressed their ideas and enthusiastic interest, privately and during workshops and lectures on the concepts of *Contact: The First Four Minutes.*

CONTENTS

Within Four Minutes
A baby is born,
A life is ended,
A heart is forlorn,
Another befriended,
One soul cries out,
Another hears,
One shares laughter,
Another fears,
A door is shut tight,
A man turns away,
Day becomes night,
And then, a new day.
    —NATALIE B. ZUNIN

INTRODUCTION

Contact: what does it mean to you?

Touching someone?

The meeting of two objects or bodies?

The command that old-time pilots gave to the guy out there spinning the propeller to start the engine?

A business connection that needs to be explored?

An encounter with a friend or stranger?

Contact is all of these, but in my context the last mini-definition is closest. Contact is the way you meet and relate with people during the initial phase of interaction: with strangers, friends, lovers, children, bosses, blind dates, plumbers, teachers, politicians—the whole cast of characters in your individual world.

Unless you are a hermit, you come in contact with family and community on a daily basis. Most of us take these routine, casual meetings or interactions for granted. If we are burdened with emotional problems, it is more difficult to see ourselves with clarity. Many people do not seem to be fully aware of how they relate to others. This is not an empty insinuation; it's the main reason for this book. As you will discover, the principles of Contact provide a mirror in which to see your reflection more clearly. This self-awareness is the first step toward more fulfilling and fewer frustrating relationships.

Do you realize how many people the typical city-dweller comes in contact with each day or week? The yearly total is more than our nineteenth-century ancestors met in a lifetime. Before our sophisticated means of travel and communication were invented, harmonious contact may have been just as difficult to achieve, but it was far less frequent. Your grandma and grandpa probably knew nothing of jet trips to Paris, swingers' clubs or freeway traffic jams.

Today, since everyone moves around so frequently, it is very important to make contact effectively with strangers, and the complexities of maintaining happy ongoing relationships are enormous. Americans change spouses, jobs or homes with startling rapidity. Parties, tours, bowling leagues, the PTA and a long list of group contact throw people together quickly and often at random. The need for instant effective contact is real and sometimes threatening.

How do you go about becoming involved, and to what degree? Are you afraid of the consequences? Do you usually shy away from encounters? What do you owe yourself, or someone else, in terms of friendly or amorous involvement?

Perhaps you know the answers. You also know that the world is full of lonely people, many of whom carry their neuroses, ego problems or childhood/adolescent scars around with them as shields—or as spears. Loneliness is the most common "disease" in the world today; I see it regularly at Contact workshops and in my psychiatric practice. Everyone is familiar with superficial contact, socially, in business, sexually or in the neighborhood. Illusions are shattered easily; meaningful contact is more perplexing.

The world is full of strangers, new faces, new bodies, new experiences. Even our intimates may be strangers after a while. Do you know what *you* are like when you meet somebody new? Do you let close friends and relatives see the real you? How does your self-esteem fit into the picture?

This book was written to help you dissolve the distance between yourself and others. One of its main goals is to inspire you to new awareness of who you are and how you present yourself. Through techniques for sensing more about yourself and others you can develop more control over the first four minutes of any contact situation.

Your relationships can be warmer, closer and more significant, if you wish.

I do not believe that loneliness "comes with the territory." It is avoidable. In gaining greater control over how you interact with people through contact experience —which means a certain amount of risk-taking—there is an investment that earns interest in love, friendship, growth and a more positive self-image.

Above all, you will enjoy more freedom—to make choices of words, gestures and depth of involvement. From understanding the principles of contact comes new freedom of choice.

Human contact is a challenge. It is also a joy, a means of self-expression and self-discovery. In these times when alienation divides and dominates, consider the power of positive contact. Your life may very well be enriched by merely exploiting the assets you already have.

BREAKING
THE FOUR-MINUTE
BARRIER

The drama of human contact is played on many stages, and you are one of countless players. In the cast is everyone you know, plus all sorts of people as yet unknown to you. Routinely, you meet and relate, often fleetingly, with a variety of emotions including fear, boredom or humor. The drama of encounter with others never ends. Do some of the following thumbnail plots seem familiar to you?

Have you ever met an attractive stranger who, after exchanging a few sentences, just drifted away—out of reach?

Have you gone for a job interview and known instinctively within minutes that you would be hired, no matter what the competition was like?

Have you awakened to hear you spouse grousing about the day ahead, or attempting to continue the argument that began the previous night?

Have you been in a classroom with a new teacher who came on with such lack of confidence that you were soon distracted or derisive?

Have you sat at a table in the public library leafing through a book, conscious of her or him across from you or seated nearby? Did you discover or search for a way to open a conversation?

When you're looking for potential romance, do they all want to be your "buddy?" Or do all your potential "buddies" want to take you to bed?

Have you ever greeted your child coming home from

school with a resentful voice that reflected irritation for which he had no responsibility?

Have you been introduced to an important new acquaintance and felt almost immediately that he or she was on your wavelength?

Do you ever greet your spouse after work with a tender kiss and loving words, as though you had been away for weeks?

No matter what your answers the questions, they all have one important element in common: You have faced the four-minute barrier, a short segment of time during which initial human contact is established or reaffirmed.

Why *four* minutes? It is not an arbitrary interval. Rather, it is the *average* time, demonstrated by careful observation, during which strangers in a social situation interact *before* they decide to part or continue their encounter. By watching hundreds of people at parties, offices, schools, homes and in recreational settings, I discovered that four minutes is approximately the minimum breakaway point—the socially acceptable period that precedes a potential shift of conversational partners. Since people are not machines run by electronic timers, four minutes is an *average,* both real and symbolic, throughout this book.

The four-minute concept applies appropriately to both casual meetings and on-going contacts, such as husbands and wives on awakening or at day's end, children and parents before or after school, and with anyone you know well and greet often. Whether with strangers, friends or intimates, your contact goals are basically similar: to create response and involvement (even superficial), to give and take, talk and listen—to communicate. In essence, getting through the four-minute barrier can be compared to a supersonic aircraft breaking the sound barrier: after the initial turbulence (of the psyche in the human frame of reference), the chance of smoother progress is predictably improved.

It has always been so. Since the caveman, through the

industrial revolution, into the era of powered flight, people have been coping with temporary relationships. Now such relationships are guaranteed more than ever. For instance, one out of five Americans will be living in a different home a year from now. Each time a family moves, it invariably exchanges many friends and acquaintances for new ones more conveniently located. As a result, it is necessary to speed up the process by which friendships are established—and possibly consummated. Since in life we often "touch and go," it is difficult to develop meaningful relationships and relationships we value for some duration.

Alvin Toffler, in his book *Future Shock* (Random House, 1970), writes of the potential directions man's interpersonal relationships are taking: "Besides losing their attachment to things and places," he says, "people are also becoming less deeply involved with other individuals. Rather than relating to the total personality of another person, the individual today maintains only a superficial and partial contact with most people he encounters."

As an example, a woman of thirty-three told me about the decline of her social life after a childless divorce. She was intelligent, well-groomed and plain. Though her face and figure were easily forgettable, she compensated with a sprightly personality. Separation from her husband after a dozen years undermined her self-confidence. She told me, "At first I kept very busy at my job, and running around with various friends. Then I noticed that some of them seemed to be taking sides. The people who gravitated towards Jim I didn't see very often. Making new friends became harder, and pretty soon I was wrapped in a cocoon of static self-pity. It was a helluva lonely spot to be in after living a so-called normal life so long."

The woman found that friendships dissolved and new contacts became unglued before she evolved enough to hold them together. Her isolation and loneliness were not self-imposed (though unconsciously many people *do* fall into such traps), but she needed to develop the means to turn casual contact into rewarding involvement.

Writer Frieda Fromm Reichman has noted that "People are more frightened of being lonely than of being hungry, or being deprived of sleep, or of having their sexual needs unfulfilled." Being alone, wishing for someone to talk to or sleep with, is occasionally anyone's fate, but when the pain of loneliness becomes intolerable, people can go crazy. (In fact, the most cruel and inhumane form of punishment is not temporary physical pain; it is prolonged solitary confinement.) In cases of forced and extreme isolation, people manifest insanity, usually through hallucinations and delusions about other people. They hear voices and see creatures. Their minds are filled and their emotions are dominated by longing for human contact. They need the presence of others and if this need is not fulfilled, their minds distort reality to make them believe people, rather than material things, are present.

Too many people endure the pain of loneliness, rather than taking steps to overcome it. Even in these fast-paced times, there is no valid reason to be lonely. The opportunities to meet, know and really get involved with other individuals are greater now than any time since Adam and Eve had only God and the serpent for conversational partners. This is so for two reasons: 1) There are simply more people on earth than ever in the history of man and 2) technological advances provide you with virtually unlimited mobility and means of communication.

Though you have occasions to establish acquaintances and relationships quickly, you also face the possibility of meeting more people than you can, or care to, develop friendships with. You may choose or find it necessary to substitute fleeting friendships or close relationships of limited duration for long-term companionship. This points up the need to develop skills, even in the first four minutes, to project your own personality while evaluating the potential of strangers.

The modern blend of friend, lover or soon-forgotten stranger is highly influenced by the extremely mobile qualities of our civilization. Nearly everyone has a car; almost anyone can fly almost anywhere. At least one-third of the earth's population have become periodic or regular travelers. You may move about on vacations, to meet business and professional requirements, to reach better jobs, change climates or improve some aspect of health or welfare. You may also travel to confront the unknown, searching for pleasure and adventure. With a couple of credit cards, a map and a watch adjustable to changing time zones, we can all imitate Gulliver without the risk of capture by the Lilliputians.

With this mixed blessing of being itinerant comes the joy of finding new friends. While viewing the Grand Canyon at dawn or lunching on French bread and wine in the hills above Nice, people are often more receptive to each other. They develop feelings of closeness and become involved more easily. "It's the people I crave, not the places," is a remark I hear frequently. A steadily increasing number of travelers acknowledge their awareness that they are seeking self-fulfillment, love, feelings of worth and individual acceptance rather than the satisfaction of status, material gain or education as they move about either locally or to distant places.

My awareness of the ramifications of human involvement began to come into focus at the time I entered psychiatric training. Later in practice, and while working with my colleague, Dr. William Glasser (author of *Reality Therapy, Schools Without Failure* and *The Identity Society*) I discovered the significance of *first contact*. In 1965 I began consulting at the Ventura School for Girls, a California institution for seriously delinquent teenagers, where Dr. Glasser had been a consultant for eight years. He stressed to me the need for becoming responsibly involved with the girls before real therapeutic progress could be expected. It took more than a four-minute contact to establish mutual trust, but the importance of initial impressions was obvious.

During my two years in the Navy as Assistant Chief of Psychiatry I helped provide psychotherapy to a continuous flow of Marines, as well as counseling for Navy and Marine widows. A group program called "Operation Second Life" began to formulate in my mind for these bereaved women. They were in the midst of shifting mental gears to make new beginnings. Here was a striking contrast: death had wiped out a precious contact for each of them, but life required making new ones and continuing the ones they already had.

There is a sequence through which all of our activities and encounters must pass. In this sequence, phase one is Contact; phase two is a midterm of varying duration; and phase three is the ending or "goodbye." While I was concerned with encouraging a new phase one for these young women, I happened to be talking to the late Dr. Fritz Perls, founder of Gestalt therapy. As I presented my ideas for "Operation Second Life," he listened intently, then responded, "This is a group of women you will have to teach how to say goodbye."

I realized how interdependent are "hello" and "goodbye," and how essential the three-phase structure can be when examining behavior, especially when trying to change and improve it. Everything we do, measured in minutes or years, can be dissected into phase one, two and three. This holds true for an Apollo launch, or the less complex activities of dressing, eating, driving, making love—you name it.

Eating begins as you confront your food and taste it. In phase two you (hopefully) enjoy the meal, and at the end you leave the table to begin a new activity. As another example, in love-making the three phases are foreplay, intercourse and the post-intercourse phase. In social encounters there are also three phases:

1. The beginning: Is it during this "hello" phase that you have the most difficulty making contact or feeling comfortable?
2. The continuance: Once you are over the initial barrier, are you stalled or frustrated in conversation while trying to remain involved for a satisfying period of time?

3. The goodbye: Are you awkward or uncertain when the time comes to part?

I have a heartening observation for you: Rarely do people have significant difficulty in all three phases. When I point this out, listeners realize with relief they are not totally inept in the "social scramble," but that problems usually exist in one phase or another. Especially, I am told, "It's the first four or five minutes that make me feel most ill at ease. I don't know what to say, and I feel ridiculous, but once I've passed that awkward point and the ice is broken, I'm okay." Take a moment and evaluate yourself according to these three phases of a social situation. In which do you shine? Which phase is most likely to hang you up?

It is my contention that phase one, contact, is the key to the door of social success, family harmony, business achievement, and to some extent, sexual satisfaction.

Let us look in at a typical party. The hostess is introducing two strangers, after which she excuses herself to circulate. The two become locked in contact according to unwritten rules of social congeniality. They tend to respond to each other, perhaps automatically, guided by conditioned cultural traditions—but for a minimum period of time (again an average of four minutes). One of them may then say, "A pleasure meeting you. I'm going for a refill," and he walks away. He has been cordial enough and socially appropriate, but most probably the two have not made an effective or favorable contact.

The average person shrugs off such a routine rejection and moves on to new contacts, which continue to range from three to five minutes, averaging four minutes. It is hardly an interval guaranteed to change your life, but what is communicated can determine whether or not strangers become acquaintances, friends, lovers, life-time mates— or remain strangers.

If a relationship continues, it is by mutual consent. If one person is unwilling, the potential relationship is lost, at least for that moment. Whether or not you are able to indicate the go-ahead signal when you feel it, may depend on your inhibitions, social taboos or special personality circumstances. The individual you may have met recently might have stayed close for forty minutes instead of four, had you been able to express your positive feelings about the contact verbally and nonverbally. More of this in later chapters. For now let us continue viewing human affinity within the four-minute framework.

At the core of a good contact situation, where two or more people are really clicking and becoming tuned in to each other, there are always present what I call the four C's. Many other elements of communication such as humor may also be involved, but you should be basically aware of these four:

1. *Confidence.* You must convey a certain degree of self-confidence as a foundation for any successful encounter, new or old, brief or delightfully lengthy. You know from experience that most people do not respond favorably to someone who is self-demeaning or overly apologetic. Such an attitude may breed a temporary sympathy, but hardly the warmth or closeness that comes from "good vibrations."

2. *Creativity.* Being creative in making contacts means finding ways to tune in to the feelings of others. Sometimes you must work through a barrage of facts in order to respond in an innovative way. Through practice observing others and learning your own strengths, you become more sensitive to a wide variety of people—creatively.

3. *Caring.* Showing another person that you are listening and interested with total attention, at least during the first four minutes, is the main indication that you care. Avoiding distraction and staying with the train of thought has surprising results, with your spouse, child, new or old acquaintances. Some people may not be used to concentrated attention, and yours adds meaning to the interchange. Dale Carnegie said, "You can make more friends in two months by becoming interested in other people than

you can in two years by trying to get other people interested in you."

4. *Consideration.* There is a believable concern radiating from some individuals which makes you feel a little better about yourself in even a brief meeting. It includes a combination of the other C's; a good self-image, a creative approach and complete attention which add up to a feeling of consideration—from someone, or from you. In reverse, some people leave you with negative feelings about yourself, such as the person who comes off as the constant critic and unconsciously makes others feel inadequate. (You may not always be able to identify why someone consistently leaves you feeling a little less adequate about yourself.) Consideration is being sensitive and aware that you are relating to another person who is unique and who also has fears, dreams, hopes and insecurities. It also involves the art of being a good listener. A good listener helps the speaker to clarify or modify his ideas in the course of expressing them, by responding with meaningful questions and comments, eye contact, and appropriate smiles.

Are you aware of whether or not your contact techniques include some or all of the four C's? Most people are not. They have developed no criteria with which to determine whether the things they say or do cause positive or negative response from others. One meeting may be successful by chance while another may miss by default. It is one of the main purposes of this book to help the reader understand these personal habits, approaches, and impressions. You should be able to *turn on* those with whom you would like to establish a rapport, or keep at a distance those with whom you desire to remain friendly and cordial, but not intimate.

In my years of exploring the four-minute barrier, I have come across many experiences recorded by well-known and unknown people about the impact of their various meetings. The two that follow are stimulating in their diversity. First, Dr. Fritz Perls discusses the disaster of his eagerly awaited and only meeting with Sigmund

Freud in Vienna from *In and Out of the Garbage Pail* (Real People Press, 1969):

> In 1936 I thought I'd make it. Was I not the mainspring for the creation of one of his [Freud's] institutes, and did I not come 4,000 miles to attend his congress? . . .
>
> I made an appointment. I was received by an elderly woman (I believe his sister) and waited. Then a door opened about two and a half feet wide and there he was, before my eyes. It seemed strange that he would not leave the door frame, but at that time I knew nothing about his phobias.
>
> "I came from South Africa to give you a paper and to see you."
>
> "Well, and when are you going back?" he said. I don't remember the rest of the (perhaps four-minute long) conversation. I was shocked and disappointed. . . .
>
> I had expected a quick "hurt" reaction, but I was merely numbed. Then slowly, slowly, the stock phrases came: "I'll show you—you can't do this to me."

Great expectations, and disappointing consummation —there may be consolation that even the most brilliant and intuitive people must sustain such contacts.

In contrast, let me illustrate a provocative meeting between interviewer Susan Stocking of the *Los Angeles Times* and writer Anais Nin:

> Talking with Anais Nin reveals only fleeting glimpses of the depths she has explored in her life-long struggles as a novelist, woman and human being. Her mind is facile and her interests broad, so it is easy to skip from one subject to another.
>
> What does come through in an interview is her unusual ability to dissolve distance. Anais Nin asks almost as many questions of her interviewer as her

interviewer asks of her. She listens intently, questions, reflects and then lets loose an easy flow of words that become more than mere answers. The words become dialogue. The distance of strangeness recedes, she inches closer on the couch, and her voice begins to lose its tremor.

Not all of us can say "hello" as well as Anais Nin. There is no valid formula for making effective contact for all people in all situations. Some methods are useful for keeping others at arm's length, for finding out about somebody without revealing much about yourself, or for promoting instant closeness. But whatever your motivation in the first four minutes of new or ongoing contacts, keep in mind that every relationship also involves saying "goodbye."

Hello and goodbye, initial and final contact. The latter is a story in itself; how to say goodbye is a mirror of how we feel about ourselves, and our lives. The burdens of goodbye can be lightened through the insights we gain in saying hello—in becoming close to others from whom we must part for moments or forever. Every goodbye can be made easier if you look toward the next hello, whether it be people or activities.

When a youngster says goodbye to kindergarten, he says hello to first grade. Saying goodbye to college, for most, means saying hello to a job. (Some have trouble saying goodbye, and become professional students.) Saying goodbye to a loved and departed spouse, after a reasonable period of grief, is followed by beginning a new way of life. Those who do not follow this pattern imprison themselves as lifelong mourners. Hence, the added significance of making contact, phase one.

In most human relationships, what happens in the first four minutes is not irreversible. In marriage, for instance, there are day-to-day contacts that become routine. What your husband or wife says as you awaken in the morning may set the tone for how you feel all day, but the mood of that four minutes can be modified. You know from the past that he or she did not mean something that may have hurt, or perhaps was not sincere about a compliment. Momentary contact may be enlightening, misleading or both. It may build hopes or start a train of thought and action that ends in bed, in the grave, or a host of locations between.

There seem to be some four-minute contacts, however, that become crucial and cannot be reversed. Most of these have a temporal quality, such as a random meeting on a trip, an exchange with a used car salesman, some job-seeking situations, or the advances of a soliciting prostitute. A kind of electronic human-data computation takes place which guides your verbal and nonverbal communication as well as your reception of impressions, both subtle and obvious. Practice in more durable contacts gives you better intuition with which to meet those occasions when four minutes may be the end of the line.

Making effective contacts in the journey through life requires "facing reality," a phrase which is not a cliché if we take it as clearly and simply as did Dr. Fritz Perls, who said: "Reality is nothing but the sum of all awareness." How do you learn to program that miniature, marvelous computer called the mind to more realistic values and to be better in touch with the sum of your awareness? Where you are at the end of the four-minute path that may lead to all sorts of roads, highways, alleys and trails in many directions, depends not only on the sum, but also on the *quality* of self-awareness you develop through living, looking, loving and learning. Eventually, you know the joy of freedom which using your full potential offers, and no four minutes, first or last, can scare you anymore. You grasp with an open hand—not a clenched fist.

Loneliness is not inevitable like death and taxes. It may be inevitable that you experience a variety of traumas while trying to develop the skills to meet the challenge of frequent human interaction. At this point you should be able to see over the four-minute barrier, if you cannot breeze through it. Here is a brief summary:

1. *Initial contact periods average four minutes*: In our culture it is apparent that a rule of social courtesy and congeniality has evolved when two strangers are introduced. Following the introduction, if neither party wishes to be rude, the two will converse for three to five minutes, or an average of four. This is the first courteous breaking-off point.

2. *Significance of the four-minute contact period*: Most people are unaware of the meaning and ramifications of those first four minutes. They sense an importance, but they do not realize that we often make or lose contact in that brief initial period.

3. *Recognizing patterns of contact*: Most people are not aware of the usual modes they use in an attempt to engage others in conversation. Nor are they aware that their patterns may even be anticipated by those with whom they are already acquainted.

4. *Impressions are based on assumptions more than facts*: When you meet a stranger, and sometimes with friends, much of the information you get is based on assumption. You form positive or negative feelings or impressions but you must realize that only superficial facts can be gathered in four minutes. Depending on assumptions is a one-way ticket to big surprises and perhaps disappointments. This topic is explored in the next chapter.

2

THE
ASSUMPTIVE
WORLD

One day, during an infrequent visit to the beach, we observed a young couple with their small child and two large dogs romping together in the sand. We were envious of their casual, carefree antics; this was the way to spend the days of our lives. Watching them enjoy the salt air and surf with delightful abandon, we *assumed* this was a routine pleasure for them until, as they approached, we overheard the woman say, "This was fun; how come we've never thought to do it before?"

What and how you assume can be of critical importance in the area of understanding other human beings—especially in the first four minutes. At the time of initial contact, particularly with strangers, you develop instant assumptions while getting acquainted; some impressions will be validated and some discarded in due time. This is part of what I call the *assumptive world,* which infiltrates behavior at different levels of awareness, and which has a number of influences that contribute to how you get along in all activities from schoolroom to bedroom.

As a normal part of life, you make assumptions. Assumptions run the gamut from far-out fantasy to routine, habitual conclusions. In the latter classification you presuppose an order in your thinking about yourself and the familiar world around you. In the same vein you plan the hours or days ahead with confidence and equilibrium, assuming the sun will rise and set as usual. These ordinary, day-to-day suppositions enable you to predict the general outcome of your actions, which actually helps give you impetus or courage to overcome emotional and physical inertia.

In other words, you may live a comparatively simple life via a highly complex blend of experience, knowledge —and assumption. A healthy mixture of these three can lead to fulfilling suppositions and behavior. An unbalanced combination may result in emotional disturbance. How can you safely distinguish between assumption and fact? It's not always easy. Sometimes there is only a faint wavering line between them, and people mistakenly treat their assumptions as knowledge. They mislead themselves with self-satisfied regularity, and drift down the line into fantasy or into other mental conditions which severely disturb people.

In contrast, the individual who copes successfully with life's complex pattern realizes that knowledge is not always wisdom, nor is sensitivity always accuracy. There are truly few absolute facts in this world, especially in the area of human behavior and interaction. Drs. George Bach and Ronald Deutsch (Wyden, 1970) advise us in *Pairing* that you "should never assume that you know what your partner is thinking until you have checked out the assumption in plain language; nor assume or predict how he will react, what he will accept or reject. Crystal-gazing is not for pairing."

But people continue to assume, because it's a trait that neatly falls within the list of human frailties. Everyone does it almost instinctively, and in reality, society functions and flourishes within the assumptive world. As you gain in education and maturity, hopefully you also gain an insulation of wisdom that may help refine your assumptions, or at least protect you in the maelstrom of life.

Here are a few familiar archetypal assumptions. How many of these types do you share?

Aunt Martha is notorious for serving everything cold, and the family is resigned to tolerating it because the old lady is an authentic eccentric. So you casually gulp a mouthful of her soup, and the burn on your tongue lasts three days.

Steve has always been a straight shooter in business deals, ever since you cornered the market in ostrich eggs together, so you read the agreement with him quickly and sign, only to discover later that Steve has duped you, and your risk is ten times his risk if the market drops.

Young Tony is bothering you again to take him to the toy store, and as usual you say, "We'll see, dear," so he becomes annoying and disruptive because he's learned to assume that means "no."

Nancy invites you into her apartment for the first time, and the lights are low and the music is romantic, but in twenty minutes an alarm clock goes off loudly, and she sends you home with a kiss.

For the last week your husband has acted strangely, and his new affection and attention is both gratifying and disturbing because you doubt his motives, until you discover by accident that he knows he has emphysema.

In childhood you find that life is based primarily on assumption: mother protects, toys are fun, rewards are as inevitable as punishments. In the process of growing you spend a lot of time and effort testing your assumptions. You may find those early influences strongly color your methods of dealing with family and friends, who all dwell in various states of the assumptive world. If a child has a rich variety of experiences that help develop his skill in relating to others, if he feels loved and his self-confidence is carefully developed, then as a grownup he is able to see himself as a capable, effective, lovable person in a friendly, secure universe, Such a person who is secure in his own sense of worth, and in his ability to receive and give love, welcomes new experiences with trust, and easily modifies his outlook or behavior when assumptions are inaccurate. He is not threatened if his personality foundation is sufficiently solid.

On the other hand, if a child is not given the warmth, support and encouragement everyone needs for emotional balance, his sense of worth and security are not fully developed, and his ability to establish meaningful relationships are hampered as an adolescent and adult. In short, his feeling of trust in himself and others is diminished, which in turn dilutes his ability to modify assumptions.

When people strive for perfection (and thus *assume* it is worthwhile attaining), they often overshoot the mark in evaluating others at first contact, or they hesitantly underestimate first impressions to avoid later disappointment. I experienced a rather extreme example of how the search for perfection seems to turn against one in an experiment with LSD in 1963 at U.C.L.A. under supervised, legal conditions. In fact, I thought I had died and gone to heaven, having lost all awareness of taking the drug. I believed what was happening to me was real. Everything around me was perfect. Every sound, every movement, every light, every shadow—all perfection. As I sat there in ecstasy, marveling that I had it made, I was suddenly overcome with an overwhelming feeling of apprehension. I'm told I said, "Everything is right, nothing *can* be wrong, and that's what makes it wrong." Soon I was plunging into the depths of depression because of my drug-induced conception that, since everything was perfect, emotions such as desire and feelings of motivation, curiosity and striving were now nonexistent. Finally, I sat in a bottomless pit of hopelessness, thinking, "You fool, when you were alive, you assumed that perfection would be heaven and now you find that it is hell."

If the goal of perfection seems atypical, it is easier to perceive how certain other assumptions govern our society and our lives by imposing "standards" of behavior and attitude. For instance:

Materialism and wealth lead to happiness.

Feeling well leads to doing well.

Cleanliness leads to good health.

A quiet child is a well-behaved child.

Keeping busy is always productive.

The printed word is accurate and true.

People are not "normal" if they don't wish to marry.

A "happily" married couple desires children.

Belief in God is a condition of mental health and normalcy.

Physicians, attorneys and dentists are happier in their careers then mechanics, printers and salesmen.

Parents and teachers often help perpetuate these assumptions, while at the same time they unconsciously advocate the contradictory idea that to be average is to be inadequate. This supposition ignores the fact that a majority of people on earth are "average," which is as slippery a word to define as "normal" since the comparisons are so relative. Yet we tend to make assumptions about ourselves, our friends, our families, culture, country, the world and the universe based on such half-baked facts, prejudices, and our own simple, hopefully innocuous, defects of personality.

When you treat an assumption as fact, you are taking a risk. Certainly, the distinction between fact and assumption is often blurred, but a substitution of one for the other may lead to disappointment, frustration and self-deception. You may be right or wrong, but unfortunately, once assumptions are firmly implanted as truth, people usually have a difficult time revising their views. As doubt finally assails a complex set of assumptions, an individual must then reevaluate his own self-image, which can be upsetting. After all, it is a reflection of your own adequacy in making contacts or any sort of judgments if you find you have been applying an erroneous set of assumptions.

In the area of contact, our assumptions, especially those called up by the sight and sound of others, always involve emotional reactions along with intellectual computations. Some induced feelings are easy enough to diagnose. Some, instilled by conditioning, are about certain categories of people and their characteristics. We all deal in stereotypes, no matter the state of our enlightenment. You've heard remarks such as, "I liked her immediately because she reminded me of my sister," or "I don't care much for that guy; he has squinty eyes like my former boss."

Here's an excerpt from a newspaper story by reporter Bill Barry, who found himself in a police training situation simulating a cop on the street with a loaded .38 on his hip. Walking in a quiet neighborhood one day, he noticed a man coming out of a clump of bushes between two houses.

He was a big, rangy hippie, wearing a sloppy Zapata mustache. In his right hand he was hefting a baseball bat. At the sight of me, he slowed a little, but kept coming. His face had a mean and nasty aspect, a tightheld scowl. He turned towards me, his hand choked up on the bat, his eyes direct at me; his stride was determined, menacing.

I cleared my uniform jacket away from my gun butt, just in case. That bat could clobber me, all right, but except for the glare on his face, he hadn't jeopardized me, yet. The question was, had he just left three dead bodies in one of the houses? Had he burgled them? Assaulted a housewife? What?

He was within striking distance, three feet away. The tendons in his right forearm rippled. My hand was on the pistol. As he came abreast, the first clear break in his manner and behavior flashed on his face; he smiled and walked on by.

Whew! I had come that close to plugging a guy who was guilty of nothing more than heading out for the ballfield. The guilty party was me, guilty of prejudice. I had gotten all uptight, just because I didn't like his looks.

So, let that be a lesson, don't project. And the

cardinal rule drummed through my head; when in doubt, don't shoot.

That's a dramatic example of reaction to a stereotype. In the following list, which stereotypes correspond to some you admit having?

Women with large breasts and/or shapely legs must be good in bed.

Garbage collectors and janitors are inevitably intellectual nobodies.

Men with short haircuts all have conservative values.

Teenagers all smoke pot or take drugs because it's part of our culture.

Wine connoisseurs are highly sophisticated people.

Men with long hair who ride motorcycles and wear leather jackets are vicious and dangerous.

Clergymen never doubt their faith.

Movie actors and actresses all enjoy casual sex lives.

All children waste their money on junk, never turn out lights or flush toilets, and go to bed without bathing or washing.

A belief in any or all of the above arrogant suppositions can make fools of us. What is more, remaining unaware of these prejudices and trying to relate to others while we are under the burden of the stereotype curse, we may cut ourselves off from rich experiences, warm and enjoyable friendships, or perhaps even be responsible for injustice. As an example, once when I served on a jury I was astounded by an "impartial" fellow juror's remark during deliberations: "I know he's guilty," he told us seriously. "He reminds me of a boy my son ran around with who was a bum."

On the basis that everyone operates at one time or another on assumptions, how can we assured that we won't over- or underestimate another individual or a group, especially during the first four minutes of contact? For one thing, we must develop values that correspond with reality, that reflect our own enthusiasm for life with a minimum dependence on wishful thinking. Further, we must remember that our assumptions do exist, that they are vulnerable, and that through a process of time and growing perception, some assumptions will become fact and others will not. As we learn to successfully predict the results of action and understanding, we gain a more realistic perspective, and enjoy more success in relationships we value as well as those to come.

Dr. George Bach's research serves as a cautious reminder. He concludes that "mainly, one thinks of others as one did on first meeting them. Initial illusions tend to be preserved."

How do we evaluate and examine the validity of our assumptions and reactions to them? One way is to retain a certain amount of skepticism about our values, or at least in the way we interpret them. I don't mean cynicism, but rather a healthy, open mind, ready to modify expectations and corresponding behavior. Otherwise, we live in illusion, having to conceal our rigidity and distort reality. All of this may take place spontaneously, below the level of acute awareness, so we can hurt or be hurt in sheer surprise.

The flexible person examines his assumptions as he registers them, during contact with others, and if there seem to be contradictions, he makes spontaneous revisions. For example, a woman once told me, "You know how worried I've always been about being seen without make-up. Men say I'm pretty, but I felt they were impressed with the skillful camouflage job I can do on my face. Well, I just came back from a cruise, and I met a terrific guy. The first time he saw me, I was coming out of the pool, and the damned salt water washed every trace of mascara, cream and all the other stuff off my face. He was looking at my naked eyes and mouth, and I assumed I was a mess. But he didn't seem to mind. Five minutes later we were in a heavy conversation about life, and two days later we were in love. I think he was actually disappointed when he saw me in makeup. Can you imagine that?"

In the lady's assumptive world she was only herself in a thin veil of disguise, but she was secure enough to react positively to being accepted unmasked. Had she been less secure, less stable, with an unconscious dedication to failure, she would have been apt to rationalize that her original assumption was true and would probably have rejected her new friend before she was rejected herself. To admit that an assumption is in error further threatens an already shaky self-image. An uncomfortable rut is preferable to change when the dominant influence is fear rather than self-confidence.

Through our five senses we all are subject to an endless list of images, sounds, smells, tastes and touches, all of which we use to form our assumptions. Many such suppositions ring true and serve us, filtered through experience and intuition. For instance, the girl you meet on a pack trip is very likely an outdoor type who wouldn't mind an unpretentious place for dinner. The person who touches your hand or arm on first meeting is unlikely to assault you. The girl who wears no perfume may be crazy about roses and gardenias. The man sitting there in a rigid position with his arms across his chest and a stern expression on his face may not be closed, controlled and uptight. That is only an assumption. He may be in acute pain, from severe arthritis for example, and that position is most comfortable for his back or legs. Or he may simply be in desperate need of a bathroom!

You see an attractive face or hear a lovely voice full of sparkling enthusiasm; you meet a withdrawn sort of person who makes an effort to communicate; you pick up a hitchhiker who babbles incessantly and says nothing. You assume the face and voice belong to someone you could love, the shy person is trying hard to make contact, and the hitchhiker was a mistake—and you're right each time. It is quite possible that assumptions made on initial contact will prove quite valid as you become better acquainted with someone.

The opposite is also true. People are continually disappointed because their initial impressions were far more favorable than time and events proved to be true. It is also unfortunate when a person continues to expect behavior or response from a new contact which is far beyond that individual's potential. A letdown is usually followed by feelings of rejection. You may not want to terminate the relationship, but you do have to adjust your expectations to coincide with newfound reality.

There is also the folly of underestimating, then later being surprised when you find you *can* trust somebody—such as the new hairdresser at the beauty shop who did a better job than your regular girl (who eloped to Las Vegas) even though she looked like a baby-sitter you once had who drank too much. People often turn out to be more pleasant, intelligent, helpful or even sexier than you first thought, and underestimating might be your way of trying to avoid disappointments (if you don't expect much, the letdown will be minimal). But you may discover when people surprise you that you are really disappointed by your own inability to objectively evaluate other people.

Obtaining more information helps you to decide whether or not your assumptions about that pretty face, the smooth manner, the "sincere" pitch, or any impression of someone, are true. You do this spontaneously by becoming increasingly friendly with others—but not to a point where your motives may seem suspicious when all you're trying to do is learn more about what makes somebody tick.

Making contacts with friends and strangers every day through a filter tinted by assumptions is unavoidable. A rose-colored filter befits the cockeyed optimist who assumes that everything on the surface is genuine, and a smoggy filter is tailored to the Scroogelike pessimist who doesn't trust anybody or anything farther than he can throw a piano. Of course, these are symbolic characters, but the world of assumptions is populated with signs, symbols and signals. Is a smile usually a come-on, or a prelude to extortion? Does the man with a large vocabulary reveal his education or his pretension? Does that lovely fragrance coming from between her breasts signal sexual adventure or indignant rebuff? Will your husband notice the delighted inflection in your voice as you ask about the raise he got, or will he simply feel that you want extra money for extravagances?

An enormous amount of information—and fallacy—can be projected and picked up in four-minute contacts between the closest of intimates or the newest of acquaintances. The more careful you are in assuming, the sooner you get through the four-minute barrier to enjoy deeper and more rewarding relationships, or successful transient contacts. You must trust yourself to effectively trust others; you must understand your prejudices and misconceptions of other people and lifestyles. With these accomplishments you can expect fulfillment from contacts, whether you are talking to a mortgage loan officer or meeting a future mother-in-law for the first time.

Kenneth Clark openly admits to an assumptive bias in his book *Civilisation*. His philosophy and values are very provocative in these times when mutual trust is ebbing between nations as well as on a neighborhood, one-to-one basis.

At this point I reveal myself in my true colors, as a stick-in-the-mud. I hold a number of beliefs, that have been repudiated by the liveliest intellects of our time. I believe that order is better than chaos, creation better than destruction. I prefer gentleness to violence, forgiveness to vendetta. On the whole I think that knowledge is preferable to ignorance, and I am sure that human sympathy is more valuable than ideology. I believe that in spite of recent triumphs of science, men haven't changed much in the last 2,000 years; and in consequence we must still try to learn from history. History is ourselves. I also hold one or two beliefs that are more difficult to put shortly. For example, I believe in courtesy, the ritual by which we avoid hurting other people's feelings by satisfying our own egos. And I think we should remember that we are part of a great whole, which for convenience we call nature. All living things are our brothers and sisters. Above all, I believe in the God-given genius of certain individuals, and I value a society that makes their existence possible.

Kenneth Clark believes in man's inherent humanity to man, and goes on to note: "It is a lack of confidence, more than anything else, that kills a civilisation. We can destroy ourselves by cynicism and disillusion, just as effectively as by bombs."

So it is with people in new or ongoing contacts. A lack of self-confidence may breed a lack of trust, thus destroying the possibility of communication. But Clark's assumption (a similar one underlies this book, incidentally) is counter to cynicism—it is a belief that most people have a basic potential to be nice, and that most intend good will to one another.

Confidence comes not from thin air, but from experiences in which we succeed. Consistent success in small routine relationships, as well as in large career goals (as in raising children, which is the toughest career of all), creates new confidence to enjoy.

But success requires venture, and venture decrees risk —of rejection and failure. Risk not, want a lot. If you wish to be assured of never having to endure the slightest hint of rejection by others, you merely avoid contact like a hermit, and the pleasures of the world are out of your reach. The average hermit may escape city traffic and the wiles of his fellow man, but he also shrinks away from reality. To experience pleasure involves some risk, and success seems clearly worth taking chances to the healthy, mature individual.

Functioning in a fulfilling way in the assumptive world means continually developing awareness of how people communicate. Appreciating the initial contact involves understanding the dynamics that drive everyone, and the misconceptions that mislead even the most wary. The assumptive world need not be populated with ghouls and knaves. Though you may expect to face uncomfortable situations when somebody is "on the make" for physical or material reasons, and there may be temporary failure in your future, rest assured that you can improve your intuition. Your memory not only stores experience and knowledge but alerts and prepares you to improve your ability, and achieve satisfying rapport with strangers and intimates. Assumptions become more accurate and relationships built on reality (to quote a phrase from the instructions that accompanied a small Japanese abacus) "Bring more joy on your life."

3.

VERBAL
CONTACT

We talk, we sing, we cry or moan, we make simple sounds of joy or despair, we read and we write; all of these are forms of verbal communication, depending on words and sounds. We also touch, embrace, fondle, gesture or merely look another person in the eye; these are nonverbal contacts discussed in depth in the chapter on body language. Our ways of seeing, listening and touching are often intertwined, and how we handle the mixture will be apparent as the Contact story unfolds.

Except in special therapeutic groups where people touch before they are formally introduced, the primary means of communication between friends and strangers is verbal. Just as there are voiceprints to scientifically identify speech patterns (so we can determine who is the *real* Howard Hughes), there is also a wide variety of conversational types. In fact, some people can be identified and classified according to certain categories of verbial initiative and response.

For example, there are the agreement addicts who nod or mumble "yes" to almost anything you say until it seems certain they are either human sponges or incapable of original thought. In contrast are the disagreement zealots who come on strong in less than four minutes, usually to inflate their own egos with bursts of hot air. If such a character happens to agree with a few of your points, he'll rearrange their importance. The conversation-dominator has a mental chart, and you may be streamrollered if you try to change the subject. You also know the jokers who take the Don Rickles approach and attempt to put you down with barbs that may or may not be poisoned.

With experience you learn to recognize these patterns in the conversation game. Some are quite fixed, some boring, others are engaging. However, as you examine the various ways people interact with words, you find several constants. First, effective communication is based on sincerity. Ways with words may be unsuccessful, even by sincere, mature individuals, if those words do not *project* warmth. Appearance is also an essential (nonverbal) influence, since the face and body create a supporting or contradictory image as the mouth speaks.

In addition, a conversational contact may win friends and influence people in one situation, while the same verbal approach in other circumstances may be disastrous. For instance, your uncle, the prominent attorney, may come on with a formal demeanor in legal circles and gain both respect and admiration. The same gentleman at a birthday party for your teenage daughter may seem standoffish or even insulting unless he tempers his formality to fit the more relaxed social surroundings.

I am not suggesting that you stand there analyzing your conversational gambits in any mechanical manner, but it seems reasonable that an awareness of the patterns you use will improve your contact with others, whether a situation is familiar or threatening.

The word-ways, or conversational techniques, discussed in this chapter apply to encounters with strangers as well as to ongoing, intimate relationships. Do you or your wife, husband, lover or good friends usually open a conversation with questions, complaints, compliments or banal observations? It may not matter, if the usual interchange is satisfying, but if your spouse is often irritated, or if you are beginning to feel indifference to routine greetings, a deeper look at the influence of communication on your relationships may be indicated. It is precisely this sort of probing which this book aims to stimulate, to help you develop renewed awareness of all your contacts, intimate, social or business.

As you consider the modes of contact examined in this chapter, weigh the effectiveness of your own conversation game. Can you allow warmth and fondness for someone to show in your voice without being threatened or threatening? Do your words and inflections create positive, negative, or neutral reactions from friends or strangers? Stop, look and listen to yourself—and to everyone you talk with. I predict you're in for some enlightening (maybe startling) surprises.

WORD-WAYS WITH STRANGERS

When you meet a stranger, the outcome within four minutes will be one of the following:

1. Both of you will indicate, perhaps indirectly, that you want to continue talking.

2. Both of you will prefer to taper the conversation off and end it as soon as it seems acceptable.

3. One of you may want to go on, while the other doesn't. (These feelings may or may not be conveyed, depending on one's skill in showing them.)

Do you recognize the symptoms of a blossoming or a waning conversation? Do you know the signals, especially those that are devious? I asked myself some of the same questions not long ago during an airline flight to a speaking engagement. I had settled down, my briefcase on my lap, going over a number of papers. The seat immediately next to me was empty. One seat over at the window was a pleasant-looking woman in her late fifties. She appeared to be reading a magazine, but I realized that, with some regularity, she was glancing my way. I saw her glancing at my papers on the seat between us; these were notes concerning a law and psychiatry seminar.

Finally, she opened up with, "You're a doctor, I see by the 'M.D.' on your briefcase. Do you do any work with the courts?"

"Sometimes," I replied, explaining that I was interested in problems of legal psychiatry.

"My son's an attorney," she volunteered, clearly hoping to continue the chat, but I was preoccupied. I smiled cordially and returned, with a nod, to my work. I had not totally rebuffed her, and it was evident her urge to continue the contact was stronger than her sympathy for my preoccupation. In several minutes she interjected, "I have another son who's a dentist."

"My wife is a dental assistant," I remarked; and we both smiled as I tried to concentrate on my notes.

Her strong desire to talk was obvious, and her congenial manner was appropriate for the situation. At that moment there was no way I could discern the degree of need this woman had to make contact with me. She returned to intermittently reading and glancing in my direction.

Then abruptly she blurted, "My brother took his life yesterday. I'm going to his funeral."

With that I chose to set aside my sheaves of paper and respond with sincere concern. She had made contact with me via a major accounting of facts, seasoned by her emotions. In our conversation, I believe I was able to give her some temporary solace, which only occurred because she clearly reached out for contact. I was glad she had.

Instinctively, this lady knew she had failed to gain my attention for more than a minute through the mode I refer to as *the search for mutual interests*. Her intuition or her experience led her to make the *provocative statement* about her brother, another approach we will discuss, and thereby she "hooked" me into her life for a brief interval. Though she could not precisely anticipate my feelings, she had apparently received both verbal and nonverbal signs that there was favorable potential in perseverance.

While human behavior cannot be programmed in computer fashion, nor can we expect sequential directions for contact such as those for building a model airplane, there are many basic modes of conversation. You may use some of these already, and others may prove valuable to break the ice with strangers. At least, the following modes will give you ideas of your own to work out.

1. *The Search for Identifying Data:* In this category fall all the preliminary questions about name, rank and serial number. If this verbal quest is stretched too far, personality characteristics and emotional overtones may be overlooked or restricted. Thus, an opening gambit of this type should be short and sweet, followed by more intimate fact-finding. Here's a digested version of a typical "I.D." conversation that seems to bloom:

J: Hello; my name is Joe. What's yours?

N: Nan.

J: That's a lovely name. Do you live near here?

N: Not far away, in the Valley. What's your last name?

J: It's Keppie. Before you ask, it's spelled K-e-p-p-i-e.

N: Thanks. That's an unusual name; is it German?

J: Yes; my dad was born in Germany, but I was born in Cincinnati. Where are you from?

N: New York City; can't you tell by my accent?

J: You've lost it—if you ever had one. Have you ever been married?

N: Nope; have you?

J: Almost, a few years ago; but we chickened out.

N: What do you do in real life?

J: *(laughing)* I'm a film distributor.

From this point he tells her the name of his company; she says some of their movies were amusingly dirty; he counters with an offer to see a preview a few nights hence; she asks a few details; and then they settle into fewer facts and more feeling about mutually agreeable subjects. They both avoid making data-gathering seem like an inquisition and seek to discover more about each other than plain facts. Joe and Nan soon find many things they have in common, which can well stimulate a relationship onward and upward.

2. *Existential and Personality Topics:* In Joe and Nan's conversation, when topics shifted to attitudes, likes and dislikes, or any subject in which they reflected an evaluation of their lives and times, they began offering insights into their personalities. Feelings you have about or get from someone are always being added to basic facts. As you discover the many views you share about everyday life, you learn something about your differences as well. Those differences may seem insurmountable or a pleasant challenge.

Alex and Cindy are in their late teens. Their first four minutes are somewhat condensed here, as an example of dialogue in this catagory:

A: Hi; I'm Alex.

C: Hi, Alex; I'm Cindy.

A: I'm having a great time, how about you?

C: Yeah, this party is groovy. Do you like the music?

A: I dig it, but sometimes my feet get tangled when I dance to it.

C: Right, I used to have the same problem. Now I improvise. I seemed to get the hang of it.

A: Maybe I could try improvising, but I'd really rather hold a girl close when I dance.

C: I know what you mean. Let's put on something slower and try.

They're dancing; they talk about singers and music for awhile. The conversation then turns to college, parents, finances, cars, television, movies and all the really important things of their generation.

By "existential" I mean subjects closely involved with your own existence which, in discussion, are colored by personality. Hints about what a person is "really like" are revealed in this way, providing someone is not trying consciously to mask or distort.

I want to stress that during and after initial contact, you must sum up all the feelings and facts you absorb about another individual and average these within your own reality frame of reference. Otherwise, you may be misled—and it happens all the time. In other words, because someone shares an interest or delight in animals, ballet, foreign films, or politics with you, your needs and values may still not be similar enough to make a binding relationship later. The first four minutes of *any* contact is a kind of audition; information and impressions are exchanged and filtered through both mind and senses. As self-confidence and self-knowledge develop, so does our ability to evaluate our assumptions. With practice, we become more accurate, thus decreasing our chances for disappointment.

A few other random questions that combine personality and existence may cover early childhood, recreation, child rearing, and anything that can be answered without statistics. Try one of these if you like: Would you consider yourself happy? Are you happily married? What would you like to do with the rest of your life? Any of them, or similar queries, can open up all sorts of personality doors.

3. *Identifying Data Offered Spontaneously:* This category is an off-shoot of the first one but may be reserved for strangers who seem difficult to turn on. If someone appears worth getting to know but lapses into silence quickly, you might open and then probe:

You: We moved from Connecticut only a few months ago, and I'm just getting used to California weather. Have you ever lived in the East?

Somebody: Yes, and I hated driving in snow.

You: I was used to it. Actually, I had an opportunity to open a new branch of my company out here, and the Coast seemed appealing. I'm an electrical engineer. What do you do?

Somebody: I'm in insurance.

You: I have a good friend in Stamford who handled all my insurance, but he's too far away to help me much now.

If that last statement, or something equally provocative, doesn't get a rise from another individual who can recognize the opportunity to make a friend and a client at the same time, the contact may be hopeless. In other circumstances, topics such as house-hunting, family vacations, or information volunteered about many mutual interests of life, may help strike a spark. Once you open, remember to give the other person a chance to talk, even if he or she is naturally reticent. There are people who might be categorized as conversational bores, but if you are adept at contact, you won't meet one. By that I mean you will be able to *manipulate* verbal communication to switch topics and hold your own—for at least four minutes. If you are really stuck, you can tactfully move away and begin anew.

Incidentally, manipulation has objectionable connotations in contemporary parlance, but I consider it in positive terms. Without approaching a semantic maze, to manipulate is to lead constructively, if not entirely altruistically. If you ask a child to wash his hands (when he's preoccupied having fun in a sandpile), or suggest to your mate that it's time to turn off the TV and make love (in the middle of an absorbing movie), you are manipulating contact for mutually worthwhile reasons. The words you choose, your timing, facial expressions, grooming, dress and body language—all are phases of creative manipulation. The word gets its offensive significance when it is associated with extreme selfish motives.

4. *Spontaneous Offering on the Existential and Personality Level:* This is a variation of the second category, particularly appropriate for the hard-to-reach contact with

whom you hope a personal note might lead to give-and-take. If both of you can be revealing without feeling vulnerable or ridiculous, there could be gratifying response. Here are a few phrases offering connotations that could be discussed in more depth:

I was always a shy kid.

I really like parties best when they're not too crowded.

I like to drink, but three's my limit.

I've thought of getting married, but I don't know if I'm ready.

I wonder what it would be like to be single again, even for a short time?

I'd love to learn to sail (or ski, dance, play the guitar, etc.).

5. *The Art of Compliments:* When you offer a sincere compliment to a stranger (or somebody close, for that matter), you are saying, "I like you," or "something about you is special." Most people react positively to compliments because it's hard to resist being liked. However, your admiration should not be expressed in phony superlatives which will seem transparent. The receiver may suspect ulterior motives which are unwelcome or, at least, premature. Everyone has some positive attributes about which you can make realistic compliments within initial contact.

In the male-female contact, compliments may carry seductive connotations, which is fine if you express them with open honesty. Here is a montage interchange that points up the potential winning ways of words:

He: (after introductions and amenities) I was noticing that beautiful necklace you're wearing. Is it an heirloom?

She: It's an ivory cameo my grandmother brought from France a long time ago. You have very sharp eyes!

He: Thanks. I like the way you wear it—a lovely setting.

She: I'm glad you noticed.

He: I make jewelry as a hobby, but nothing as fine as your cameo.

She: How interesting. Do you make it for fun or to sell?

He: Just for kicks. I'm a dentist and I have all the equipment in the office for casting in gold to make rings and things.

She: I'll bet you're very good at it. Do you have any samples here?

He: My wife's wearing a pin I'll show you later.

At this point mutual admiration has flowered, and they continue to converse about hobbies, children, and a cruise one couple is planning. They like each other and they show it before the four-minute mark. This is not necessarily a seductive exchange; it represents the warmth and interest which people can offer and enjoy in a short interval.

6. *Talking about Here-and-Now Surroundings:* This is another spin-off from the search for personal and existential information. You attempt to make contact through comments on the moment, usually not controversial. At a party, for instance, he mentions how casually everyone is dressed, and she says it's nice to be informal. She complains about cigar smoke, and he offers to put out his cigarette, though she says it isn't necessary. They talk about the furniture and the food, the hostess and her problems, or the background music. A quick survey of the milieu in which they live indicates enough in common to continue contact in a more congenial setting.

You can consciously originate conversational topics about the here-and-now shared temporarily with someone, and expand the scope of verbal communication to the outer limits of serendipity.

7. *Focus on the External World:* A conversational path sometimes leads away from the personal and into the

world around us. If it isn't bogged down on an unreward-
ing topic, such an exchange can also reveal things not
easily apparent about other people as well as ourselves.
Often this sort of encounter occurs in the midst of another
conversation (which I call the *Third Party Contact*, discussed further in Chapter 6), and the external world
becomes an excellent vehicle for initial involvement. Later
you might segue into more familiar topics with emotional
overtones.

I watched a foursome interrelate recently at a reception
that followed a lecture I gave. Two men were talking about
an automobile race, and the wife of one accused them of
being fascinated by blood and guts of accidents. A third
man nearby countered that it was the driver's skill which
most men found exciting, leading the first man to ask if
the newcomer drove a sports car. He admitted owning a
Jaguar XKE, and was thereby included in the conversation with little more effort. They went on commenting on
TV coverage of races and the highlights of a Can-Am
competition that had been run a few days before. I drifted
away as they were telling the woman that movie stars
rarely do their own driving in the racing movies she had
seen.

This group shared opinions and took impressions of
each other according to values expressed about a sport in
which none of them participated. World affairs, local
scandals, space exploration, the ups and downs of the
stock market, and dozens of other "out there" subjects are
also handy ways to make verbal contact, which can refocus
on the personal later.

8. *The Search for Mutual Interests or Acquaintances:*
One of the most frequent modes for establishing communication with a new acquaintance is to find friends or
interests in common. Your son goes to the same school
his son does; she lives in a neighborhood where you have
friends; he knows a doctor who plays tennis at the courts
where your daughter plays, etc., etc. There's always a link-
age in every crowd between strangers who have seen, or
been, or know, or have dealings with someone you know.

If a proud father shows you some good snapshots of his children, even when you have no offspring to compare, you may discover you both enjoy photography or use the same brand of camera.

Mutual friends or interest are a temporary device, however, and contact that begins in this category usually needs more depth to continue. There's a reverse twist as well, when you search for the similar and come up with opposites that may breed antagonism. Bach and Deutsch mention this in *Pairing:*

> We do not encourage pairers to seek out differences. But we tell them not to shy away from potential partners just because great polarities exist. When they do exist, we advise that the pairers not sweep them under the rug and emphasize what similarities they find between them. If the differences are confronted, the interest that is generated is likely to be warm and intriguing. The experience can be enriching because each is attempting to pair not only with an individual, but with another world as well.

9. *The Creative Gibe:* There's a bit of sarcasm in us all, and the urge to greet others with benevolent insults sometimes seems fitting. I call this the *creative* gibe because, to have a positive effect, it must be well-intended and have a touch of humor. It may also be the technique by which a person of limited self-confidence feels he can "come on strong," but such gambits may be embarrassingly transparent. However, pleasant sarcasm helps open a contact to a more revealing dimension than innocuous chatter.

Keep in mind that every gibe or playful insult involves a risk. People can be turned off or embarrassed by what sounds like your lack of sensitivity. It is advisable to have the measure of another person, at least through instinct, before resorting to sarcasm in the first four minutes. On the other hand, you might *enjoy* taking chances. A friend once told me how he met his future wife over the punchbowl at a wedding reception, which is usually a delightful place to make new contacts. He related, "I had seen her from a distance and thought she was gorgeous, but a little haughty. We finally met at the punchbowl and I guess I was trying to cover a lack of self-confidence when I asked, 'Do you always drink so much?' She was startled but answered, 'How would you know? Have you been counting?' I was actually being presumptuous, but I came up with something flip that kept the conversation open, and she was intrigued. I knocked off the insults pretty fast, but the first one worked!"

Many characters in fiction or on TV seem to relate swimmingly through sharp quips, but only professional entertainers and the lighthearted young can pull off the creative gibe with that kind of consistency. However, it's one way of seeking new acquaintances if you're willing to take that kind of risk.

Barbara Walters summarized this scene well in her book, *How to Talk with Practically Anybody About Practically Anything* (Doubleday, 1970), and her observation applies to both sexes: "Don't make the adolescent mistake of trying to impress a man by insulting him. It doesn't demonstrate that you're hard to get, just hard to like."

10. *The Humorous Approach:* Choosing something funny you saw or heard as an entree to conversation in the first four minutes can smooth the way to further contact, if your remarks are in good taste—and really humorous. Most people respond well to the light touch, though it is advisable not to stay with jokes or comic remarks very long. They are often impersonal, and could keep others at a distance. Most people avoid the traveling salesman prototype who comes on with vulgar and boring jokes, though he still appeals to kindred characters. If your humorous monologues last a while, and you can hold an audience, perhaps you should consider a career in show business!

11. *Social Graces in Action:* The most elementary display of courtesy or social grace is as nice a way as any to make contact with friend or stranger, though it may only

be the prelude to a four-minute interval. Some word-ways include:

May I light your cigarette?

Please sit next to me—I've been wanting to meet you.

That glass looks very empty; shall we wander over to the bar?

May I get you a chair?

You have a couple of buttons undone in the back of your dress; may I close them for you?

12. *The Hobby and Fad Approach:* While youngsters may still play party games, unfortunately adults usually don't feel relaxed enough to enjoy themselves in such ice-breakers (though charades may make a come-back someday). As a substitute, you might pursue your own hobby-game-fad interests through conversation about handwriting analysis, astrology, palmistry, the psychological effects of color, or improvisational theater games. Because these reflect your personality and tastes, they can induce others to open up more freely than a discussion of the weather can. Personal diversions and interests find response from strangers, either because they have similar interests or are intrigued by yours.

For instance, a couple meet at a social gathering and he remarks on the beauty of her hands. "May I hold one?" he asks, "Palm reading is my hobby." She willingly extends a hand, and borrowing on his amateur knowledge of palm reading, he says something like: "These lines show you're a fairly outgoing person, and that long curve indicates you have a warm personality." He may take a few guesses that she was once a tomboy or has philosophical leanings, and they both play the next stages of the conversation game by ear.

Just talking about a hobby or a current enthusiasm that you share with someone can be an excellent means of positive contact, even if you don't get everyone in the room involved.

13. *Can You Tell Me . . . ?:* Spontaneous contact through asking for help or information might be functional (you may just *be* lost and need directions), or it could be

an opening gambit that is sincere but unnecessary. It does give the other person a chance to show how clever he is by offering aid, which could begin to close the gap you had as strangers. There are a number of "Can you tell me?" openings for the social situation, including:

—where you got that cigarette case? It's beautiful.

—who your veterinarian is, the one you mentioned cured your dog of worms?

—the best way to get home from here? I had an awful time finding the place.

—how you mix these drinks? They taste just like the ones I had on an Italian cruise last summer.

Everyone enjoys a situation in which he can show off naturally, even if the subject is trivia. However, don't use this gambit too often, or you may find yourself catalogued as a "professional waif." You don't need the helpless game to make contact with a legitimate question.

14. *Verbalizing the Nonverbal:* Since people are usually flattered when they are observed and/or admired, indicating this can be a conversational opener. "I notice that you seemed so quiet sitting here in the corner of the couch. Is anything wrong you'd like to talk about?" That may be a nosy way of encounter, but everyone is looking for a shoulder to cry on at one time or another.

You might also comment on clothes and grooming, the fact that somebody talks with their hands, or any other feature of gesture which deserves a positive response. The fact that you *noticed* is the key to many a contact door. Of course, you must be sincere; you shouldn't be critical. And if you start with flattery, keep it crisp and ringing true. How you verbalize about the nonverbal can turn a four-minute contact into a decisive friendship or even more.

15. *You Remind Me of . . .:* This opening phrase is rather lame if not in earnest; but, when someone says, "You remind me of my sister (brother, boyfriend, uncle or army buddy)", your interest perks up long enough to find out why. But the person who is often told he or she looks like Paul Newman or Raquel Welch may not be

surprised; the reply you get may indicate whether the conversation is worth continuing. A sincere "You remind me of . . ." works best when the reference is unfamiliar to the other individual and you add a few exotic details.

16. *Self-Apology:* Opening lines such as—

I didn't realize how people would be dressed here; I feel so uncomfortable with this dress on.

I'm sorry to be so late but the television was broken and I had to wait for the repairman.

I don't know anything about animal behavior so I can't really join your conversation.

Please don't ask about my hands; I'm a mechanic and I can never get the grease off them entirely.

None of these sincere regrets are prone to generate much interest from other people so avoid them if possible. You tend to demean yourself. Apologies are appropriate for many situations, but don't lean on them expecting sympathetic response; there are many better ways to achieve positive contact. On the other hand, such an opening gives you the opportunity to put somebody else at ease if that gesture seems temporarily useful.

17. *The Effective Accident:* The cliché in this category is the lady who drops her handkerchief, hoping it will attract the attention of a charming gentleman whom she would like to meet. An "accidental" collision with someone in order to make verbal contact is another sally. Any casually planned mishap may backfire because it seems contrived, but in fact and fiction this mode has launched many four-minute meetings which grew into more intimate relationships. This approach also offers the bumper and the bumpee immediate physical contact, which could result in solace being offered that might bring people closer together.

18. *The Whimsical Hook-In:* The most prevalent use of whimsy is "putting someone on," usually by distorting reality in a humorous way. By exaggerating we gain attention and individuality, *providing* we are not malicious or harmful to anyone. Friendly teasing often results in friendly response. In a short time, the deception is usually real-

ized or signaled, and the aftermath of your gambit is enjoyed out in the open. Of course, if you deceive someone intentionally only to impress them, feelings will be hurt because of your dishonesty, and you are more apt to make an enemy, not a friend.

The put-on can also be useful to "steer" a conversation that you find turning in an unpleasant direction. For example, at a party I met a woman who was so vehement in her fact-gathering that it seemed like a cross-examination. She had heard me mention Puerto Rico, and when she asked bluntly what I had been doing there, I told her I was lecturing to the crime commission, which I was. She bore in with more questions, turning me off further. I elected to tell her I was an experienced criminal who had never been caught, but was so expert that the authorities called upon me to brief law enforcement officers. She was impressed enough to take a step backwards. Later I told her who I actually was, and she apologized for coming on so strongly. (Again, this gambit was placed in the open because the attempt was whimsy, not deceit.)

Many put-ons center around identity misrepresentation or far-out observations ("This is the best coffee I've had since my outfit captured a cappucino machine in Naples"), reversals of role or opinion, or excessive flattery. References to physical attributes (beautiful legs, handsome profile), or sexuality in its many forms ("My wife knows about my mistress, but says . . .") can be intriguing in early conversation. How you handle the subject of sex in good taste will depend on the time, place, and company you're with. You run the risk of discovering, after it's too late, how your whimsical hook-in was accepted or rejected if people are reluctant to continue the conversation or invite you back again.

19. *The Provocative Hook-In:* Both whimsy and the creative gibe are forms of provocation, but the shading in this category is concerned with a projection of identity or personality impudence. You may recall the meeting of Jenny and Oliver in *Love Story*, by Erich Segal (Harper

and Row, 1970), which is a classic of deft provocation. The Harvard hero meets a "bespectacled mouse type" girl in the Radcliffe library where she's working behind the desk. He asks for a certain book, and she counters by suggesting he look in his own school library. He ruminates to himself that Radcliffe girls have an exaggerated impression of their own intelligence, and asks for the "goddamn book" again. She cautions him about using profanity, calling him "Preppie," and adds that he looks "stupid and rich." He is challenged to rejoinder:

"What the hell makes you so smart?" I asked.

"I wouldn't go for coffee with you," she answered.

"Listen—I wouldn't ask you."

"That," she replied, "is what makes you stupid."

Segal uses the creative insult to provoke and hooks the reader into his story just as his protagonists hook in to each other.

Provocation can also have negative aspects, as a friend once explained when he said, "I tell myself I'm testing response and learning more about people, which is partially true; but I can't escape the realization that provocation is also an attention-getting mechanism. Why not just say what's real and not fall into this exaggerated pattern?"

Provocation, whimsy, humor and the creative gibe are all approaches to contact which I would label, "Handle with care," though they can be fun and effective.

IN SUMMARY

If your manner of verbal communication expresses genuine interest in someone else, in their work, clothes, travels, accomplishments, lifestyle, physical appearance, values, etc., and you approach with warmth, contact is easily extended beyond four minutes. Since interpersonal relations can't be scored like a basketball game, you have to *sense* how a contact starts and proceeds. You know that modes of conversation are intermixed. Questions, answers, compliments, jokes, opinions, and careful listening as well, all add up to making a connection—finding things and feelings in common. If there were actually a rigid, step-by-step formula for applying contact modes, we'd all be bored quickly and look for variations. The modes described above merely point out directions contact may take, based on typical situations. Your own self-confidence is also vastly important and will be discussed later.

Here are three outstanding aspects to understanding all verbal contact:

1. *Recognize the importance of the initial few minutes.* We tend to take contacts for granted, especially with close friends and relatives. We need to realize the significance of words, inflections and subliminal signals others give us— or we give out.

2. *Be aware of your word-ways.* Most of us meet and greet—and we may realize what we're saying and what others tell us—but we are not fully conscious of the modes applied as described in this chapter or of the possible variations and alternatives. It's a little like knowing all the moves of chess, but using only a few of them to play the game.

3. *Evaluate your word-ways and make changes.* If we do take initial relationships for granted, and we are not aware of contact techniques, we may be making ineffectual contact in the same way, over and over. Try to analyze the effectiveness of your verbal approaches. Do you converse according to an automatic pattern? You need to know the way of words and your own ability to use them with hard-to-reach strangers, loved ones who seem to talk but say nothing, or whenever verbal relationships seem to need improvement.

Think about this: It is impossible to be in the presence of another person and *not* make contact. Even in total silence, in open hostility, in any effort to be left alone, there is contact, however tenuous or strained. Sitting next to a stranger on a plane or a park bench, there is always an atmosphere of awareness, even without verbal communication. Add words and feelings, realize how many people relate from beneath masks they try to keep invisible, and think of the many options for contact which we enjoy —and which can motivate us as we try to move others.

Vicarious experience helps boost morale, so I'll conclude this chapter with a story I found heartening. It concerns an Eastern college dean who visited me in California to discuss setting up a workshop program in his hometown. He arrived at lunchtime, checked into his hotel, and proceeded to the large restaurant where he sat alone. Nearby he noticed three men in animated conversation. Casually he approached their table, with drink in hand and a smile on his face, which is a blend of Richard Burton and David Niven. "Excuse me," he said cordially, "would you mind if I joined you just for the company? You all sound so congenial."

Before he could offer another word of introduction, one of the three stood up, tossed his napkin on the table, and hissed fiercely at the dean, "You damned people from L.A. are all alike! I'm getting the hell out of this place!" With that, he left abruptly, followed by his two companions, all of them glaring as though they had been kicked in the shins.

"What did you do then?" I asked. With a wry smile, he told me, "Well, I saw three other men at another table, and slowly—a bit more cautiously—I made the same request of them."

"What happened?" I asked with hesitation.

My friend smiled and responded, "They said, 'Yes, please sit down and join us,' and introduced themselves. I spent the time very pleasantly and I appreciated even that brief contact with some of the natives."

The dean had refused to accept the first rebuff as a token of his own inadequacy, and, like the rider who is thrown, he got back on the horse. He had both confidence in his ability to make positive contact and motivation to continue his quest for simple social exchange. It is evident that he had been successful in meeting strangers in unfamiliar surroundings before, or he might have retreated and perhaps brooded alone, or, at best, withdrawn to ponder ways of amending or improving his approach to launching the first four minutes with complete strangers.

4

VARIATIONS
OF THE
VERBAL THEME

Words, words, words. We rely heavily on verbal communication for first impressions and long after. Although we usually react to someone visually (even for mere moments) before conversation begins, words are the medium for our most important contact perceptions. Here, therefore, are additional variations on the verbal theme, examined separately, though they often overlap and support one another.

ROUTINES OF CHAT

At Contact workshops some people ask, "Which verbal mode is best for most occasions?" Just as there is no best way to make love, I believe there is no best way to make contact effectively with another person. If there were, it would soon become a monotonous formula. How you feel about yourself, someone else, or the specific occasion affects the choice of modes you employ, and your words are dynamically affected by facial expression, tone and inflection. Think of the verbal mode as a vehicle: how it is driven, at what speed, on which side of the road, how good are your turn signals, is your mental engine tuned— these are far more significant than the brand name of your oral chariot.

Before dissecting "chat" into categories, I want to share some thoughts by Hugh Prather in *Notes To Myself* (Real People Press, Lafayette, Calif., 1970), which seem to crystallize the feelings of many people:

At first, I thought that to "be myself" meant simply to act the way I feel. I would ask myself a question such as, "What do I want to say to this person?" and very often the answer was surprisingly negative. It seemed that when I looked inside, the negative feelings were the ones I noticed first. Possibly I noticed them because of their social unusualness; possibly they stood out because acting negatively was what I feared. But I soon found out that behind most negative feelings were deeper, more positive feelings—if I held still long enough to look. The more I attempted to "be me" the more "me's" I found there were. I now see that "being me" means acknowledging all that I feel at the moment, and then taking responsibility for my actions by consistently choosing which level of my feelings I am going to respond to.

Not everyone is sufficiently in tune with "self" to make conscious choices of the "me" presented to strangers or intimates. You may have a flash of personal intuition in which you almost see yourself on a movie screen, talking, initiating, reacting. In such moments you *sense* the way you are projecting certain facets of your personality to someone else. Such insights are valuable to any contact.

A friend once told me, "At a party where I had good reasons to feel at ease, I could feel myself responding to an attractive man with what I'd call 'cool intimacy.' I wanted him to know he was fascinating, but I needed to give the impression of my own verbal competence as well.

"There have been times when I feel haughty or removed from a crowd, but that evening I was close to humanity, and my urge for articulate give-and-take was strong. We were immediately talking about feelings, and I enjoyed being conscious of his appreciation that I was sexually attractive, too. Verbally and nonverbally we challenged each other, but not as if it were a contest.

"I found out later that Michael (that was his name, and we're now close friends) caught the exact 'me' I was projecting. Sometimes you have to imagine how others see you without being able to verify it. Lately, I know how I'm coming across in initial contact."

This woman improved her contactability by tuning in to herself and carefully listening to and observing others' reactions to her.

Do you sense your own wavelength when interacting with friends or strangers? It's a form of being self-conscious (but I don't mean shy). In this context self-conscious denotes *in tune with yourself enjoying the benefits of positive awareness*. I'll have more to add in a later chapter on self assessment on the analogous subject of role-shiftability.

Whether or not you consciously choose which facet of your "self" to be, there are various levels of sincerity and openness in conversation, which I have divided into four categories. Three of these are symbolized by winged creatures which represent flying at different levels of communication, from the skittish and superficial to increasingly rewarding and meaningful.

A *fly* flits about, is hard to follow, practically weightless and usually quite annoying. A *sparrow* is hard to touch, but has an air of friendliness in its cautious manner. A *canary* is a domesticated bird with a sweet song; it allows occasional proximity, but offers only unpredictable friendliness.

Can you sense which creature represents your most frequent conversational flights? How often do your words soar above sincerity?

1. *Fly-chat:* This term describes the lightest, most shallow chit-chat, including social amenities such as, "Nice weather we're having," or "Aren't the draperies just beautiful?" Fly-chat has little meaning or personal relevance, but typifies conversation born of incidental necessity, unnourished by involvement. When you are fly-chat-trapped, courtesy is probably a seemly social necessity. You may also perceive nonverbal signs that reveal the encounter will soon evaporate without a trace.

2. *Sparrow-chat:* One step above fly-chat, this is a

somewhat more genuine form of communication, showing a moderate interest and involvement. It's the sort of conversation you have with a neighbor you see occasionally, or a friend with whom you've never developed much affinity.

The depth of sparrow-chat may suit an occasion, or it may indicate a reluctance or an ineptness about being more open.

3. *Canary-chat:* In this stage you begin to give or get the feeling of involvement. You are tuned in to a degree, but you may sense a few sprinkles of superficiality. Particularly, canary-chat connotes a semblance of *feeling*, below the surface of mere chit-chat, which could inspire you or another to seek more depth in due time.

In another shading, John Powell, S.J., in *Why Am I Afraid to Tell You Who I Am?* paints a sensitive picture of tentative exposure this way: "There is some communication of my person. I am willing to take this step out of my solitary confinement. I will take the risk of telling you some of my ideas and reveal some of my judgments and decisions. My communication usually remains under a strict censorship, however. As I communicate my ideas, etc., I will be watching you carefully. . . . I want to be sure you will accept me. . . . If you raise your eyebrow or narrow your eyes, if you yawn or look at your watch, I will probably retreat to safer ground . . . . or worse, I will start to say things I suspect that you want me to say. I will try to be what pleases you."

And finally:

4. *Nonchat:* The ultimate step on the verbal stairway to friendship and intimacy, nonchat means you are in touch with genuine feelings of being together. The elements of flightiness are grounded. You sense that someone is listening and trying to understand; that you are involved, if even for a short time. You are accepted—and you accept—and you share the excitement of entering into another's mind and emotions while yours are being explored at the same time. Such a blending does not always imply full agreement, nor does easy agreement always

mean real rapport and trust, but the way is open for all three.

Hugh Prather expresses this so well, saying: "For communication to have meaning it must have a life. It must transcend 'you and me' and become 'us'. If I truly communciate, I see in you a life that is not me and partake of it. And you see and partake of me. In a small way we then grow out of our old selves and become something new. To have this kind of sharing I cannot enter a conversation clutching myself. I must enter it with loose-boundaries. I must give myself to the RELATIONSHIP, and be willing to be what grows out of it."

Granted, we all chat from time to time. However, the leap from empty chatter to full-scale verbal contact *can* be made in a mere four minutes. Those of us in whom life has developed a certain mellowness leave a bit of ourselves as we absorb something of others while investing the effort to really make contact, even if it's brief.

INTRODUCE YOURSELF

People are lonely because they build walls instead of windows. Show me a person who claims he or she has *never* been lonely, or has never longed to meet somebody and muffed the opportunity—and I'll show you a person who needs more windows. Loneliness can be anyone's curse, but from it can spring the positive and progressive urge to make contact. Listen to the words of today's popular songs if you want a sampling of the sentiments to which a large number of people are responding. Though there is some monotonous repetition, there is also great poignancy of longing, and stark descriptions of men and women, young and old, failing to communicate.

Of course, satisfying our emotional needs in a healthy and fulfilling way has never been—and still is not—hopeless. I believe anyone can find, or nurture, the courage and motivation to make the most of his or her best aptitudes. Whether you seek the services of a computer-dating organization, or initiate contact on a one-to-one basis, a combination of courage and awareness are the main components of your do-it-yourself introduction kit.

"Courage," said Winston Churchill, "is the first of human qualities because it is the quality which guarantees all the others."

I believe that courage is all too often mistakenly seen as the absence of fear. If you descend by rope from a cliff for the first time and are not fearful to some degree, you are either crazy or unaware. Courage is seeing your fear in a realistic perspective, defining it, considering alternatives and choosing to function in spite of risk.

Whether you are single or married, attractive or plain, rich or poor, young or old, you may face opportunities without feeling you are prepared. Keep in mind that everybody has felt something of the same fears and reticence at times.

Let us investigate do-it-yourself techniques for self-introduction with settings such as apartments, parties, cruises, encounter groups and clubs. For some people, the single world is a bonanza, a happy hunting ground, but for others it is a hangup because there is stiff competition. Some people may be more aggressively competitive than you care to be, but you can still often make effective contact with the ammunition you may already knowingly possess.

The goal here is self-introduction, for personal or professional reasons, when nobody else will do the honors. Mainly, I want to stress the mood and attitude you convey. You can be a magnet, even of low power, to attract someone else into conversation. Your mind and body can be charged by a positive self-image, by pride in your appearance, voice, education and other personal assets, and by an ability to convert quickly the image and fantasy of thought-feeling into the reality of action-conversation.

No matter how secure other people may *seem*, almost everyone is eager to meet new people for friendship or intimacy. Most everyone also harbors a fear of rejection or exploitation which leads people to launch into new contacts somewhat cautiously. As Bach and Deutsch put it in *Pairing*, when people "find a potential intimate, they want to get insight rapidly into what sort of partner he or she will make, and how to convey something of their genuine selves to him or her at once. In other words, they want to know how to make intimate love begin with a stranger."

All acquaintances were once strangers, and every new contact is a kind of test and challenge. You may be rejected, and you may learn how to reject gracefully. If you are rejected, it is like paying a premium on an insurance policy which will protect you as you gain more contact experience.

It is probably easy to think back to a time and place where you were reluctant to introduce yourself to someone—and that moment was lost. Your fears, for whatever reasons, may be stronger than your eagerness to make contact. In the past you could not be sure which opportunities would have been fulfilling, but you *can* determine to venture today and in the future.

Following are a number of items to help you apply your built-in, do-it-yourself introduction kit. You are free to rearrange and modify them in order of personal importance:

1. Talk. Period. It is the most important rule of self-introduction.

2. Show genuine concern about others in a way that indicates something special about them. Offering compliments, listening intently or asking for information all demonstrate interest in the other individual. Defenses begin to melt when people perceive the message, "I am interested in you."

3. Remember the three P's: *Positive, personal and pertinent.* A positive approach is a magnet; a personal touch lends a feeling of intimacy; and pertinent conversation assures a here-and-now hook-in.

4. In loneliness you are not alone. Everybody is looking for involvement in friendship, business, love or sex. Take your pick. I have rarely met a person who does not have room for another good friend. Have you?

5. Other people are more likely to respond favorably

when you approach them directly and honestly. If you do not turn somebody on, at least those who are aware and sensitive will usually make it evident in a pleasant way.

6. Almost everything of importance in life involves taking risks. If a contact is disappointing or aborted, the experience of a self-introduction that did not work out is unlikely to undermine your whole life. You'll still be alive and well, hopefully ready to make new contacts. Strangers are very unlikely to slug you, spit in your face or call the police when you attempt conversation in a social situation, or even in an airport waiting room. Rejection is transient. You can easily rationalize that it is easier to be turned down by somebody whom *you* might have wished to reject later, than by a close friend or loved one.

7. The worst you can feel, when a self-introduction does not come off, is temporarily injured pride, or a minor dent in your self-esteem. Listen to Hugh Prather in *Notes to Myself* (Real People Press, 1970): "Because the results are unpredictable, no effort of mine is doomed to failure. And even a failure will not take the form I imagine. The most realistic attitude for me to have toward future consequences is 'it will be interesting to see what happens.'" A pleasant social success is delightful padding for an extrasensitive ego.

8. After a self-introduction, do not be distracted by figures or fancies. Do not start checking your hair or your shoes instead of listening or talking. The best conversationalists have a knack of ignoring the clock or outside pressures, at least for the initial few minutes. Even a dull person who introduces himself to you may take on a different aura in the spotlight of your total attention.

9. Even though a smile is nonverbal, its place is within the conversational territory. A pleasant expression, a grin, a real smile puts your best face forward. Later in this chapter are some pointers about jokes and humor, for now, remember that a laugh begins with a smile, which need go no further to be effective as a friendly response or quiet come-on for the conversational novice and veteran alike. While some people may fear becoming entangled

in their own words, a smile defies such hazards, and may draw verbal communication from others that helps set you at ease to start or continue talking.

Psychiatrists, social scientists and clergymen, who daily delve into the complexities of human contact, believe that loneliness is *the* malady of our age. Loneliness consists not so much in not knowing others as in *not being known* by others. But with a smile you begin to tip off your identity, whether you or another is lonely or depressed, and by that much you have enriched the atmosphere between yourself and strangers.

There's a song that says, "Let a smile be your umbrella," which is a pseudo-negative way of suggesting that bad news may be deflected by parting your lips and showing your teeth. Outwardly, this gesture may help, but I'd rather imagine a smile as the prow of an ice-breaking ship making its way through potentially hostile surroundings. Smiling creates goodwill and promises many things, in both reality and fantasy.

10. Say or ask something that will project some aspect of your personality, and will provoke response. Some people have a way of stimulating conversation; it may be sexy but not blatant, informed but not pretentious, interesting but not egotistical. Aware conversationalists leave an opening for you to expose yourself. In four minutes two people can make each other feel comfortable and accepted—even without ulterior motives. Try to avoid questions that can be answered yes or no, rather phrase your questions to give the other person a greater freedom of response. For example, contrast "Do you like Chicago?" with, "What do you like about living in Chicago?"

11. Men, come on gently and accent your sincerity. As Eric Weber says in his book, *How to Pick Up Girls* (Symphony Press, 1970), "Remember . . . nice guys finish first." A girl or woman who is alone may feel that the unsolicited advances of a man, especially in public places, are a veiled invitation to sexual fun and games. Even if her intuition is correct, a conversation can begin if a man uses finesse and is warm and friendly.

If you use compliments, be sincere and try to find something to praise which the person may not have heard innumerable times. You may also search for a way to make contact with humor, rather than choosing a compliment. Look for an emotion or a crisis you have in common and offer understanding. When you reach out to give, chances are you will also receive.

12. Women, a pleasant hello from a stranger is not the prelude to vulgarity or rape. Listen a moment, as long as you have not just met in a dark alley. Maybe he is as lonely as you have been.

You might consider at times such as these the provocative words of Dory Previn as she sings the last verse of "Scared To Be Alone":

> I think perhaps tomorrow
> I'll try to make a friend
> To really get
> To know him
> Instead of pretend
> I'll ask him if his feet hurt
> Has he burdens to be shared
> And if he doesn't walk away
> I'll ask him
> If he's scared
> And if he doesn't walk away
> If his eyes don't
> Turn to stone
> I'll ask him
> If he's scared
> To be alone.

The burden of appearing "forward" is still being borne by the American female. Consider a subtle approach; overhear a conversation in which you join; ask for a light; make a casual comment about the wallpaper or refreshments. Or simply open with direct honesty, "Hi, you look interesting. My name is . . ." No red-blooded male will reject such a contact, even if his wife is watching. It won't take you four minutes to add the impressions that you are *not* (a) going to drag him immediately to bed, (b) on the make for a free dinner or a ride on his sailboat or (c) desperate to marry and quit your job. Even if all these are true, the tactical female (and her male counterpart with parallel missions) need not reveal her ultimate motivations until—much later. Depend on it, the average unattached male without immature hangups will respond within the framework of your approach unless he has just been released from prison or is still living at home with his folks.

Using any self-introduced technique, try to be creative and inventive. Be direct but tactful; be positive and as revealing as seems appropriate. Don't invent a lot of fiction you'll have to retract, and don't try to be slick. Above all, don't apologize for making the contact in the first place.

The art of contact takes practice. A journalist friend of mine told me he is rarely uptight in any professional or social situation, because he has confidence in his reception based on meeting people for twenty years or more. He agreed, however, that practice cannot prepare everyone for anyone. In other words, the variables of human communication make perfection impossible, and probably undesirable. Self-confidence and sincerity are the ideal bases for meeting new people. When your own ego is comfortable, you can say in the face of rejection, "It's their loss."

In the process of developing the ability to meet people, feelings of awkwardness come from anxiety. If you are nervous, you are too involved with thinking about the impression you make. Too much concern with the mechanics of contact can undermine the assets you *have* developed. If you are inept at first for whatever reasons, in four minutes you may sense this and conclude the contact as gracefully as possible. If you tend to be somewhat phony or excessive, the other person will probably feel it and fend you off.

Once you learn to approach people openly and honestly,

and have been accepted often enough to start building a foundation of self-esteem, you will instinctively feel you are okay. In taking the risk, you give the impression that you like yourself, which helps improve a stranger's self-image.

Remember the four C's to self-introduction:

1. *Confidence* in yourself.
2. *Creativity* in what you say.
3. *Caring*—give four minutes of your total attention.
4. *Consideration* for the other person as an individual.

Successful contact requires that you be familiar with the meaning of your own motives as seen or assumed by someone else. If you are lonely, it may show, but if you are not trapped in a shell of self-pity, honest vibrations of *needing* contact should bring empathetic response. If you are moved to exploit another person, even unconsciously, and for whatever trivial reasons, it is likely to be noticed, and perhaps rebuffed.

I am reminded of an anecdote from a *Time* story (February 28, 1972) about Liza Minelli, who, as a young girl, stayed up to mingle with guests at her mother's (Judy Garland) parties. Judy often invited Marilyn Monroe because she felt people treated her "rottenly" and, Liza recalled, "Marilyn talked to me a lot, and I remember knowing why; because no one else talked to her. We were really good friends when I was about ten. She used to tell me how lonely she was. I told her that she had to talk with people and let them know she didn't want anything from them." How's that for irony!

Especially if you're lonely, meeting someone new can be exciting, so approach self-introduction with a sense of discovery, not of disaster. Why miss opportunities when you know that being positive, pertinent and personal may trigger a like response from someone whose need is similar to yours, no matter what you assume? Your assets should potentiate the adrenalin of courage. Learning to introduce yourself is like exercising a muscle. The more you do it, the better it works.

THE THIRD PARTY HOOK-IN

Being introduced by someone you know to somebody you don't know is a customary way of making contact. It happens all the time, and is often accompanied by phrases such as: "He's an old friend of mine; we were in the Navy together"; or "Mary, this is Jack. You've both been to the Netherlands and loved it, though I think Jack was there a year before you were."

When descriptive information is passed on about yourself or another person, the initial grounds for conversation are established. You almost always begin at that point. If the talk wanes, you usually switch to another topic to keep things going—if that is your urge. Introduction by a third party is often comfortable, because it offers a kind of script to follow, which can be a security blanket if you are still building self-confidence. It is the technique used on blind dates when two people are drawn together by a mutual friend who is certain you have something in common.

By following some of the techniques of self-introduction mentioned previously, you may also draft a third party into service either by asking him or her to make the introduction, or by hooking-in to two strangers, one of whom appeals to you. For instance, at a party:

You: Excuse me, but I heard you two talking about the Involvement Center; have you both been there?

First Man: I have, but I don't know about Phil.

Phil: No, I've only read a couple of books about sensitivity groups. Have you been there?

You: Yes, a few times . . .

In moments you introduce yourself and have a conversational ball rolling. Of course, it is not always so easy, and some individuals may resist being interrupted, but the same social graces, warmth and honest projection that can make self-introduction a pleasure instead of a task operate in this situation as well. Even the most confident conversationalists may be ignored as third-party intruders. If others do not extend the courtesy that you might under the same circumstances, try one more polite thrust to make a connection. If that seems unacceptable, politely excuse yourself and leave. Venture elsewhere.

As a third party, don't try to dominate the conversation at first, unless convinced your words are immediately fascinating to others, and that everyone is tuned in effortlessly. Be more subtle; let someone probe your mind and interests for starters, until you are clearly accepted and no longer the outsider. At that point, four minutes will have passed, and you can run with the ball in whatever direction the goal posts seem to be.

Whatever you do, don't interact as the third party with alibis or "pity signals" about people ignoring you, or your response will be an unspoken, "No wonder."

FIVE CONVERSATIONAL DELUSIONS

If you hope the first four minutes will be the prelude to something more, there are several myths or pitfalls to keep in mind:

1. *Advice:* People do write to Dear Abby because they want counsel, but, as a psychiatrist, I have discovered that unsolicited advice is rarely appreciated. How often have you been given little tidbits of guidance by strangers about your business, love life, or any subject under discussion, and come away feeling rewarded? It seldom happens, and for the same reasons that *you* may have felt inundated by self-appointed experts, you should avoid being one yourself. A flood of helpful hints about how to run your life is usually presumptuous, often off target and frequently a turn-off, especially during initial contact with a stranger. Advice that is less personal, about travel plans, apartment hunting, department store sales or things equally unemotional, may be safer to offer, but stop at a sign of boredom or resistance.

When somebody *asks* for advice, that is a different matter, but even so, it should be given sparingly. If your help is acknowledged, you feel comfortable to continue and to share your information or experience.

Close friends may volunteer advice during the opening of a conversation, because there is a framework established for give and take. Love and friendship thrive on intermixing parts of our lives, but good lovers and good friends know how to pose advice while rationing it. Even friends meet pitfalls, as illustrated a few years ago when a friend told me he was buying a new home. His words and tone indicated the decision was made. I kept my minor reservations about the house to myself. I could not be certain he was making a mistake, and his enthusiasm led me to be reticent.

Weeks later he told me that after careful thought he had decided not to buy the house, after which I told him about my previous doubts. His anger with me was surprising. "I'm disappointed," he said, "because if you had told me before, I might have realized it was a mistake much sooner." I explained that he had not asked for advice, and I had assumed the die was cast. He said he assumed an old friend would give advice unsolicited. Fortunately, this is a rare occurrence, and I note the incident to point out that between good friends a certain amount of counsel may be appreciated, even when it is not asked for directly.

On a business or professional level, whether you are talking to a barber, a shirt manufacturer or an attorney, try to resist the temptation to make suggestions about hair styles, clothes, or esoteric points of law. As Barbara Walters wisely points out, "Most advice is criticism, and criticism from someone who cares is hard enough to take. Criticism from a stranger is rarely appreciated, rarely followed and rarely stimulates good feelings between people."

2. *Questions:* Perhaps you have spent four annoying minutes with someone who came on socially like a public opinion poll or a market research interviewer; his questions hardly left time for your answers. It is normal and acceptable to ask identifying data from a new contact,

plus questions to clue you in on more than name, rank and serial number, but limit your interrogation to essentials. Avoid personal queries at first, if you feel they may be considered prying. Of course, a nosy inquiry can be posed in a humorous way, and be answered in the same light vein.

Behind most questions there is a statement. Consider rephrasing to make your inquiries more welcome and provide your partner with responsive "elbow-room." For example, "Where do you live?" becomes "I'm interested in where you live"; or "Do you like champagne?" can be something provocative such as "I like champagne, and I hope you do, but three glasses can knock me on my ear." Listen to prospective questions in your mind and decide if they might pay off more effectively as assertions.

In *Notes To Myself*, Hugh Prather speaks tellingly about the delusion of interrogation: "If I want to communicate with you," he says, "I must keep you informed of my feelings. A question often hides my feelings. It is sometimes my attempt to discover your position before I reveal mine, or it sometimes hides a criticism I don't want to risk stating. If I ask you, 'Why do you say that?' or 'Is that what you really think?' I show you little of what I am feeling. Instead, I put you on the defensive without making clear what it is in me I want you to respond to."

3. *Silence:* Talking and listening are both essential elements of good conversation; silence is not golden except when you are being a good listener. Shy people are sometimes advised, "If you're not clever at talking, you can compensate by being a good listener." You can't take that literally, for a worthwhile contact requires a meaningful give and take. Prolonged silence may unmask you as a one-way radio: all receiver and no transmitter.

The "good listener" is always a welcome social asset, when certain limits are observed. Even the most relentless talker will find an obsessively cocked ear oppressive and boring. Most people enjoy talking with others who offer conversational feedback. Some contacts are stimulated by jockeying for verbal supremacy, and are challenged to direct the talk to favorite subjects.

To gain the attention of interesting people, you must offer some verbal magnetism of your own. Learn to please the ear as well as the eye. Words pave the way for non-verbal communication.

4. *Fact-flinging:* You may have heard someone remark (about their inadequacy in the conversation game), "I don't know what to say—I don't have many facts at my disposal, and other people seem to be so well informed." This is usually a deceptive excuse for lack of confidence caused by other personality problems.

Any knowledge you have is an asset to conversation. By contrast, incessant fact-flinging is usually a bore and can easily label you as pretentious. Certainly, good conversation includes factual give and take, but not to the exclusion of talk about personal experience and feelings. The latter are the essentials for friendly or loving relationships between people. Don't be a one-volume walking encyclopedia which has limited value. Be a multi-volume human being.

5. *Self-focus:* People love to talk about themselves, and you may get high marks for encouraging them at times. But they also want to hear from you. I am sure you are familiar with the boor who dominates a conversation opening with a personal outpouring that usually has no mutual relevance. Many older people fall into this pattern, recalling the past with an eloquent display of non sequiturs. More youthful types may simply be egocentrics, fascinated with the sound of their own words.

When you walk away from contact with a self-centered new acquaintance who offered no chance to "get a word in edgewise," it can be akin to feeling robbed. If you failed to volunteer something about yourself, you are also guilty of at least a misdemeanor.

Overwhelming verbosity is comparable to blood flowing unchecked from an open wound; however, nobody wants to stick around with a tourniquet to stop the flow. Neither party to an initial contact should feel cornered by a barrage of words nor a frustrating silence.

Another brand of self-focus is to pretend authority in an area where you have no real depth of experience or knowledge. It should not be a handicap to admit not being authoritative; people feel good about explaining things they know well. However, the person who invades the beginning of a conversation with a mixture of facts and opinions that seem superficial soon sounds like a fool. You, or someone else, will see through his facade. If you want to be part of an exchange beyond your ken, ask a few questions. Don't apologize. People will respect your honest approach.

It is also annoying when somebody tries to switch attention to himself in the presence of famous people, by (a) asking about others even more famous, (b) trying to establish contact with silly remarks to show his own accomplishments, or (c) outright adulation which has to appear somewhat phony. Even celebrities enjoy being admired for themselves, and most of them recoil from a trivial attempt to find friends in common or from attempts of an egotist to grab the spotlight.

Writing in *Cosmopolitan* magazine, (July, 1971) Veronica Geng offers this: "Now, one last word applicable to every conversation, whether you're chatting with Mr. Big or a high school chum—for heaven's sake, stay loose! Keep reminding yourself that conversation is not an information-retrieval test or a tournament of witty sallies; talking is just a way of making comforting noises while we try finding out, in ways often mysterious, what we really want to know about each other!"

FACTS vs. INVOLVEMENT

In general, all communication between people has two purposes. One is the gathering, sharing, giving and receiving of facts. The other is the establishment or continuation of emotional and personal involvement. Fact-seeking and involvement-seeking intermingle in widely varying degrees, depending on who is talking to whom, where, when and why.

Because this book is devoted to techniques of communication, I make the above distinction to underline the point that *meanings* can be clear or cloudy, in verbal or nonverbal contact. For instance, remember the recorded dialogues of Mike Nichols and Elaine May? Their words tumbled and their facts were coated with humor, but, primarily, they sought involvement and the fact-seeking was secondary. Did they project realistic feelings to each other, or to the listener? Were the meanings of their words open to interpretation? Listen to them again, if you can, for the answers will not be the same for every reader.

A letter can be one example of fact-seeking or sharing with minimum emotional involvement. Business letters are often called "impersonal," though a personal hook-in is prevalent today, especially in advertising and promotion when the writer (whose signature is printed on a form letter) seems to care about you and your problems. Involvement sells, and a love letter, at the other end of the spectrum, can be the proof. Words of love on paper have tangled many a couple into the marriage knot!

Whether spoken or written, communication is always open to interpretation. "What did he mean between the lines?" is asked of a letter or written message. "The real message of his speech was unspoken," is a common comment in politics, for instance.

Though people are more apt to communicate initially on a factual level rather than in emotional terms, in most contact situations especially with one's spouse, children or in social and business encounters the significant role of communication should be involvement-seeking. Using a chemical analogy, it might be said that language is the medium in which human contact is suspended and contained.

Many activities draw people together, from playing bridge or tennis to attending a meeting. Within the sharing of these experiences, enjoyable human relationships are the primary goal. If they are not now, they should be, for even if you intend only to gather facts, some projection of personality will assure more satisfying success. Verbal communication can be mechanical or it can be touched with warmth, followed by physical contact or nonverbal interchange as well.

The conversational medium is not the message; the relationship is the message, even if feelings are initially disguised. The cool fact-seeker is disconcerted when confronted with an involvement-seeking situation. A corollary to this is the difficulty of showing your feelings with somebody who wants to remain insulated.

I have seen many intelligent, sophisticated individuals who have difficulty chit-chatting. Some explain that they choose not to because it seems so meaningless. "I don't learn anything yakking with people at a cocktail party," one may say. Others with a bit more insight will explain in private, "You know, I wish I could chit-chat, but I have trouble making light conversation. I just don't know how, so I'm usually very uncomfortable in social situations."

This indicates that someone has learned the fact-seeking function of language well, but lacks the awareness and/or skills to make verbal contact lead to the joys of involvement—even if it's minimal. "Involvement" may have overtones that seem threatening until one has the self-confidence that comes with actually being involved.

Ramifications of involvement-seeking are treated in Chapter 6 under a topic I call Sensory Involvement. With this term are the many shadings of sexuality which draw people together during a four-minute contact and beyond. Of course, there are some people who skillfully evade involvement by focusing others' attention on charm or verbal glibness, like a magician distracting his audience while his hands prepare a trick for delivery. However, the magic that I am talking about is that which radiates from our senses of the sight, sound, smell, touch and, perhaps, taste of another person.

5

TO THE
CONVERSATIONAL
NOVICE

This is addressed to beginners, to people who are exceptionally shy, and not to individuals sophisticated in making contact and communicating with people in an effective way. For readers who are inexperienced in the social scramble, a conversational guide can help ease you into comfortable communication. The following suggestions for the novice are not magic formulas, but they can stimulate temporary security while you prepare to engage with others and become more relaxed.

Your preparation, however, must be dynamic, meaning that it changes continuously according to your lifestyle. Otherwise, people may feel that you have memorized a script. You should soon realize how to vary and enhance these items and update them.

1. Search your mind for at least three interesting, stimulating or exciting things that have happened to you recently, which you feel others will appreciate hearing and can identify with. Choose incidents which are complimentary to you without having to brag. If you need to, practice telling these stories briefly in front of a mirror, and then to a close friend or relative. Keep in mind that many people find emotional and physical hazards colorful, especially if you have braved them successfully. Be careful that exaggeration does not make you sound ridiculous.

2. When you hear a joke you like, jot down the punchline, or try to remember it. You need not copy the traveling salesman with a whole repertoire of comic repartee, but inserting humorous stories, or referring to something

funny you read or saw, can be an apt lubricant to smooth contact. Caution: Although this is listed as a suggestion, joke telling involves a risk, timing is critical and there is no absolute formula. If an attempt at humor is not communicated with a certain ease and grace, it is usually better untried, for it may serve to increase, rather than decrease, distance.

Practice, because being humorous is one of the most difficult communicative skills to master. It is akin to learning another language. Freud characterized humor as a rare and precious gift, and Thomas Hobbes spoke of humor and laughter as "sudden glory." Humor always has an element of kindliness and respect for human dignity; some wit or cynical comment may lack those qualities. Humor conveyed smoothly triumphs over your anxieties, fears and foibles.

Marcia Davenport offers an appealing description: ". . . by humor I do not mean the capacity to be funny. I mean that breath and tolerance, that warmth and ease, that gleam of cynicism without which an understanding of human nature is impossible and without which we are devoid of the power to see ourselves, even in fleeting glimpses as others see us."

Humor is a useful contact tool, and a most desirable channel in the complex network of human intercommunication.

3. Things you read in books, magazines or events of general interest are all excellent springboards to conversation. If you've only read a *review* of a book, admit it. Keeping up with fact and fiction is beneficial, whether you intend to discuss them or not. At the right moment, you are ready. Try to keep current with at least one "best seller" every two or three months. How you read a book is important. I suggest you read not only for enjoyment, but also for recollection. Try to remember—even jot down—incidents or special points in an appealing book. Keep in touch with your own attitudes, opinions and feelings as you read.

4. There is an enormous amount of public identifica-

tion in movies today. Everywhere you will hear real people and events compared to characters and plots seen on the screen, both theater and TV. Since cinema offers a slice of life, make a point of seeing outstanding films, because familiarity with them offers a means of verbal connection. Remember, if you are viewing a film for discussion background, you need to retain more than if diversion is your main goal.

5. Current events are excellent conversation-starters. It is de rigueur to keep abreast of newspapers and magazines, TV news and in-depth programs as preparation for mixing in social or business circles. Choose one important current event of maximum interest to you, whether a political crisis, a prison riot or the current drug-abuse scene, and make it a point to be able to talk knowledgeably on that issue. Do not ignore other topics, but know the score on one or more. People will enjoy hearing your thoughtful views, and sharing theirs with you. If others are less knowledgeable, do not turn them off by acting superior, such as by saying, "You mean you don't know about . . ." Share without pontificating.

6. You are likely to hear a person's name within the first four minutes of meeting him or her. Remember it; use it several times in conversation. Most people are flattered that you picked it up quickly, and most like to hear their names. Calling someone by name indicates that you are interested in him, that you like him, that you are aware of him as an individual.

7. Make an effort to learn something interesting or important about the other person's life. See if you can discover things or accomplishments of which he is proud. Talk about these points. If you hear someone has been on a trip to Europe, or anywhere you have been, pick up on it, identify with it and share the experience. An interchange seems certain, unless your conversational partner is a complete egotist.

This list of things people talk about is endless, and everyone enjoys expounding on his own thing. At a recent gathering I recall discussions about children, a Ph.D.

thesis, a new wine from California, fantasies about sex, and how crowded Waikiki has become. No matter what the topics, sharing information and feelings makes you and former strangers feel closer. When you pick up this vibration, it increases your confidence to initiate further involvement.

8. Try to stay calm. That is easy to advise and sometimes difficult to achieve. If you stay with the here and now, and have prepared some of the other pointers in this section, you will dilute your anxiety. Fear itself is your biggest enemy. Ignore what may happen in the near future, and do not make an inventory of mistakes you might have made, or of personal hangups such as your prominent nose or receding hairline. Instead, make an effort to *relate*. Keep your eyes on the other person's eyes and face, stay with the flow of talk, enjoy the sight and sound of *that* person before you.

If you appear anxious and uptight, it may turn others off. Make a herculean effort to control the butterflies in your stomach, and concentrate on the conversational moment at hand. Think involvement and it can help wipe out thinking fear. If panic still prevails, try to postpone it, or admit aloud that you are nervous, without self-condemnation. This may just endear you to some protective type of person.

Look around the next group of friends and/or strangers you encounter. Notice that the dominant, self-confident individuals seem calm, while the uptight unfortunates scratch their heads, tug at their noses, lick their lips, flutter their hands or do something that signals their tensions. Such activities are distracting and make others wonder if a person has something to hide or is just scared. If you are a jumpy sort, get a firmer grip on yourself as you practice conversation contact. Be aware of your own tension signals.

9. Here are a few conversational openers on which to improvise your own phrases to help build confidence out of chaos. If these appear to you to be trite suggestions—

good. Those who are at a total loss for simple opening phrases may say:

How's your day going? How did your day go?
What's happening? What's new?
Do you know what I learned (or did, or saw) today?
You really look good today! (only if they really do)
I really like your . . . (select something specific)
What would you rather be doing now?

10. Start now. Emerson said that consistency is the hobgoblin of little minds, which may be so, but procrastination is the bugaboo of the whole human species. "I'll start tomorrow," is the stock remark of the person "going on a diet," and tomorrow rarely comes. Only now, in the present, before the urge to put it off gets any stronger, can you start reading more books, learning the finesse of good humor, seeing movies, practicing in front of a mirror or begin polishing any of the techniques that catch your fancy because you believe you can make more successful contacts—and thereby be more appreciated, and less alone. In the process you become better aware of yourself, and perhaps drop a few of the facades that even you realize are pretty transparent.

Fritz Perls once said, "Friend, don't be afraid of mistakes. Mistakes are not sins. Mistakes are ways of doing something different, perhaps creatively new."

I can add, when you *listen* to your mistakes, you grow.

Today's novice is tomorrow's veteran—if you have the courage to try. As you take risks, smile, give of yourself, listen and respond with feeling as well as facts. New contact experiences are near at hand.

6

NONVERBAL CONTACT

Across a crowded room a pair of eyes set in an attractive face seem to be sending an invisible beam your way. He or she is a stranger—but not for long.

A close or intimate friend or relative sits slumped with head resting on open palm. He or she seems dejected. Though neither of you have spoken, you are aware he needs comforting.

The child is questioned directly about a missing wallet or a broken vase, but he only averts his head and turns away, anxious to retreat.

All the above, and a whole vocabulary of *kinesics* (the study of body motion as related to speech) are modes of nonverbal communication which account for at least half of all contact between people within four minutes or longer. Julius Fast called kinesics *Body Language* in a book of that title (M. Evans and Co., 1970) which deals with understanding nonverbal communication. Fast notes that "our nonverbal language is partly instinctive, partly taught and partly imitative." Only recently has the importance of nonverbal encounter come to be appreciated, and the basics related to contact are within this chapter. A subordinate category that includes grooming, dress and scents is covered in Chapter 8.

We have dealt at length with the meanings and the uses of words, which are obviously quite dependent on the accompanying attitudes and expressions of the face and body of the speaker. Contact may *begin* nonverbally, but it is rarely limited to sight and touch, for words and actions are as interwoven as threads in a fabric. Though the real significance of one's spoken word is sometimes difficult to determine, the body language is not as aptly disguised, and understanding it abets communication.

Though Fast divides the body into specific parts, each with its own subtle actions, I will deal with larger anatomical sections since whole sections of the body—head, eyes, nose and mouth, for example—usually act or react in unison. Of course, the actions and motions of the entire body communicate a great deal to us, and must be considered congruous (or incongruous) to the verbal message delivered or received. For instance, a parent may shake a judgmental finger at a child, and with a stern face be saying, "You know I love you, but . . ." This nonverbal attitude is incongruous with the word-message, and the child is most likely to respond to the parent's stance (body language), rather than to the words he hears. It is easy to see that the most meaningful communication occurs when both physical and verbal expression reinforce one another and present the same statement.

THE BODY SPEAKS

Clearly, *the eyes* are our primary medium of nonverbal communication during the first four minutes of contact. Visual encounter can be direct or subtle, and depends on the length and depth of gaze, as well as use of the eyelids. Great attention is devoted to the eyes in our culture, including makeup (shadowing, false lashes, eye liners, and even change of color using contact lenses). Racks and racks of spectacles are available so we can "decorate" or accent our faces with flattering frames. Far-out sunglasses as big as dessert dishes are not uncommon these days. In other words, to make a pun on parliamentary procedure, the eyes have it.

Julius Fast notes that there are various formulas for the exchange of glances, depending on where you are and what sort of contact you wish to effect. In simply approaching someone on the street, you may alternately focus on his or her eyes and look away when you are within eight or ten feet of one another. Before that time, if collision seems possible, each of you is likely to signal to which side he will turn. Passing is accomplished smoothly after glancing and veering in that direction. During this kind of encounter, Dr. Erving Goffman in *Behavior in Public Places* (Free Press, 1963) says that a darting look and lowering of the eyes is body language for "I trust you," or "I'm not afraid of you." To strengthen this signal, you look directly at the other's face before turning away.

"It's impolite to stare," is a tenet of our culture's social etiquette. Julius Fast tells us that a gentleman is not supposed to look steadily at a woman longer than a few seconds, unless she gives him license with a smile, a backward glance or a direct meeting of eyes locked to his. It is also inappropriate in America for two men to stare at each other for more than a brief instant, unless they intend to fight or seek closer rapport.

Among other eye-to-eye conventions is the look-away priority. If you find someone staring at you, it is his responsibility to look away first. If he doesn't lower his eyes, and you maintain the visual engagement, then you begin wondering what he has in mind. At the same time, you are aware of whether the contact feels personally agreeable or not. This situation may become embarrassing or annoying, or it can be enticing, depending on time, place and person. Certainly, the mature person with a well-developed self-image can make more of initial eye-to-eye contact than the shy individual whose interior doubts make direct behavior threatening. Also, a conducive setting for any meeting which begins with a steady, open gaze is as great an influence on our reactions as the appeal of the visual contender.

At times, following conventions is less fitting than heeding instincts which move one to verbal exchange. Of course, there are a number of other qualifying factors which automatically modify a choice, such as appearance, projected mood or warmth, and specific emotional needs of the moment. Sexual or sensory connotations are hard to define verbally, but they are undeniably there when eye contact with a stranger is a potential challenge.

A meeting of the eyes may start in motion a fast train of assumptions. "He was undressing me with his eyes," is an old expression, or "She seemed to look right through me." Eyes appear to be warm, liquid, bright, darting, mysterious, penetrating or revealing—all words on the worthy fiction writer's list to endear or expose his characters. A person accomplished in eye-power is likely to appreciate other forms of sensory contact as well—without many hangups.

Once people are talking, they look at their partners less often than when they listen. To look away while speaking is natural, as topics shift and thoughts are collected. A pause while glancing away usually means an incomplete phrase, signaling, "I have not yet said all I want to say; don't interrupt." However, looking away while listening may signify, "I'm not completely satisfied with what you're saying. I have some reservations." However, it could indicate habit, nervousness or lack of interest in the person or subject under discussion.

Just as the hipbone is connected to the thighbone, eyebrows are linked to the eyes. Eyebrows raised and lowered, plus a smile, may show agreement and interest. The same movement accompanied by a frown could mean puzzlement, surprise or disagreement. Eyebrows lowered and eyes narrowed might be considered seductive; added to a slight squint the signal could be intense interest, or perhaps even dislike.

A wink without a smile usually says, "I've got a secret," but a wink-and-smile combination is a come-hither look. Eyes narrowed in a frown may indicate suspicion or caution, while wide open eyes accompany pleasure, surprise, agreement or disbelief. A movement of the eyes up with brows furrowed for a brief period often implies thinking, but without furrowed brows the gesture could connote disinterest, or a ho-hum look. A quick eye movement, perhaps with a hand to the head or a shaking of the head, may denote an expression such as "Oh, no."

The movement and expressions of eyes tell us about people more graphically and dynamically than a seductive perfume or a neat haircut. Unless we *look* at others as we experience life, we miss the potentials of nonverbal communication. We may see things, scenery or abstract humanity at a distance, but we don't really see others with whom we interact. The physically sightless must develop their abilities of touch, and their perception of voices and sounds becomes enhanced, but those of us who are sighted may enjoy the full advantages of eye-power. But only if we look! You need only look "over there" at another human being, friend or stranger, to realize the implications of a single glance. Multiply that look by four minutes and you may preview many of the pleasures and problems of a lifetime.

These reflections about the power of positive seeing are meant to provoke thought about your own or another's feelings and mental perceptions. They are only guidelines, not absolute rules, and they may change from culture to culture or as time passes.

Let's consider the nonverbal cues of *the head* before we examine its other components in detail. A single nod says "yes" or offers specific agreement, while a slow, repeated nodding indicates encouragement or more general affirmation. Nodding is an invitation to continue talking or action, a technique which therapists often use with patients. A nod may also mean, "Yes, I'm listening, though I don't necessarily agree or disagree, but do go on." Swayed side-to-side, a head movement says "No," or "I disagree." However, a slow sway of the head could also signify, "I'm not sure I understand what you're saying."

Confronted with a rigidly held head and stiff neck, particularly combined with a blank facial expression, one is unlikely to make effective contact unless extreme loneliness, curiosity, challenge, danger or sympathy are the motivation. However, a tilted head may show curiosity; combined with come-on eyes, it would be coquettish and seductive, particularly as a feminine gesture. With eyebrows raised and/or eyes narrowed, a tilt of the head signals disbelief. A sudden jerk of the head backwards while frowning may imply disagreement, or without the frown, surprise. In contrast, a forward lurch of the head pulled back quickly means, "I've got your point;" but drawn back slowly, the gesture may mean a growing interest and acceptance in you, or by you, or even amazement.

Though *the nose* contributes to facial communication, it adds a secondary and sometimes humorous component. To wrinkle your nose and maintain that pose for several seconds usually indicates dislike or even a malodorous situation. It is usually a spontaneous reaction, as is a quickly wrinkled nose accompanied by a smile and a direct look. To someone of the opposite sex this gesture says, "You're cute," or "Hi." To "lift one's nose in the air" is a sign of haughtiness. Holding your nose with thumb and forefinger indicates "it stinks," a sign that seems unique to our culture, and one that is learned by assimilation rather than by instruction. In fact, many of the winks, nods, shrugs, glances, nudges or leers of body language are similarly learned by reflecting other people.

At this point I come to a phenomenon which I find both amusing and provocative, but for which I have found no specific origin or explanation. Let's investigate what I call the personal debris syndrome.

In the presence of others it is rude to pick one's nose, ears or a corner of the eye, and during the first four minutes of contact with a stranger this faux pas is an avoidable blunder. However, I have discovered there is a remarkable and seemingly cultural format to the personal debris syndrome. It seems that most people cannot blow their noses, pick at their eyes, forage in their ears or pick their teeth without then looking intently for a moment at the "gem" they have discovered. This phenomenon is poorly understood, and may hark back to man's primate heritage when keeping clean must have been a recreational diversion.

I might facetiously suggest that if one insists on continuing this common (in a dual sense) behavior, perhaps one could make it trigger further contact by sharing the examination of the gem with the other person. (He or she may be able to produce debris equally as precious or even larger than yours!) From that point of intimate disclosure, one might develop a very meaningful and close relationship based on "common" interests.

Except for the eyes, *the mouth* offers more variety of nonverbal communication than any other feature of the body. Remember "making faces" in the mirror as a child? It was your mouth that changed most readily to make you laugh or feel sad. A partial list of mouth messages: tightly pursed lips, with a slight grimace show determination or anger; a gentle grin denotes agreement or a favorable impression of someone or something; open-mouthed laughter is indicative of joy and happiness which is often contagious; and the smile comes in as many models as a popular motor car, from the mini or compact size, to the medium easier-to-maneuver model, to the full-sized luxury expression that envelops you softly and warmly.

A turned-down mouth communicates disapproval or sadness in any culture. Smiles and tears are also universal symbols. From Alaska to Zanzibar a picture of children and parents smiling or crying together signifies the same thing. They are either happy or they are suffering. We are all born with certain forms of nonverbal communication such as these, while others are learned, as mentioned before.

Like legions of songwriters, I am tempted to rhapsodize about the connotations of the smile, because it is the lubrication for words and the collaborator of the eyes in contact. A halfhearted smile may turn people away quickly, but a smile that exudes warmth and positive response is a magnet. Smiles can be misleading, but they can lead, as well, to some very lovely interchanges with strangers and friends alike.

The kiss is a welcome form of nonverbal exchange, when the mouth offers a wordless message that is sometimes open to stimulating interpretation. In the first four minutes with a stranger a kiss is unlikely, but friends and intimates enjoy kissing as part of hello and goodbye. People who kiss often and deeply do so for pleasure, but inner moods can be sensed or expressed by the variation of lingering kisses. Couples who wish to be closer can let each other know via lips and tongue, and intrigue is often initiated by a kiss that is more intimate than expected. When two people kiss, and one or both respond with less than usual enthusiasm, it is often a signal of unspoken disturbance. In healthy relationships, verbal communication will be used to probe for the reasons.

A man who kept a diary while involved in group psychotherapy shared this pertinent excerpt with me:

I asked the women if they feel their bodies are precious. I noticed while this was going on that peoples' mouths were betraying them. The tight-lipped, pursed-mouth people were all pent up and rigid, and the loose-lipped, easy-mouthed ones were open and exploratory. One woman never stops smiling; I can't stand that. What's going on under that fatuous defensive smile—not that I care about her and her problems, but I have to observe that she isn't letting anything through. Think I'll start a new science: mouth reading. Here we go again.

A person's *shoulders and trunk,* among other things, communicate control and self-esteem. Stooped shoulders and posture are a well-known indication of diminished self-image (the most typical exceptions are stooped shoulders caused by physical disease, or by occupations such as dentistry or shoeshining). A chest thrown forward and a backward tilt of the shoulders shows pride, self-confidence or even narcissism. Shrugging the shoulders is a clear symbol of "I don't know," while a swing of one shoulder with accompanying head motion says, "Come here," or "Come with me."

Body build, as in football players or other athletes, or the well-defined leg muscles of a dancer, can be a clue to profession, though a broad-shouldered man of more than average height may not be rugged nor well-schooled in self-defense. While a man's shoulders and trunk may communicate indefinite signs about his personality or disposition, a women's chest is usually given sexual connotations in our society. The cult of the large bust, thrusting breasts, or well-formed bosoms is fundamental to our fiction, movies and other printed media. Not only are full, shapely breasts considered definite symbols of active, joyful, even aggressive sexuality by both men and women, but the latter are prone to accent the breasts in keeping with current fashion, whether their feelings about sex are forward or timorous, in order to be "with it" in the social or business whirl.

A photographer friend of mine who has shot nudes and pin-up pictures for years coined this phrase for his models: "The thrust of the bust is a must." He knows as well as you and I that the nonverbal message of a woman's breasts is open to as varied interpretation as the smile on her face. However, in these times of increased sexual freedom, women are apt to emphasize the breasts by wearing deep-cut blouses or dresses, natural-look brassieres or no bras at all, a phenomenon we will examine more closely in a later chapter.

Hands and arms can communicate receptivity or inner tension or rejection. When upper arms are held closely against the sides of the chest or arms are clasped in front of the chest, there is projected a closed feeling, a standoffishness. In contrast, free and spontaneous movement of the arms, wrists and hands enhance communication, signify openness and self-confidence, and can indicate a nonverbal welcome short of embrace during initial contact. Excessive movement of hands, arms or trunk can signify restlessness, insecurity or a certain sense of immaturity in adults. Minor versions of these actions in young children, when they may be just random motions, are without specific interpretation.

Open hands versus closed hands may disclose a person's feeling of receptivity, as well as strength, firmness, conviction and poise. In a portrait photograph a man is usually asked to close his hands to denote masculinity rather than spread his fingers, while a woman's hands are open to symbolize femininity.

In some people, crossed *legs* or *ankles* while seated typify an uptight individual, but in others these attitudes may merely manifest relaxation. Women have always made a conscious effort to keep their legs and knees together, or ankles crossed, and with the advent of the miniskirt it is even more reasonable and appropriate. In fact, in a recent medical "discovery" known as the "miniskirt syndrome," muscle spasms and pain in the upper legs are attributed to ordinary efforts to maintain modesty by miniskirt wearers.

When a man sits with legs open or spread, it may indicate a sense of personal freedom, sloppiness or just casualness. Of course, tightly crossed legs in a man may simply mean that he has a full bladder and is waiting for the right time or place to seek relief. I want to emphasize again that body language simply provides a basis for making reasonable assumptions and not for concluding facts.

A fund of fantasy has been accumulated about the position, shape and degree of revelation of women's legs, just as there are sexual connotations about the size and shape of breasts. A woman wearing slacks has approximately the same lower trunk freedom of movement as a man, though certain unfeminine poses are considered uncouth, where a man would not be criticized. However, the shape of a woman's ankles, calves and thighs, which send sexual messages to many men, are disguised, regretfully or charitably, in pants.

The nonverbal sexual implications of bare legs, or legs in sheer hose when a woman wears a skirt, are basic to male fantasies. Legs are classified according to the woman's age, the degree of revelation, the shape and position of the legs and, of course, the concomitant attitudes the owner of the legs projects. A young girl (from teens to early twenties) in a short skirt with "good" legs (a relative term you'll have to define for yourself) that she shows casually almost to "the limit" is not necessarily signifying any single message about her sexuality or openness to intimate contact. Personal freedom, based on experience and sexual self-confidence, may be indicated, but it is not certain. Some young ladies simply enjoy the feeling that their legs are being admired; others, however, make sure their legs are well revealed to be attractive—in order to attract.

A more mature woman in a short skirt, or with skirt high enough when sitting to show off her legs, may also not be an "easy mark"; she may be signaling a sense of physical well-being, that she appreciates her body and likes others to do likewise. The girl or woman whose body seems "precious" to her, as the diarist wrote, is likely to keep pulling her skirt down in order that no one get "a birds-eye view of the promised land."

In other words, a woman's legs, as well as her breasts, can express sexuality in our permissive society, and you might examine your own attitudes and/or fantasies. Is the nonverbal information you deliver or receive appropriate to your own state of sexual evolution and sensitivity? Are you likely to misread or be misread? Do you realize how dynamically important the body can be in the impressions it offers during the first four minutes—or the assumptions you make which may be accurate or simply derived from literary images?

The feet also speak in body language. A rapid up-and-back movement when legs are crossed can display impatience, nervousness or boredom. Some people are prone to play "footsie" under tables when verbal communication is restricted, but the messages from foot pressure and movement must be analyzed according to time, place and personalities. "Footsie" can also be damned annoying, in the manner of groping hands making unwelcome overt assaults.

The *whole-body* posture of frequent and excessive shifting or twisting can denote discomfort, boredom, impatience or irritation. A young child who rocks back and forth in a stable chair can be showing signs of underlying emotional problems, while an adult might be signaling indifference during a verbal exchange. Some people who are fearful and nervous cannot disguise their trembling, which in business or social situations is indicative of illness, extreme insecurity, anxiety, or perhaps even the use of certain drugs.

In contrast, a rigid body posture may reflect an effort to conceal feelings of fear, or show inhibitions above and beyond the requirements of time and place. "Hang loose," is the common expression to someone whose doubts of the moment may seem overpowering.

EATING AND DRINKING

In our society, how someone imbibes food and drink communicates quite a story nonverbally. People eat in ways that evince coarseness, gentility, good or slothful manners, presence or absence of education, social status, timidity, aggressiveness, and even highly charged sexuality. The latter was dramatically illustrated in the classic scene in the movie *Tom Jones,* where lust and seduction were openly implied as Tom and a recent female acquaintance gazed at one another across a table while swallowing raw oysters, sensuously gnawing turkey legs, and otherwise making dinner symbolize mouth-to-body contact.

Real-life men and women who cannot enjoy instant rapport via a cinema script can yet convey a great deal of their feelings about one another and their own self-images while dining together. They exchange visual expressions while they watch methods and manners of eating or drinking. How one sips or gulps water, wine or other beverages may be subtle dramatizations of such statements as "I am well-bred," "I'm my own man," "I'm shy," or "I intend to get drunk." How one seasons food, asks for the butter, handles his napkin, or chooses a fork mean more than just knowledge or ignorance of good manners. These may seem like superficial symbols, but many people are unaware of their habits and behavior and don't realize they are being silently evaluated—either positively or negatively.

At my workshops on Contact, it is now traditional to bring sack lunches which participants are requested to share. I recommend that those who neglected to bring food be invited by others, at random, to share their food as a source of contact and interchange, while everyone is expected to exchange morsels with anyone who wishes to accept or trade. If the way to a man's heart is through his stomach, the way to anyone's esteem or affinity may open with as simple an involvement as offering or accepting a couple of grapes or a bit of cheese.

THE POWER OF TOUCHING

Every time you pat someone on the arm or shoulder, you are sending a psychic message such as "I like you," "I agree with what you're saying," "You have done well," or "All is well; don't worry." If you back off from someone's touch, the hand-off gesture is as strong as any words. Touching can be intimate, and sexy as well. But in initial contact, in the four minutes when friends or strangers exchange tokens of their own well-being, the power of touching is limited—but dynamic.

In *Intimate Behavior* (Random House, 1972) Desmond Morris comments that one of the several reasons why adults are inhibited in the expression of physical contact stems from the need to avoid "sexual implications." He notes, though, that "the basic urge to touch one another remains, however, and it is intriguing to study how we go about this in our day-to-day affairs outside the bosom of the family." He believes we "formalize it. We take the uninhibited intimacies of infancy, and we reduce them to fragments. We set up rules of etiquette, and we train the members of our cultures to abide by them."

In some ways this is a shame, because most people enjoy being touched-and respond to it affirmatively. For maximum benefit, touching must be aptly and carefully timed. A man touching a woman on the upper arm during first contact can enhance and catalyze their meeting beyond the possibilities of mere verbal communication. If his timing is off or this body language is misinterpreted, the woman may be turned off and will endeavor to keep a certain distance between herself and her "aggressor." A touch on the arm or a caress of the cheek, for instance, speak a world of words, but carried beyond a few seconds, the message may become antagonistic.

Although most people enjoy being touched and respond well, whether they admit it to themselves or not, it takes a perceptive and sensitive person to know within the first few minutes with a stranger the right move at the right time to accomplish better intimacy. Touching can break invisible barriers between people where words fail. A handshake comes first, but a lot more can be said with the hands. Psychiatrist Bruno Bettelheim says, "The ability to experience touch as pleasant must precede any human relation." In a perceptive article about touching in *Cosmopolitan* (July, 1971), writer Laura Cunningham notes that former President Lyndon Johnson once said: "I must feel a man's skin to know him."

Miss Cunningham makes some telling points about the significance of touching:

> Not to touch would be not to live. You spend your whole life reaching out for people, animals, and objects that delight you—and cringing back from those that repulse you. . . . Edward Hall, a Northwestern University anthropologist, maintains that a girl can feel heat radiating from a sexually aroused (or angry) male standing *three feet* away! He also says you can tell a good party from a bad one *through your skin* (clue: the good parties feel warm

because of the excitement they generate. . . . Touch is the razor's edge between life and death for infant human beings. . . .)

We are taught to hold ourselves in—to avoid contact if possible. Don't you say "Excuse me" if you accidentally brush up against someone?

In various cultures, Miss Cunningham points out, attitudes towards touching are strikingly different. She notes that Florida University psychologist Sidney Jourard observed couples sitting at cafes in four cities. "In Paris the average couple came into physical contact 110 times during an hour (and they were just having a conversation!)" In San Juan, Puerto Rico, couples patted, tickled and caressed 180 times during the same interval; but the typical London couple never touched at all, and Americans studied patted once or twice in an hour's conversation.

Touch *will* bring you closer (physically and emotionally), so loosen up, warm up, touch more, try *not* to shrink back. Most important, don't wait for people to approach *you*. The power of touch lies in its being generously proffered—be the first to offer contact and you'll not often be rejected. . . . Touch, after all, is the most *intimate* of the senses. Use it to your advantage! It isn't enough to look, sound, and smell—even *taste*—nice. The most powerful impressions you make will be by touch.

I fully agree with this sensitive advice from Miss Cunningham.

Between strangers, acceptable touch may first be transferred to material objects. For example, a woman tells a man she likes his jacket, and then strokes it gently and seductively, commenting on its softness. A man may exclaim about a girl's lovely earrings, or a locket, or a pin, and ask to touch it. In each case, the object may be a surrogate for touching a part of the other person, which may come about in due time. However, if a man reaches for a piece of jewelry tucked into the cleft of a woman's breasts, he may be considered vulgar or intrusive if their relationship is new and untried. "How you react touchwise in your social life is plenty important to your sex life," Laura Cunningham warns. She adds that the less inhibited you are about touching and kissing in a social setting, "the more fun you'll have in bed. The *best* lovers are those who are extremely *tactile*. They *adore* the feeling of other people's bodies, and aren't ashamed of their own."

A new countermovement in psychotherapy has been sparked by Paul Bindrim, a clinical psychologist who deals directly with problems of touch in his nude therapy groups. Basically Bindrim approaches contact through the assumption that "the more you're repressing, the more is brought out by skin contact and real warmth and closeness with others." Closeness in his context excludes "overt sexual expression" which is defined as any sexual activity which would be unacceptable in a group wearing clothes. In his groups, talking, touching, hugging, or even wrestling are encouraged to help people experience their own senses as well as sensory contact with others.

When we touch someone or are touched, there is usually a feeling of admiration, of desire to communicate beyond the veil of words, behind the touch. Though strangers may be suspect in most hand-to-body contact, physical embrace among friends and intimates is more widely accepted in our culture today, as it has been in European societies for generations. Says Laura Cunningham: "A more exuberant form of touch is the hug, a gesture reserved for people you know very well. (You *can* hug someone when you're introduced for the first time, but he'll probably be stunned and back off.) It's a great way to let a good friend know he (or she) is special."

It has long been acceptable for women to hug one another as part of a greeting, and it is now becoming more common for men to do so as well. This has been engendered in great part by the encounter group movement, and it is being eagerly accepted by our younger generation.

Men and women involved in friendly or intimate relationships have hugged each other for generations. Physical embrace between men and women who know each other only casually is not only acceptable, but is acknowledged as highly desirable.

How people hug, how long they continue the embrace, and where they touch (face, hair, neck, arms, back, etc.) indicate nonverbally the intensity of their involvement. Accepted touching or hugging between newly acquainted people may reveal to both that a closer relationship is possible and desirable. How a husband hugs his wife—and kisses her—when he returns home from work may stimulate the affection they feel for each other, or it may frustrate and annoy either of them when response is disappointing. In parallel, how an adult hugs a child may tune him in or turn him off. The key is to pay attention to the child's response to the hug, and responded accordingly.

Though styles of dancing seem to be in constant evolution, even the younger generation today seems to be exploring the pleasures of slower, more intimate modes in preference to the separated gyrations of rock and roll. As I mentioned earlier, dancing is the only social situation in our society (except perhaps for some types of group encounter) when two total strangers, after an exchange of perhaps ten words, find it acceptable to move about and hug one another for a period of three minutes or more. There are just two prerequisites for the occurrence of this phenomenon: music, and feet in motion. When the music stops, or if the couple stops moving, it becomes a sticky situation for them *as strangers* to continue to hug in the presence of others. If the same two people who had never seen each other before were to meet while shopping, and he asked her, "May I hug you for three minutes?" she would like be embarrassed, insulted, or at least think he was deranged.

Dancing is one pleasant way of realizing the power and pleasures of touching. Holding hands can be even more persuasive, though opportunities during initial contact with strangers may be quite limited. However, even with casual acquaintances, a lot of warmth and various signs of intimacy can be transmitted by the amount of pressure and the nature of intertwining of fingers and palms. Without eye contact, you can show someone how you feel about him or her, or discover the same, before you ever have kissed and perhaps before any words of endearment have been exchanged. One may fondle another person's hand in a way that is quite acceptable and may be the prelude to beautiful familiarity. Try it, but stay in tune to the response you obtain or don't obtain and react to it appropriately.

Dr. Owen Williams, a dentist in Tucson and a friend since college, noted in a letter to us:

> I think we grew up at a time when society said it was bad to touch. I would have felt too threatened in college to have touched or hugged either one of you. Now we do it easily, freely and beautifully with expression and a great deal of meaning.
>
> I use touch in my practice. A reassuring touch on the arm or a pat on the shoulder tells a patient, "Relax, I know what you feel, I'm here, and I care."
>
> I feel sorry for people who are afraid to touch.

OUR PERSONAL AIRSPACE

Another important aspect of nonverbal communication is our personal zone: the space immediately around us or the varying distance between us and others. Do you understand how these zones are assigned, how you and others adjust to and even defend them?

Plants and animals require a certain amount of space around them for growth or personal security. People have the same needs, often intangible, but always present. No matter how open or crowded an area, individuals try to maintain a zone around themselves which is really a basic part of their individual human identity. It may sound odd, but your physical identity includes more than just your anatomy and the clothes which cover it. Identity includes an airspace around you, and if certain zones of that space seem to be violated, you may react (or expect reactions from others) in ways which are similar to how you respond when threatened by touch. How we deal with these zones of airspace is integral to our contact relationships with others.

Anthropologist E. T. Hall has defined four distinct zones or distances relative to most people:

1. The intimate zone—our own faces and bodies plus a few inches. If you stand too closely to someone, just inches away, you are invading a part of them. At least psychologically, we feel we *own* some of the space around us, for both comfort and security reasons.

2. The personal zone, where you can be close to someone in what may be termed a personal distance, for conversation perhaps, but intimacy is not invaded.

3. The social zone—a few feet perhaps, in which you can interact with someone appropriate to time and place.

4. The public zone, in which you are not close to people but are aware of them.

Notice that intimacy increases as airspace distance decreases—with one exception: To Hall's classifications, I have one of my own to add:

5. The ambivalent zone, or the airspace between people that is in doubt or dispute. As examples, the armrest between two movie or theater seats, or the space into which you tilt an airline seat, also "owned" by the passenger behind you. Armrests may be shared by alternate use, or fought over in a bickering sort of way. I'm sure that armrests and tilted airline seats have also become contact modes for people who turned dispute into rapport. Elevator space, bus or subway standing room, and other public places also present ambivalent zones, which are dealt with according to the character and personality of the individ-

uals. Four minutes could be the start of a pleasant relationship that starts with a potential dispute.

Incidentally, it is an interesting experiment to sit next to someone in an area where you might have planted yourself many feet or yards away, say in a park with lots of empty benches. Watch the other person's reaction. This kind of exercise is part of the practice of *stepping out of role*, which is not only fun at times, but can be very useful in teaching you more about yourself and others. I have an excuse when I step out of role because I am always "researching modes of contact." I may sit beside someone for a few minutes, and then turn and explain my ploy, asking for their comments. In hundreds of such incidents, I've never had anyone refuse to level with me. They tell me how they felt when I sat down, and this approach has led to some fascinating conversations.

In considering Hall's theory of personal airspace, how is it relevant to ongoing or new-found contacts you make daily? For instance, married couples (or the live-ins who may be sharing space and each other temporarily) may have difficulty, about which they are usually not aware, in finding a suitable and mutually agreeable "arguing distance." In a therapy exercise, if a woman is asked to face a man and determine the spatial interval she would prefer if they were to have a heated argument, the distance between them will usually be several feet, somewhat beyond the possibility of physical contact. A woman's choice in the same exercise is often more distant than the man's. Yet in reality, couples often tell me, "He stands too close," or "She keeps backing away" when they're having a verbal dispute. Perhaps a woman feels a potential physical threat, and a man feels the alienation of too much space. In any case, while trying to work out a mutually comfortable distance, perhaps a couple's mode of arguing may be improved. I suggest you discuss this concept with your spouse—of course, at a time when you are not arguing.

In agreeable communication, couples may also analyze

the zones which they enjoy—and ones they may not harmoniously share. For instance, a woman once told me, "When my husband and I really get into a heavy conversation, I like to be close to him, even touching, but he seems uncomfortable. It's almost like being in bed when I may press my body against his, and he seems startled or reluctant at first." People may be unaware of why they feel uncomfortable or irritated, when really their emotional reaction is not related to the topic but rather to the distance between them. Often greater understanding develops between couples when they begin to define to each other the compatible zones between them during verbal communication, whether arguing or in agreement.

A minister once asked me to help him understand why his parishioners seemed to back away from him during their tête-à-tête talks. The man had a strong appeal from the pulpit and on the phone. He was a perceptive, cordial, knowledgeable man, but insensitive to the personal airspace of others. I watched him during the intermission of a meeting one evening, as he interacted with members of his congregation. Amazingly, he usually stood so close to both men and women that they were forced to retreat a few steps. I later explained what I had observed, that he was violating their zone of personal distance, uncomfortably close to their intimate airspace. He then realized his friendly proximity was not mutually agreeable, and after adjusting his stance to a personal, rather than intimate distance, people could then exercise their option to move closer to him. (I should add that this minister was not a victim of halitosis, a common curse that forces the widening of any person-to-person span.)

The intimate zone, and probably the personal as well, appear to be closer between women than it is between men or newly introduced men and women. However, the limits change as human encounter becomes more informal, less hung up on puritanical fears and phobias. Ponder your own zones of airspace required for comfort, and at the same time, observe how others move toward or away from you. A small shift during conversation can com-

municate increase of interest or the beginning of indifference; you can infer closeness and trust within someone's
personal zone if they stand pat and talk with their eyes
as well as with words. You may discover that your contacts need to be reevaluated according to the distance you
perceive to be agreeable between yourself and strangers or
lovers. Try standing closer and see if people back away, or
stand further away than usual and observe if your partner
steps toward you and reduces the space.

INTERPRETING BODY LANGUAGE

Nonverbal communication is rather like a code which
we must learn, analyze, refine, modify and enhance to
achieve more satisfying relationships. It is sometimes difficult to be certain that we know precisely what someone
means in words and sentences. Inflection can shade verbal
exchange positively or negatively. Add to this the combined messages of gestures, eye contact, facial expressions
and anatomical shifts; the mixture can be confusing and
lead to what can be called "a breakdown of communications."

When a listener disagrees with you, he may shift his
position or raise his eyebrows; he may frown, raise one
hand or open his mouth slightly. He is preparing to rebut
your opinions, but to what degree? Will his physical
gestures mean your contact is doomed, or perhaps through
mild controversy it will be strengthened? Compound and
expand the codes of nonverbal communication to national
and international levels, and you begin to fathom how
millions of people within one set of borders can misunder-
stand and mistrust millions of others under foreign labels.
I also believe that a portion of the problems between
various ethnic groups in our country is related to subtle
conflicts and differences, culturally conditioned, that
happen during contacts with each other. Many break-
downs of communication and misunderstandings seem to
begin at this initial point of encounter.

Both body language and spoken language must be

related and interdependent to deliver the full meaning and message between people or groups of people. Listening only to words can create distortion, and observing only gestures and expressions can be just as misleading. Have you ever tape-recorded a dynamic speaker or singer in a live performance, only to be disappointed to find on play-back later that it is not as exciting, amusing, provocative or meaningful as it first seemed? Personal presence is lost; the sound of words or music is coming from plastic tape and paper loudspeakers. Body language, the physical projection of words, is integral to the complete pattern of interaction—making contact and communicating.

Some people rarely see themselves in a mirror; they may look, but they don't *see*. I believe that the time spent and the way one looks at himself in a mirror can be a good measure of his own positive or negative self-image. Those who avoid mirrors except for minimal periods of grooming and do not gaze into their own eyes or observe their faces and bodies often seem to have a poor self-image. As the egocentric opposite, individuals who con-stantly stare at themselves in the mirror, primping and doing a modified ballet routine, either need a lot of re-assurance or are basically self-centered. Between these two extremes of mirror-users, there is a happy medium. We all need to look at ourselves intently, into our own eyes, at our own faces and bodies, periodically. How else can we evaluate and increase awareness of who we are—and physically what we want to be? As a therapist I often advise people to study themselves in a mirror a few min-utes each day, with and without clothes, changing facial expressions and trying various body motions, to help learn their personal code of nonverbal communication and to get "in touch" with their own bodies.

When two individuals look into the same mirror while talking to each other, they become aware not only of verbal give and take, but of their own gestures and gri-maces and whether they seem congruous or incongruous with the implications of their words. Many a mother has used this technique to show a dirty-faced child who is screaming or crying the truth of his appearance. It is more difficult to continue histrionic behavior when confronted with your own face! Married couples could benefit from this technique. In fact, I sometimes use it in conjoint marital therapy.

On occasion, I have asked patients to look in a mirror during a therapy session. They often exclaim, "I've never really looked at myself this way. I use a mirror all the time, but I've never seen *me*!" Have you seen *you*? Other people are trying to read your nonverbal code, and they'll be more accurate if you are more familiar with how it (you) looks to them.

TO DISCOURAGE COMMUNICATION

Words, gestures and expressions discussed to this point and hereafter are all used to enhance and encourage contact. There are times, however, when we deliberately wish to discourage someone's attention, a delicate matter of fact for sensitive people. But it *can* be accomplished both verbally and nonverbally.

Without finesse, one can say, "Go away," or "Get lost," or one can simply turn and ignore another person—all methods of hostile encounter used by intimates, unfortunately, but unthinkable in polite encounter. Most of us are unwilling to inflict damage or insult on another's self-identity, and we prefer to drop verbal or nonverbal "hints," hoping they will be received and understood.

My investigation has shown that few people are able to handle the turn-off situation effectively, either when trying to discourage communication, or in being rejected themselves. Most people are aware, however, that a lack of response or an obvious indifference through words or gestures sends the "I'm not interested" message clearly. To this, I will add only a few thoughts.

In his book *Awareness* (Real People Press, 1971), John O. Stevens points out that *it is impossible not to communicate*. He illustrates with a story in which a man writes, "I have written you 71 letters and have received no answer—this, too, is an answer."

Stevens continues:

> When a person refuses to express himself directly in words, or when his words are used to disguise rather than communicate, his voice, body, position, and movements often give a detailed statement. Anything that is not expressed openly seeks expression in other ways. We learn to lie mostly with our words and, to a much lesser degree, with our nonverbal expressions. We learn to lie somewhat with voice tone and facial expressions, but these nonverbal lies are usually caricatures of reality. . . . Our nonverbal expressions are usually much more honest than our words, and often there is a large discrepancy between the two. A man might say, "I'd like to get to know you better," while his shoulders lean back and his hands make small pushing motions as if saying "Go away." A girl might say, "I don't want to see you again," while her shoulders and hips wiggle in sexy invitation.

The art of discouragement in communication comes with practice. It takes empathy for the feelings of others and conviction about our own feelings to be left alone.

You want more significant contact with people, those you live with, and those you haven't met yet. Most nonverbal communication can be learned if there is willingness, openness and real motivation. We can learn to reveal verbal messages with more gusto and effectiveness and communicate with more accuracy in order to achieve intimate, social, and business goals. While we study the code—ours and theirs—we discover ourselves.

7

THE
HANDSHAKE

Except for the occasion when it is socially acceptable for two strangers to hug each other while dancing, the handshake is the first and sometimes the only body contact one makes in four minutes, or even in longer periods. Just as hands come in all shapes and sizes, the grasp of the hand can be firm and friendly, soft and delightful, moist and chilly, aggressively phony, or as incongruous as a paw or a flipper. The handshake is of special importance in initial contact with a stranger or a friend, between men, women, or one man and one woman.

It is expected that men shake hands when they first meet. Along with visual communication, the degree of firmness of the grasp, the duration and the type of interlock all form parts of a message. The way one hand responds to the other may indicate either a retreating or controlling nature, though the process is usually taken for granted and connotations are not recognized in the average meeting. Either party can terminate the handshake by loosening his or her grip, at which time the other usually makes a corresponding move. When someone insists on keeping your hand locked in greeting after you loosen your grip, it may cause embarrassment and annoyance. (In late winter of 1972 when President Nixon arrived in Peking, he engaged in some of the most prolonged handshakes with Chinese officials that have ever been seen in public. Whether his hosts' grips persisted, or the President wished to convey extra cordiality, we may never know, but the TV images via satellite left me with a distinct impression of an attempt to convey goodwill by both parties.)

Young boys are often taught by their fathers or other grown-ups "how to shake hands like a man." Instructions always include the stipulation that the grip be firm, if brief, conveying strength and friendliness without bone crushing, and release be in response to the other hand or self-initiated. Girls may be shown how to shake hands in a more dainty way with less pressure and duration. Business-women and most mature females today seem to prefer a firm handshake in natural response to the male world, though aspects of femininity often give way to expected custom.

Whether or not women should shake hands with men is still a question in the process of cultural change. This simple contact seems increasingly appropriate, though a proper ladylike shake is not yet clearly defined. Should a woman respond as firmly as the man? Should she offer just a finger-grasp or her whole hand? Is the woman expected to initiate the handshake, since man-to-woman shaking is still a confusing protocol? At any time a handshake between sexes seems expected, I recommend that a woman offer a moderately firm grip, keeping in mind that she is confirming her femininity rather than demonstrating physical strength.

As an example, some time ago my 13-year-old son and I met Mary Hemingway (widow of Ernest Hemingway) after she had given a moving lecture. We approached her to speak only briefly, and she reached out to shake our hands in turn. As we walked away, Ira responded, "That's the best handshake I've ever had from a woman. It was firm but ladylike."

Women shaking hands with other women also do so with the attitude that warmth and sincerity are expressed by limited but undeniable pressure. Sometimes women, when expressing feelings to other women during a crisis, do not shake hands. They soothingly hold the other's hands in theirs, while they verbally, and with facial expression, communicate their interest and concern.

On special occasions a greeting that includes a handshake is explicitly dictated by protocol. Sally Raleigh, writing in the *Seattle Post Intelligencer*, described her meeting with Queen Elizabeth II: "I knew what I was to say and do. I was to shake hands (gloved) and say 'Your majesty,' when I met the Queen and then Princess Anne. . . . The handshake was approximately one downbeat."

The original handshake of primitive times probably originated when men showed each other open palms to indicate they were unarmed. During Roman times, men grasped each other by the forearms; today the meeting of hands is a gesture that accompanies verbal interchange, though it may not be cordial. However, in ancient Rome the handclasp was used as a pledge of honor. Desmond Morris, in *The Disguises of Intimacy*, notes that the handshake "did not gain wide usage until almost a hundred and fifty years ago." He explains that "the cause of this change was the industrial revolution and the massive expansion of the middle classes." Businessmen and tradesmen were frequently "doing deals" and "making agreements" with a handshake. As industrial urbanization increased, the handshake invaded the realm of social greeting.

When people wish to show closer affinity, they shake hands with the right and grip the upper arm above the elbow with the left. This may be a welcome and closer form of contact than just grasping one-to-one. The "peace" handshake which appears to be increasingly accepted is also closer. The mutual grasp of thumbs is combined with a bending of elbows which requires closer physical proximity of the bodies.

A special variation is what might be called the "politician's" or "good friends'" handshake: the left hand covers right hands that are clasped, or left hand grasps the other person's right forearm or shoulder. This entanglement may be reassuring to close friends, but strangers usually find it a suspicious attempt at instant ingratiation.

Writer Steve Harvey made an interesting survey of the political handshake for the *Los Angeles Times* in which he quotes author Theodore White as saying, "There is something about shaking the hand of a candidate that gives people the feeling they are wired in to history, a part of it all." White classified people as "squeezers, supporters who look you in the eye," and "grabbers" who may come on suddenly and refuse to let go. Though some presidents have had to bandage their right hands after grueling contact with the public, Harvey discloses that Calvin Coolidge enjoyed hand-to-hand meetings, and opened the doors of the White House daily just before lunch to all visitors. Coolidge proudly claimed in his autobiography that "on one occasion I shook hands with 1,900 in 34 minutes." He added that, ". . . listening to their greeting was often a benediction." FDR terminated the Presidential open house, and often sent Eleanor to substitute for him after half an hour of handshaking at a reception. She became a master of the art, developing what came to be known as the ". . . Eleanor whip. With a quick flip of the wrist, Mrs. Roosevelt would guide each well-wisher down to the next dignitary in the receiving line."

James K. Polk headed off what he assumed would be bonecrushers by "seizing him by the top of his fingers, giving him a hearty shake." Harry Truman adopted the same strategy much later, explaining, "If you clamp down first, ahead of the other fellow, you'll never have your hands hurt." Dwight Eisenhower was known for his handshaking fortitude, but when his hand became sore, he simply wandered, chatting, among his guests. According to Theodore White, Lyndon Johnson was the most enthusiastic handshaker of recent Presidents. "He liked what he called 'pressing the flesh,' and would grab four or five hands at once in a crowd. Both Kennedy and Nixon were more restrained, according to Steve Harvey's account. "I don't believe either one liked to be touched," White said, adding, "Kennedy, especially, disliked the old habit of some politicians who would grab his collar while talking to him."

In a footnote on wholesale handshaking, Harvey says Teddy Roosevelt holds the White House record: in 1907 he shook 8,513 hands on New Year's Day! However, like so many other human endeavors, there is a world champion handshaker, one George Borkowski, a Briton, who pressed the flesh 37,750 times in 7 hours and 15 minutes in 1967, and Harvey adds, "He wasn't even running for office."

The one type of handshake which inevitably turns people off is usually termed "the dead fish." Whether the hand is dry or clammy, a flaccid grip connotes indifference, an impression that may be reinforced in far less than four minutes. However, a moist palm may merely show someone is nervous, a symbol which automatically eliminates any job applicant at at least one large company of which I am aware. Its personnel director once told me that regardless of the qualifications of a man he interviews, "If his handshake is weak and clammy, he's out." Such reaction to body language is probably far more prevalent than we realize, as others assume many things about our glance, stance, or advance.

We shake hands thousands of times in a lifetime, and it is unfortunate that most of us get little or no feedback on whether or not others like or dislike our handshake. In Contact workshops I direct large groups of individuals to circulate, shaking hands at random, being aware of eye contact, and grading the handshakes immediately. On a scale of one to five, one is the least meaningful and five is the most warm, friendly, sincere—even enticing— handshake-eye contact combination. After shaking hands and exchanging numerical ratings, people discuss the reasons for their opinions. Many are astounded because they have always felt their handshake was adequate and may exclaim, "A dozen people rated it 'one' or 'two.'" From this feedback, people have the opportunity to develop a more effective handshake that better conveys real feelings, while learning to size up others.

These workshops have also shown, through polling over 500 women, that the majority prefer a moderately firm handshake from a man. Interestingly, most women also felt that either sex should have the option of being first to extend a hand upon meeting or departing. The long-established custom that a woman should be the initiator of the handshake is disappearing. I feel this is appropriate and consistent with the current recognition of male-female equality. Man's superiority over women per se is rapidly becoming an archaic notion and if either has the option of offering a hand first, it is one form of confirming equality. In contrast, in the military the person of lower rank is expected to originate a salute in passing.

Even in the days when men kissed women's hands, the lady had to offer it first. Only an uncultured male or a raw knight fresh from dragon-slaying would grab her hand without asking permission or waiting for a sign from the lady. You recall that women were then clearly considered inferior and thus had control over initiation and acceptance of the hand-kiss greeting. There is also a parallel in the sealing of pacts; the weaker or inferior male usually offers his hand first. In a contest, it is usually the loser who offers his hand to the winner, which is both a sign of grace and an affirmation that the contest was won fairly. It also emphasizes a continuing bond of friendship or cama-raderie.

The evolution of the handshake protocol seems incongruous and odd. If the woman was inferior, why did *she* have the initiative? Because the man delegated it? Because men were such gentle lads? Because of the protocol of communication between sexes? I do not understand, but that's the way it was and still is for many.

We make contact through a handshake for numerous reasons; as a greeting, to say goodbye, to confirm a pact, to congratulate, to accept a challenge, to give thanks, to commiserate, to offer good luck, to end a disagreement, to comply with simple courtesy, and, as a corollary, to evaluate or take the measure of someone's anxiety or sincerity.

I believe that, excluding verbal or physical attack, the most rejecting insult one individual can offer another is to refuse to shake an outstretched hand. It is equivalent to spitting on someone. In fact, spitting on a spouse's shoe was part of the divorce ceremony of the ancient

Hebrews. I have seen movies that included both physical and sexual violence which did not evoke audience response as strongly as when one actor spit in another's face.

A handshake refused is so powerful a response that most people have never experienced it or tried it. Many of us may have had the discomfort of a hand offered and ignored because it was not noticed, or another's hand was taken instead. In such an event, you quickly lower your hand or continue to raise it until you are scratching your head, making furtive glances to assure yourself that no one saw! When two people want to shake our hand simultaneously, we may grab both, one in a handshake and the other in a kind of reverse twist of the left hand, which serves very well as a sign of cordiality and saves someone embarrassment.

Sometimes I think that if everyone treated others with the respect and sensitivity with which they shake hands, there would be far less violence and war. The usual give and take of clasping hands and shaking, and the immediate sensitivity to another's response, are truly beautiful.

As a parting shot, I want to share a short episode in a book called *The Desert* by Alan Wheelis (New York: Basic Books, Inc., 1969, 1970) where Aeriana and her lover are surprised one evening by the sudden presence of Aeriana's husband, Scott. As narrator, the lover explains, "I go down the steps, hold out my hand, saying, 'Hello, Scott.' He stares at the hand, then my face. 'But don't overdo it,' he says with calm malice. 'Hypocrisy is no doubt necessary, to lubricate the gears of society, but in moderation. No reason to shake the hand that plays with my wife's genitals.' "

8.

SURFACE
LANGUAGE

We are all born naked. Most of us have added clothes, decorative accessories, grooming and fragrances, which combine to become a secondary mode of nonverbal communication. Body language is usually of prime significance, but grooming and dress are not necessarily subordinate. They both give rise to what may be called the *surface language*, a pattern of immediate impressions conveyed by appearance. How these impressions are relevant, or influenced by the folly of assumptions, are the targets of this chapter.

Consider the nudist man or woman lounging at the edge of a pool, from which someone of the opposite sex emerges. He or she is pleasing of face and figure, and, if female, her hair is awash and her makeup almost dissolved away. If male, his hair is in certain disarray. This recent swimmer wanders over to the lounger and sits nearby. They introduce themselves and start to talk. As the wet person dries in the sun, he or she also finds the lounger personally appealing.

You may instantly surmise that a man would react primarily to the comeliness of a woman's body and face, while a woman would also intuitively compute the anatomy of a man and respond according to both intellectual and sexual conditioning. You may be thinking, "What a terrific advantage nudists have! No mask of clothing to distort an image, not even the veneer of a beauty shop to disguise nature." However, the entire area of nonverbal self-expression via grooming and dress is excluded. We clothe our bodies, style our hair, make up our faces or frame them in hats, groom our nails, disguise our natural odors with chemicals and even reshape our noses or breasts to conform with contemporary standards of allure and/or to reinforce the personal image we want to convey to others. We depend on this surface adornment, processed according to chosen lifestyles, or according to criteria that seem to create images we would rather project in order to augment (or perhaps overshadow) the sound of our words and the movement of our faces and bodies during the first four minutes of contact—and long afterwards.

Is your usual nonverbal communication through grooming and dress:

1. honest and congruent with your self-image?
2. primarily dictated by current style rather than personal taste?
3. aimed to complement your positive attributes?
4. designed to make others aware of you?
5. tailored to make you inconspicuous?
6. inconsistent with your basic self-concept and uniqueness?

There's obviously nothing wrong with dressing and grooming to please ourselves and to be attractive to others. However, no matter what our taste at the moment, no matter if the goal is camouflage, revelation or somewhere between, we should be aware of the impression we make. Even more important, we should realize that the surface appearance of others is computed in our minds and through our senses via assumptions as well as facts. Our freedom and control during initial contact with friends, and especially with strangers, may be highly influenced by our own dress and grooming.

To illustrate: In a newspaper article profiling a female social worker, the writer noted, "Miss ————, hard to picture in her present role, is pretty, vivacious and blonde. She could double as a model or an actress." I don't know this individual, and she represents only a prototype of beauty which may be amplified by fantasy into a possibly deceptive stereotype. In everyday fiction, blonde beauties with brains, or even blondes treated merely as sex objects, often switch roles to perpetrate nasty surprises on handsome heroes—and trusting readers. In real life we are also prone to rely on stereotypes, an addiction that can give a painful twist to initial contact.

Supporting and amplifying this thesis is an article by Ellen Berscheid and Elaine Walster in *Psychology Today* (March, 1972), called "Beauty and the Best." For several years the writers investigated the impact of one aspect of appearance—physical attractiveness—upon relationships between people. At first they "shared the democratic belief that appearance is a superficial and peripheral characteristic with little influence on our lives." Perhaps, they wrote, we have assumed in error that most people hold "internal attributes" as more significant than external attractiveness in making value judgments.

Drs. Bersheid and Walster discovered that "beauty not only has a more important impact upon our lives than we previously suspected, but its influence may begin startlingly early." Teachers of young children have admitted ranking pupils by appearance; the best-liked kids in class are often the most attractive. In the same nursery school survey, it was shown that parents "assumed that the unattractive boys and girls were chronically anti-social in their everyday behavior." These ominous expectations, were echoed in research on fifth-graders evaluated by teachers who assumed that the attractive children had higher intelligence, related better to others and were better candidates for the honor roll—though statistically the children were nearly equals.

Studies that prove surface appeal in children elicited special attention from adults were paralleled in further findings about college-age students. It was no surprise that beauty influences social relationships, the writers said, but physical attraction overshadowed the desirability of dates from a similar social level—at first. Eventually, young people introduced on blind dates tended to use wider criteria than just looks if they continued relationships. About this the authors decided, "Apparently, even in affairs of the heart, a person is aware of a credibility gap."

Continuing their investigation on the importance of physical attractiveness on popularity, Drs. Bersheid and Walster found that although men admitted valuing beauty more than women did, students of both sexes ranked intelligence, friendliness and sincerity first. Why the discrepancy? "Many students seem to believe that it is vulgar to judge others by appearance. They prefer to use such attributes as 'soul' or 'warmth' as bases for affection," at least when publicly polled.

In another study the authors found that young adults "thought good-looking persons were generally more sensitive, kind, interesting, strong, poised, modest, sociable, outgoing and exciting than less-attractive persons." That "beautiful persons" were considered "more sexually warm and responsive" is not unexpected, but it was also learned that good looks were expected to lead to better jobs, happier marriages and more fulfilling lives. To this they add, "If we believe that a beautiful person embodies an ideal personality, and that he or she is likely to garner all the world's material benefits and happiness, the substantial lure of beauty is not surprising."

Understandably, the article asks, "Is there any truth to these stereotypes?" To some degree, they assert, in that beautiful or handsome people have a wider range of social activity, more chances for contact, sexual experience, and, I might add, for acceptance, which helps develop a good self-image. However, interview data from women in their late 40s and early 50s showed, "The more attractive the woman had been in college, the less satisfied, the less happy, and less well-adjusted she was 25 years later." Husbands become disillusioned with their former reliance on surface charms, which tend to fade with the passage of time. In my experience, women, as well as men who place a high value on physical attractiveness to the exclusion of the development of personality, have serious difficulty adjusting to life in later years. But physical attractiveness is a significant standard by which we form our first impressions. The whole process by which political figures become products of media, subject to lighting, makeup and diction lessons, is one extreme example of how a human surface can be refabricated to impress masses of people.

Perhaps, the writers say, someone with a beautiful personality is also seen as more attractive than he or she actually is. Research did not show the source of our stereotyped images of beauty, but it is suggested that "it might be the instinctive nature of any species to want to associate and mate with those who are the healthiest of that species." Since health and beauty are not always synonymous, I might add that we are conditioned since ancient times by facial and anatomical symmetry celebrated by painters, photographers and today, advertisers. Artists might rightfully claim that personal beauty is judged by basic elements of design that are modified through time and cultures, but have not changed radically since history was first recorded. Taste about surface decoration *has* tended to fluctuate widely over the centuries, from the flamboyant to the antiseptically plain, but underneath, the structure of face and figure we call attractive has been consistently variable (from the "plump" Renoir beauties to the "twiglike" Twiggys—from "ice cream cone" breasts to flat chests to the "natural look.") Hence, perhaps, our preoccupation with surface language.

It has been my experience that how one reacts to specific physical characteristics, which might be considered outside of the usual range of attractiveness, can determine whether these characteristics become attributes or liabilities such as Theresa Brewer's voice, Jimmy Durante's nose and Goldie Hawn's giggle. However, I feel, it is generally better to enhance your attributes rather than attempt to change your liabilities into attributes.

In addition, I do believe that in many cases those not born with "contemporary natural beauty standards" try harder with both their physical appearance and personality—and do succeed.

FOR WHOM DO WE DRESS?

"Clothes make the man," is probably a slogan coined by the fashion industry, which at one time had most people convinced that some things were "in" and some were "out," and that if we didn't heed the temporal styles we just weren't "with it." Today it's not so easy to make predictions about people from what they wear. (Though you can still make some assumptions about their employment.) At the office a man may dress conservatively because it's expected, or it is appropriate to his work, but socially his style is "mod." Women seem to be less afflicted by conformity in the business world; skirts are short, midi, or long, and pants and boots are becoming acceptable even in the offices of blue chip companies. There is only a smattering of the no-bra look behind counters and desks, but women and girls in revealing clothes are quite acceptable in many metropolitan social and daily-life situations.

There is some reasonable evidence that nonconformity in dress indicates a casual lifestyle—which implies personal and possibly sexual freedom. This is hardly infallible, since taste may be based on current trends rather than values reflecting the intimacy an individual allows, enjoys or expects. Certainly, however, a square-looking person, someone dressed in hippie or mod style, a woman with ever hair in place or one with free-flowing hair, a man with beard and mustache, or a girl in hotpants, all paint pictures of personalities and lifestyles to which we react.

The colors of clothing, as well as design, can signify the ease or seriousness with which one takes oneself; most of us have favorite colors that may or may not become us. Much of culture has been rich in associations to color. Faber Birren, in his book *Color in Your World* (Crowell-Collier, 1962), points out that "a man sees red, feels blue, is green with envy or purple with rage. He talks of yellow cowards, white hope, black despair, pink tea parties and brown tastes. In his flags and emblems, religious rituals, customs, superstitions, he uses color as a reflection of his feelings, for these colors vividly portray the emotions within him."

Blue, red and green, according to Birren, are the colors most individuals prefer, and in that order. Red he feels is positive; blue, tranquil; and green, a balance between the two. Preference for red may mean an outwardly directed, or extroverted personality, or even exhibitionism, whereas pink not only reflects mellower qualities of red, but until recently has been distinctly feminine in connotation.

Preference for yellow often reflects imagination, and search for self-fulfillment. Introspection, thought, theorizing and contemplation may often take precedence over action.

Green connotes balance, harmony and reasonable conformity and respect for others.

Blue preference, Birren suggests, "is the color of deliberation and introspection, conservatism and acceptance of obligations."

Every color and mode of dress can influence the direction of contact, regardless of whether or not the assumptions we make are correct. Since we dress to please our own self-image as well as to influence the impression others will have, choice of clothing goes beyond whimsy. It tells others a great deal about our tastes, which are integral to personality. Today we are not bound by narrow standards of dress. There is enormous variety for both men and women. Hard and fast rules are no longer possible or desirable.

Perhaps the one distinction to be made (and it's not always definitive) is that between clothing and costume. An outfit that seems exhibitionistic on one person may be judged a costume, but on someone else it is not so show-offy, depending on age, place, circumstances and personality. What you usually wear can also be a portrait of your self concept.

Style does telegraph messages, daring or not: fashionable or funky, fun or functional, plain or vibrant colors—all offer instant impressions to and from others. Any distinct type of dress or grooming meets with immediate associative response from others which is partly assumptive. In our minds is a fat file of cultural conditioners and personal experiences that call up associations through which we label and categorize. We all make fast references to that mental file; the point is not to be overly dependent on it, at least during the first four minutes.

During Contact workshops a favorite nonverbal exercise is based on two strangers visually assessing each other after no more than a verbal exchange of names. Each fills out a questionnaire of observations about the other, and later another estimate of what might have been written about himself or herself. You probably won't have a similar opportunity when you meet strangers, but you might keep some of the following points in mind. Essentially, these are deductions and assumptions about someone based on physical presence, dress and grooming. Along with basic details, I'll pose a few hypotheses which could well occur to you during initial contact.

—Estimate age, marital status, number of children, if any, occupation, economic status and educational level.

—What sort of activities does he or she enjoy, e.g., dancing, camping, gambling, reading, sports, artistic or creative activities, politics, etc.?

—How is he or she dressed and groomed? Does he or she "look the part" of any specific stereotype?

—(about men) Does his hair, beard, shirt, trousers, shoes or any other accoutrement indicate something unusual or specific about him?

—(about women) Is her hair, blouse, skirt, slacks, shoes or other clothing and makeup indicative of certain characteristics she may have? Is she wearing a bra? If not, does the image of her nipples under blouse or sweater imply something about her sexuality? Is her skirt fashionably revealing or modest?

—From outward appearances, would you say he or she is aggressive or passive, permissive or rigid, extrovert or introvert? What other personality traits can you estimate?

If and when you get to know someone about whom you've mentally filled out parts of this questionnaire, you might try to recall where your assumptions were on the beam, and where you misjudged widely or to a degree. Of course, body language and verbal communication will be added to the store of data you receive from strangers in social or business situations, but a total of facts and assumptions will still be enlightening if and when you are able to make comparisons with reality.

In my group encounters I have considered evaluating reactions of people, using videotape playback, after they have interacted wearing several sets of clothing. Group members would be asked to bring favorite clothes for relaxing, and for formal and informal social contact. Hairstyling and makeup might also be altered during the videotaped exercises, which could then be discussed frankly in relation to varying personal impressions gained as people dressed in one role or another. Comment and feedback would be illuminating, since the impact of personality and character seems to shift according to changing garments and grooming.

We all dress to play a role which may be quite authentic and natural. Wardrobe and accessories can make actors of us as well. This excerpt from "The Gambling Den Guide Book" *Aloft* magazine (Spring, 1971) by John Keasler underlines my point: "Your wardrobe expense to look like a high-roller is, strangely enough, negligible. The male needs only a black shirt and white tie. Nothing else counts." In a casino Keasler claims this is the essence of a "sharp" gambler's clothes. He continues: "The lady who wishes to look like a Mystery Gambler should obtain a long cigarette holder and an orange lipstick. It is not at all required she actually smoke. Merely hold the cigarette holder in the teeth at an upward angle. . . ." These sartorial props, says Keasler, will not impress casino employees nor actual gamblers, but *other* visitors will make the properly outfitted "high-rollers" a center of attention!

Society is changing rapidly, and values are so assorted that "being different" is no longer the impairment it was a couple of generations ago. The latitude we have in choosing clothes (or costumes) is delightful, but at the same time, it makes typing people more difficult. Contact may be more complex, but inhibitions about appearance are less restrictive. Like the jet-set swinger or the small-town merchant, we discover who we are and with whom we want to associate by analyzing how we express ourselves with our own surfaces.

GROOMING

That which we apply to our faces and bodies, and the way we arrange hair in particular, is the core of grooming. It is clear that the makeup women use on eyes, brows, cheeks, lips, and even as camouflage for the nose, may all have a positive effect on appearance—when used in moderation. The points I've mentioned about distinguishing facts from assumption when trying to delve into the truth about someone are all appropriate to grooming. Beauty cannot be applied, but it can be enhanced. Lovely nails, skin or hair are plainly desirable, and should always complement the picture of the "total you."

Accent or highlight your physical strong points and deemphasize the significance of your less attractive qualities. For example, a girl who worries because of deep, dark circles under her eyes can cleverly conceal those shadows with a cover cream and perhaps highlight her natural eye attractiveness. A man or woman uncomfortable mentally and physically due to skin blemishes can and should use skin-care treatment to help clear up an oily condition, or acne or blackheads. Do not hesitate to consult specialists such as dermatologists, cosmetologists, hair stylists or even electrolysis experts.

According to Kathleen Olsen, a cosmetic executive of Saks Fifth Avenue in Los Angeles, "How you look often affects how you feel. It is psychologically pleasing to look your best. Understanding cosmetics is to know what's right for you and what you need. If you don't know, seek professional advice from cosmetic consultants or books. Enhancing the true you can give a sense of physical and psychological well-being, a more positive self-image which you project to those around you."

For men, beards and mustaches are contemporary marks of distinction, but the college professor, the sandal-maker, the student activist, the psychiatrist, some businessmen and lots of people in the arts all enjoy the look once reserved for the ancient and wise. As for long hair, it seems to be most popular with youth. A few years ago long hair was shocking to older people, who associated it with effeminacy, but today shoulder-length hair, with or without a bearded face, merely indicates a certain freedom of spirit, or perhaps symbolizes an anti-establishment attitude.

Grooming with a natural look is indigenous to pride and a healthy self-image in men or women. If one intends to look theatrical in terms of makeup, it may fit an occasion (such as a far-out party), or it may simply seem weird.

In "Beauty and the Best," the *Psychology Today* article quoted earlier, writers Berscheid and Walster note that our billion-dollar cosmetics industry may soon capitalize even more on *their* thesis that physical attractiveness is of prime importance in contact between people. I do not agree with this thesis. Physical attractiveness, in my opinion, is only one facet of good contactability. I have been under the impression that the power of cosmetic product promotion has been shaping our lives for generations. We may gain personal appeal from creams, sprays and other odoriferous chemicals we see advertised and buy, but we may also tend to substitute idealized illusions for facts. We can't all look like sixty-dollar-an-hour models, no matter how deeply we go into debt.

Any significant shift from the acceptable dress and grooming of "the times" most usually begins with the young adults considered "antiestablishment." High heels were first worn by so-called "loose women"—as were bras. The Beatles began the long hair loog for men. It is only after a period of time and perhaps some "getting used to" that these unconventional ideas begin to become acceptable to those who represent establishment. The military has given official sanction to longer hair for men. The "radical" new styles of today may be what the well-dressed will wear in the not too distant future! So be tolerant.

THE WORLD OF SCENTS

At one time only men made contact with women by sniffing their perfume and exclaiming about the pleasure it gave them. Today men smell as spicy and seductive as women. This delightful change of events gives the woman an excellent opportunity to counter with her comments about his aroma . . . for better or for worse.

The human response to aroma or odor seems primarily to be conditioned by our culture. For instance, babies do not react instinctively to the odor of a full diaper as undesirable, but the message gets across after an infant senses a mother wrinkling her nose, and quickly washing and throwing away evidence of excretion. Psychological experiments have shown that it is possible to recondition people to like odors which were once offensive, and formerly sweet aromas can be made to seem repugnant.

Just as humans want to exude an appealing fragrance, on a more fundamental basis, animals rely on natural odors for sexual stimulation and for other nonverbal communication. When two animals meet for the first time, they are apt to sniff at each other. Farley Mowat, in his book *Never Cry Wolf*, (Little Brown, 1963) observes that wolves urinate around the edges of their territorial areas, and he himself used the same method to set boundaries which the animals acknowldeged, "staking out" for himself a geographical island in the midst of a single wolf family's large territorial area.

Over the years, people have become slowly conditioned to dislike various natural aromas of the body, a process which has produced a vast industry making and selling deodorants and deodorant soaps. Some of these sound as though they make perspiring impossible. Other cleverly packaged preparations are available to deodorize the mouth, feet, and genital areas. And one step further, there are also perfumed, flavored douches on the market to conceal natural odors behind a mist of wildflowers or lime ice cream.

Since sexuality may be turned on or off through our sense of smell (as well as through the other senses), perfumes, lotions, mouthwashes, toothpastes, underarm deodorants and other spray-on fragrances are part of the nonverbal language of successful contact. Natural body odors in our society have become largely undesirable, and if one is to make contact effectively, it is important to exude appealing fragrances, in social or business situations, at home, or almost anywhere. The financial drain is minor but the effects are major. Just as unisex has invaded the apparel market, it has also occasioned aftershave lotions to smell like Chanel No. 5, men's hairsprays to be scented like women's, and various other preparations such as mouthwashes and deodorants to be completely interchangable so men and women smell alike—and like it!

Ron and Susan Pursley of Don Loper Cosmetics and Fragrances, feel "personal choice of aromas portray an extension of a man or woman's personality, true or fantasized. Sometimes the same man or woman may use different fragrances for different moods."

However, nature's own aroma is fortunately still a turn-on to some people. In *The Sensuous Couple*, Robert Chartham explains, "There is a school of experts who maintain that sex odors, among which sweat is included, are quite powerful stimulators of Sensuous Men and Sensuous Women *once they have been turned on. . . .* I have met men who agree that they are stimulated by genital odors, and women who have found the distinctive musky smell which the penis of some men gives off after some minutes of arousal very exciting." He adds that other equally sensuous people "react violently against the suggestion that sex odors are aphrodisiacs."

In any case, fragrances can convey things which hopefully are consistent with (or may be one step ahead of) verbal and body communication. The *presence* or *absence* of your grooming, dress and aromas make a statement about you in the first four minutes. Others naturally and spontaneously draw assumptions about your statement. Are you sending the kind of statement you want others to receive?

9.

SEX REARS
ITS LOVELY HEAD

Almost everything you always wanted to know about sex (and most of the things you didn't) has been written, discussed, debated, researched and analyzed. Many who were "afraid to ask" may be learning at this moment by experience, hopefully with patient, loving teachers, which is how those of us who are fortunate "students" learn anyway. However, the closest most authorities come to writing about initial sexual contact in the first four minutes, both vertically and horizontally, is advice about foreplay, which is sometimes rather clinical. Here I intend to probe the sexual encounter on several levels, with the focus on beginnings—since beginnings have an enormous influence on how two people (limited here to a male and a female) "make it" as comfortable, meaningful, exciting, satisfying sexual partners.

VERTICAL SEX

I do not mean to be funny, nor am I about to list new positions for intercourse while standing. By vertical sex, I refer to the varied sexual overtones of encounter in social situations, or anywhere when man and woman, boy and girl, male and female happen to meet as strangers, mates, or "great and good friends," a phrase *Time* used to refer to intimate unmarried couples.

Many of the verbal and nonverbal cues exchanged between people have already been covered: scents, seductive dress and grooming, words of endearment, touching, embracing, etc. Granted, there are meetings between the sexes which are never intended to include sexual overtones, but vibrations between the sexes are almost always there. In women they are thought to be manifested as "wiles"; in men they may be called "tactics." No matter how you regard the sexy glance, the seductive touch or the affectionate words that people exchange, they can all be media of successful contact.

Some individuals are afraid their sexual allusions will be misunderstood or repulsed, despite their subtlety. To them I say, the basic warmth that people show each other by words or gestures is partly a product of sexual attraction. Do not be afraid of being warm, if you are also sincere. A look straight into the eyes of someone newly introduced, a smile, a few words of acknowledgment that indicate you find *that* someone attractive—and your message will be clear, honest and complimentary, and almost certainly appreciated. We all enjoy admiration, and part of the freedom I feel everyone can develop in making contacts is the ability—actually, the joy—of expressing positive feelings, or accepting them.

Sexuality and its symbols are everywhere, and I do not just mean in print or movies, but in person. When you feel warmly about someone new or someone close, show it. Both of you may then depart the contact glowing—and good feelings about yourselves will be enhanced.

HORIZONTAL SEX

In the first four minutes of a sexual encounter, foreplay begins with the eyes as well as the hands and body. It is important to let your partner know how much you enjoy looking at her or him. We all respond to visual appreciation, which often in turn inspires a more exciting sexual experience. Make a random habit of watching your mate undress, telling him or her by your gaze, and verbally, how much you like his or her body. For example, a man may tell his mate how stimulating it is to see her breasts move, or the thrill he feels letting his senses ponder the triangle between her legs. We know that words are a sexual turn-on; they need not be four-letter words or direct expressions of passion. A woman may also tell her partner how his physical gifts enrich her sexual desires. Incidentally, people find such words of admiration not only sexy, but positive reinforcement to keep their bodies in good shape.

One of the essential learned skills for developing mutually satisfying sexual relationships is the ability to "tune in" and "be aware" of the various, sometimes subtle clues and signals radiating from your partner, heralding his or her desire for sexual encounter. It has been my experience that people have felt rejected when they assume their cues have been received and subsequently ignored. Be certain your signals have been received before you conclude they are being ignored. I would also suggest that if your subtle clues do not get results, don't be so subtle—talk, touch, and, if necessary, take the risk of being the aggressor.

As eyes enjoy and words whet sexual appetites, hands begin to fondle and caress. At the same time one is receiving sensual pleasure by touching face, breasts, chest, legs and genital areas, one also strengthens the feelings of primitive excitement and the bonds of interdependence which two lovers share. Couples who make love frequently must renew the stimuli on a regular basis. I have frequently heard the opinion that "it's impossible to sleep with one partner for several decades without a certain boredom setting in, which leads to infidelity, or at least experimentation with someone new." For people who seek variety in their sexual techniques, this need not be true, but the fact remains that sex does not renew itself. It has to be fired and constantly restored by us, by stimuli within us (some of which stimuli originate in sexually provocative words we may read and images we may see that become part of our fantasies and keep the fires going).

Couples who are beginning sexual encounter need to develop some of the same approaches as longtime lovers. But they also require special empathy to overcome apprehensions which naturally tend to flaw the harmony that people ordinarily take time to develop. It is likely that couples who have achieved gentle, loving rapport through conversation and physical contact short of intercourse will meet in bed, be aroused and consummate their mutual passions more smoothly. However, in these accelerated times, sexual activity may begin with little preface. When people are experienced and understand the fine art of making love, whether they are in love or not, the chances of beginning and ending the contact in satisfaction and fulfillment are better. When there are sexual hangups to dissolve, it is even more important that the first four minutes be filled with warmth and mutual appreciation.

As for couples who have sex almost without learning each other's names, the first four minutes may be so close to the final few minutes that observations about subtle and ego-stimulating encounter are really academic and irrelevant.

People develop verbal and nonverbal patterns in approaching sexual intercourse, some using strangely crass questions that begin, "How about a little sex tonight?" or some employing maneuvers as delightful as the woman lying nude in bed, casually reading, when the man arrives to join her. Partners in ongoing intimate relationships are apt to give each other signals, some of which can stimulate arousal and indicate interest in love-making. A man once told me he always knew when his wife wanted to have intercourse because she perfumed her neck, breasts and genital areas on those nights. He added that they also had spontaneous sexual relations when only their natural aromas were present, which provided variety and an exchange of initiative. Women should be aware which perfumes their husbands respond to most lustfully—and where they enjoy the scents to come from. Men can also stimulate their partners with a variety of aftershave lotions or colognes, on face and neck, and daubed into pubic hair as well. A woman who is attracted by the fragrance arising from around her mate's penis may be inspired to turn him on orally, which in turn should provide reciprocal interest in her own sexual charms.

In other words, the subject is arousal, both emotional and physical, in the first stages of sexual encounter. We have all heard case histories about men who kiss quickly or not at all, are ready for intercourse long before partners are turned on, mount, move, climax and fall asleep in a routine without passion. They have sexual intercourse as if they had been motivated by a computer punchcard inserted into the feeling lobes of the brain. The sexual mates of such men may believe that the first four minutes is the *whole* contact, though it is likely these women become bored quickly without fulfillment, and probably without orgasm.

In contrast, an attractive woman once told me that her husband was an ardent lover who "tries everything he can think of to please me, to get me hot, and many nights, nothing works. I lay there thinking of twelve other things. Sex just isn't rewarding with him anymore, but he keeps trying." She discovered that her husband had been very inexperienced when they first married, and she had nurtured his sexual approaches and techniques until they were both satisfied. But she suddenly was disenchanted, as though she had created a copulating puppet, and she longed for men such as she had known before who "took her in hand," as she put it.

Kissing is a primary pleasure in the initial stages of sex, but most people feel they know how to kiss well. However, many a sexual engagement has been delayed or lost when one or both partners either kissed with too little feeling or so ardently that one of them felt devoured. At first, people discover how each already kisses, and slowly, but immediately, one or both should interchange impressions and suggestions, by mouth and by words. Kissing has variety, just as intercourse has its diversity of positions, timing and styles. Gentle lips can also be firm, a probing tongue should give way to reciprocity, and sexual energy will circulate through the body.

Most people enjoy being kissed on the neck, breasts,

thighs and genital areas. The mouth is a surrogate sex organ in the beginning of sex play. Lovers should make it a point to explore their partner's face and other points of erotic stimulation in dynamic and exciting ways. It may be true, as a mature woman once told me, that "a woman's kiss is the invitation to her bed." Once they are *in* bed, both partners' kisses, plus caressing by hands, starts their body chemistry into preparing sexual secretions (as well as the male erection), while the closeness of flesh, the taste, the smells and the words of pleasure and love all stimulate a man and a woman into the ultimate sexual joining.

All the senses should be alive and active as intercourse becomes imminent, and experiments in pleasure-giving and receiving help stimulate the inhibited, the cautious, the cool or the fearful lover. Some women adopt various ways of teasing their mates to arousal by body movements, sexy words, erotic touching, and even by playful delays. Men use their own teasing methods, including sucking a woman's nipples, sensitively finger-probing the vagina or running their hands lightly over a woman's body.

Certainly, between partners who make love regularly, the use of fantasy is a positive beginning, which can be continued through sexual exchange. The answer to, "What are you thinking about, darling?" could suggest words or activity to enhance sexual fantasies that are so often drawn from aberrations or exaggerations which we read about or have seen in various media. Occasional role-playing in bed, providing it is mutually agreeable and not painful, is a prevalent practice that keeps the fires of desire burning indefinitely.

Long before women's lib was a common term, the illusion was fading that men were expected to make initial advances in sex play. In healthy relationships, I feel that mates will take turns stimulating each other, since variety is also the spice of sex. The shift of initiative adds excitement and a certain mystery to contact, and helps avoid routine that can blanket the fires.

Along with disclosures of erotic fantasies and the interchange of opening advances are other stimulants to successful sex, namely lighting, music and setting. Total darkness illuminated by several candles can be a turn-on; brilliant, indirect artificial light, sunlight and any other kind of light that interests you, all spur new sexual awakening. Soft music, classical baroque, the sounds of Rachmaninoff or rock-and-roll can stimulate people initially. I know a woman who told me the most feverish intercourse she could recall took place on a well-carpeted floor, while she listened to *Carmina Burana* with earphones! While a bed is probably the most comfortable place to make love, a change of pace such as in a swimming pool, a car, a waterbed, or on very isolated soft grass under a blue sky may add new interest to lovers or recent strangers.

These are the preliminary activities which start sensory wheels in motion and generate the responses necessary for optimum excitement and satisfaction in a sexual relationship. The goal is richness and variation, which may reflect a couple's day-to-day relationship and very likely amplify their caring.

A PERSPECTIVE OF LOVE

In contemporary relationships, sex without love is not uncommon. It may be rated, according to individual response, from gratifying to superficial to offensive. Without any attempt to dissect the pros and cons of sexual mores, which are best guided by conscience rather than external authority, I feel that a short discourse on love is fitting here. Contact in four minutes may grow to contact for a lifetime, during which the influence of love has more impact than all other human emotions combined.

Love has been defined by poets and philosophers, explained by lovers in every language, and used as an alibi by murderers. In my view, the definition of mature love between two responsible people is quite personal. I do not choose to categorize in terms of human vs. divine, family vs. friend, enduring vs. transient, emotional vs. intellectual, or within any other rigid framework. However, there are certain qualities to the emotion of loving that I believe are universal.

In contrast to some human characteristics with quantitative limits (e.g., the amount of food one can eat or the distance one can see clearly), the amount of love one can give and take has no quota. For example, if a person has one child, he does not pro-rate his love for the child according to a total "child-love" ability. If one has five children, each is bathed in total love, not one-fifth of a hypothetical "child-love" capacity. In other words, the human capacity to love is not limited, except in terms of available time and proximity to express it.

The more one loves, the more one is capable of loving. Love breeds love; the more individuals we love in many different frameworks, the more our capacity increases to love still others.

Love is not static. It is a dynamic emotion that grows, diminishes and changes in a constantly fluid state. Love endures, and yet you may love someone now, love him or her in a different way an hour later, and still in other ways tomorrow. But love is not subject to a strict time clock; it is as present and ever-changing as the endless panorama of clouds and sun in the sky.

Love is one of the few things in life that we can best keep by giving away. In general, the less one gives of love, the less one receives. You cannot secure the emotion of love by trying to possess it, any more than you can grab a handful of air. Love is never unconditional except for transient periods. For, along with love come inherent expectations for those we love and for those who love us.

It is difficult—actually rare—that anyone continues to love another person whom he feels dislikes or even hates him. Feelings of love must be relatively reciprocal or they cannot be permanent. Do you know anyone that you love who dislikes you intensely? In reverse, is there one person you dislike whom you know loves you? Some relationships can be twisted into a love-hate situation, but not for long.

Love fosters qualities of forgiveness, tolerance and compromise. Love also involves a willingness—not a desire—to sacrifice and even suffer temporarily. Classic lovers in fiction and operas "die for love," but in real life, real lovers more appropriately turn their energies to living for love.

Mature and responsible love requires a sense of freedom, for oneself and from another person. In other words, healthy love means possessiveness is limited by mutual consent within a harmonious arrangement. A dubious love is reflected by the man who says, "I love my wife so much, if she ever has an affair with another man, I'll kill them both." That man's wife runs the risk of becoming a chattel.

Well-balanced love involves a strong desire for the other person to be happy, with no implication that you are the only source of fulfillment but, rather, with welcome latitude to satisfy his or her own desires and needs. One hopes to be the center of love gratification, but to demand it is to undermine love's footing. To create synthetic dependence fosters an atmosphere of fear, jealousy, domination, possession—and eventually love dissolves in the acid of anger.

In the course of emotional growth, the concept of love and the capacity to love goes through various stages. By the time one is mature enough to know the depth of love, one is usually able to give and receive it with a minimum of pain and a maximum of pleasure. Sexual compatibility is often mistaken for an interchange of love, though it may be a limited physical manifestation that tapers off in ratio to real caring and involvement. Casual sexual contact with limited commitment often flourishes to become satisfying love, when the quality of unselfishness is unstrained. However, neither love nor sex "falls like a gentle rain from heaven," in Shakespeare's words. Love may be mild or stormy, but it must find a natural climate of mutuality to endure and be meaningful.

This is not an attempt to define love but to describe it. Love is a feeling of the present that can be enhanced or neglected, enduring or transient. It is related to both the mind and the heart. Love must be demonstrated through involvement with others. As an abstract concept, it is but a word on a page, with no link to the human circulatory or nervous system which carries its impulses from nerve ends to feeling and action.

In this brief consideration of love there are only brief hints of the many sexual hangups people suffer. This is neither a clinic nor a couch where such problems may be worked out. Sex can appear to be many things. It is often a pathway to frustration; it has been called a weapon and the bed its battleground. In the first four minutes of sexual encounter, it may be clear if emotional pressure will forestall gratifying physical contact.

The erotic is too often flavored by the neurotic, though both horizontal and vertical sex are the principal—and wonderfully primitive—ways to exchange the gifts of creation and affection.

10.

MARRIAGE AND COUPLES: FOUR MINUTES X 2

At the end of an all-day workshop on Contact, I asked members of the audience for final questions. We had only a few minutes left, and there was a silence until a hand was raised timidly at the back of the room. A small, pretty woman stood and asked, "Dr. Zunin, will you tell me in one sentence, what is the best thing to do when my husband comes home from work?"

"In one sentence?" I repeated, and added, "I'll tell you in two words: be nice!"

I elaborated for her, "If necessary, be 'phony.' Even if you don't feel like being nice, do it anyway, at least for four minutes. It's a good investment, and the dividends you and your spouse collect may be a lot more valuable than you'll earn in the stockmarket. In addition, if you act nice, good feelings often follow along and phoniness may fade into sincerity."

Why? Because the success or failure of a marriage, which today includes couples living together in a serious ongoing relationship, can depend on what happens between a husband and wife *during just eight minutes of the day:* four in the morning upon awakening, and four when you are reunited after the working day. During the years of a marriage or the interval when cohabiting lovers share bed and board, these crucial eight minutes may set the tone of a continuing alliance. Certainly, they symbolize the manner in which a man and a woman integrate their lives, either in loving empathy or masked hostility.

133

You may now be thinking, "It's a routine; we get up and get going," or "So, he comes home, and we talk a little and have dinner—what's the big deal?" Coming and going *are* a big deal, because below the level of ordinary awareness, in spite of what appears to be a casual procedure, couples literally bombard each other with cues and messages. Husbands, wives or lovers usually don't realize they are making swift, durable impressions on each other's minds in the morning and evening—impressions which influence the day's work and activities, the night's sexual encounter or evasion, and a lifetime of relating.

Perhaps half the messages exchanged are spoken, and the remainder are projected through body language. Physical movements, a glint or squint of the eyes, neat or crumpled clothes, a scent of perfume or B.O.—all of these can provide significant and obvious impressions of moods and attitudes to contradict or augment words of affection. Chapters 6, 7 and 8 discuss nonverbal communication more fully.

I have found that the interaction of a couple (married or not) during the morning and evening contacts is a revealing portrait which discloses their concern for each other, their mutual interests, and particularly, their self-concepts. During workshops and with private patients, I have said, "Describe in detail that daily eight minutes when you meet in bed at dawn or greet in the kitchen at dusk, and I will tell you what your marriage is like."

Let me give you the keys to examining your own contact patterns via case histories and observations. Though you may be used to thinking of long-range, far-reaching therapeutic study of your lives, with the help of books, psychologists and psychiatrists, groups and other means of self-help, you may be astonished to find how far an understanding of the four-minute contact periods will take you on the road to self-discovery.

I recently asked an attractive married woman in her early thirties to recount the usual pattern of the first four minutes with her husband as they awakened each morning. She hesitated for a moment, and then with obvious discomfort replied, "Oh, I'm too embarrassed to tell you." I had visions of a pleasant positive physical encounter which she wanted to keep to herself, but she went on, "I never thought about it before, but the first words I utter to my husband are 'Please help me up; my back hurts.' I'll never do that again."

Without getting into all the ramifications of the aching back, I suggested, "Why not? If you really have a back problem, I know how stiff and painful it can be when you awaken. Your husband must know it, too. Perhaps you can establish a four-minute massage pattern which would start you both off in a better mood. Rather than making an annoying complaint to him, you would enjoy the touch of his hands on your back, and the sounds you make or the expression on your face could compensate him. At least, your need would be directly met without the overtones of bitchiness that you seem to feel your first words implied."

It came as no surprise to me, and probably won't to you, that people persist in using words that alienate their partners. Instead of those eight minutes bringing them closer together, these contact periods drive them further apart. When couples analyze their contacts objectively, they are often embarrassed. It is obvious they act out of habit and conditioned ritual rather than out of a sense of awareness, concern and sensitivity.

Some couples who have had disagreements the night before will consistently forget them in the morning and look forward to the new day. Others may continue the conflict as soon as their eyes are open. Since people usually start the day following somewhat set patterns, it is important to realize that these routines create satisfaction and enjoyment from closeness, or unhappiness and frustration from loneliness. If you can constructively examine your patterns of the early morning, you will discover that concern for your partner's feelings can be shown in a variety of ways, all of which spark an intimacy and empathy to be enjoyed at home or through positive by-products at work all day.

Let me describe some of the ways couples respond in the first four minutes of the morning:

The Silent Partner—"Don't expect me to talk until I've had my third cup of coffee," he groans as he rejects his wife's attempts at friendliness. He is unaware of his grumpy attitude and places his faith in a magic chemical guaranteed to soothe his disposition.

The Commander—He awakens giving orders. His spouse feels as though she should salute. "Okay, we have ten minutes to get into the kitchen. I want scrambled eggs, crisp bacon and half a grapefruit. Come on, get up. You take a shower first. I'll give you eight minutes. Then I'll shave, etc., etc."

Compulsive Groomer—She leaps out of bed as the alarm rings, and rushes to the bathroom. Her spouse is not allowed to see her or touch her until she has combed her hair, brushed her teeth and rinsed her mouth. It's probably a syndrome that originated in a TV commercial.

Efficiency Expert (her)—"You know, George, I tell you every morning, if you'd wake up at seven instead of seven-thirty, you'd have five minutes for your hot shave, seven minutes to shower, six minutes to shine your shoes, eight minutes to dress and four minutes to comb your hair. Then you could come to the kitchen just as I'm putting the eggs on the table. Now, why don't you listen. . . . I tell you this every morning."

Efficiency Expert (him)—"You know, Helen, if you got up twelve minutes earlier, you could have the coffee ready by the time I was through shaving. Then while I showered and dressed, you could make my lunch and finish making breakfast. We could chat for three minutes and I'd be in the car by seven-fifteen."

Affectionate Aficionado—"Come on, honey, don't pull away; you know I enjoy making love in the morning. The kids can wait a few minutes for breakfast." Not a bad way to start the day if both partners have the same urge and make time for sex without disrupting other routines.

Obviously, if a couple awaken and embrace, four minutes of kissing and fondling is very likely to launch the day positively.

Trivia Trapper—"Good morning, I'll be home at five today. Have dinner ready because I have a meeting at seven. I left some clothes for the cleaners on the chair by the window. Don't forget to renew our subscription to *Time,* and have the mail sorted by the time I get home, please. . . ." A guaranteed way to make your spouse feel like a hired hand.

Panic-Stricken Pessimist—"Oh, this is Wednesday. What a terrible day it's going to be. I have a deadline to meet [or three kids to drive three different places] and I haven't even started. I hate Wednesdays!" Tuesdays, Mondays or even Sundays can also be equally cursed.

The Complainer—"Roz, did you know I've been up all night? These sheets are filthy; why weren't they changed? And there's dust all over the night stand. When are you going to learn how to clean?" On the other hand, Roz might open the day with: "Harold, did you know I didn't sleep a wink? It's all those damned bills we haven't paid. Why can't we balance our budget? Haven't you asked for a raise yet? I'm going crazy thinking about money, and I need a new dress for the Carsons's party."

There are many variations on these themes, including the husband or wife who always wants to sleep five more minutes, the partner who opens with an argument over the temperature of the electric blanket or the couple who immediately fight about who was pushing who out of bed. Some couples do awaken intertwined and smiling, while others begin with a soft conversation about activities upcoming that day in a kind of sharing mood. In any case, you may see yourself in one of the categories or even think of new ones not listed. Are you aware of how the morning contact sets the pace for the hours that follow, and often symbolizes the kind of relationship you enjoy—or dislike—with your spouse?

Let's take a closer look at a few couples:

Phil and Renee are in their early thirties, have two

youngsters and the usual middle-class problems of child rearing, job status, etc. In nine years of marriage they have managed to magnify their differences, which are rarely tackled directly. From the start their relationship was a continuing battle for dominance, and each morning begins with some variation of disagreement such as:

R: Why don't you make coffee today? I got up first yesterday.

P: It won't hurt you to make it two days in a row.

R. Why don't you ever do anything nice for me? I know lots of husbands who make coffee *every* morning for their wives, and bring it to them in bed!

P: Maybe they have wives who don't pester them all the time.

By the time Phil leaves for work, his thoughts about Renee are usually negative. "Why won't she get off my back?" he ponders. "Why can't he be considerate?" she asks herself. They will plague each other indefinitely unless both see how the pattern can be changed, or until something drastic happens—such as divorce. They are both building up resentments, and instead of discussing them issue by issue, as objectively as possible, they take out their frustrations by needling each other. Renee thinks of herself as the "unappreciated wife," while Phil considers himself the "badgered husband."

Strangely enough, married people in conflict unconsciously *plan* how they will "dump" their bad feelings on one another. It takes new insights for them to discover they can also plan in advance to be loving and kind. Couples get into ruts under the guise of comfort, security and being "very married." Their actions and reactions become predictable, boring and eventually destructive. It's impossible to examine a whole marriage relationship under a single spotlight, but concentrating on the first four minutes of contact, morning and evening, can help reveal symptoms and perhaps start you on the way to solutions.

One of the hindrances to a good morning contact is the time element, illustrated by this short account from a woman who was recently divorced.

"We slept in a comfortable queen-size bed, but our marriage was going nowhere. You want to know how the morning started? Ken woke up before I did, but he'd stay in bed a while. It got so I couldn't stand the aggravation of just turning to look at him. It wasn't anything he'd done then—in fact, he was sometimes nice and warm. If he put his hand on my thigh or my breast, I'd reject him instantly. If that didn't discourage him, he'd offer to make me breakfast, and asked what I wanted. My constant answer was 'No.' It didn't matter what, he turned me off by that time."

Grim, isn't it? I discovered their timing had usually been off. In the past he had one pressing goal in the morning: to dress, eat and run. With this focus, he rarely took the time to be loving or concerned about his wife. When he finally realized the chasm between them, it was too late.

Whatever you do in the morning's opening minutes, it should be mutually satisfying. Caressing is almost always welcome by couples with a healthy sexual rapport. A conversational exchange can be just as rewarding. Talk about dreams, about plans, about anything that lends itself to an exchange of good feelings. Or if possible, go outdoors and inhale the freshness of the day together. Have a leisurely cup of coffee, watch early morning TV in each other's arms. Try anything which will bring you closer together, and vary your patterns from time to time.

Look for signals within the first four minutes of awakening each day, signs that intend a message. A husband —from a marriage considered by both parties to be a good one—related the following, almost daily, morning pattern, characterized by his wife's consistent headache:

He: Good morning, dear. I'll get the paper and start

some water boiling for your tea. Do you have a headache this morning?

She: Yes, dammit.

He: Well, tough shit; I'm going to get my coffee and I'll see you at the table.

She: But my head is splitting, worse than it's ever been.

He: Too bad; maybe you'll feel better later. Are you going to class today?

She: It's not till 8:30, so let me sleep another fifteen minutes.

He: Okay, but what seems to be your problem?

She: I don't know; I just have an awful headache.

He: Why won't you see the doctor?

She: You're always telling me that, and it's not so serious. It'll go away.

He: Fine, I'll see you in fifteen minutes.

She: Thanks.

(Later at the table, having breakfast):

He: Darling, you look great! Your head must be better.

She: That fifteen minutes did it, like it always does, you know.

The morning headache is a signal, even more transparent than the backache, that something is being left unsettled between people. In the above dialogue they were learning to be direct. He didn't over-indulge her and she had no cause to whine extensively. When we examined the manner in which this couple interacted on awakening, she admitted her headache was a gambit to gain a little extra sleep, and he admitted to a need for her to jump out of bed when he did. When they realized their first morning needs did not have to ¡coincide precisely, she stayed in bed her fifteen minutes without a headache, and he understood that patterning his wife after himself was not the happiest manifestation of love.

To give you a sampling of the multifarious forms the first four minutes of the morning can take, here is a list of some ways people handle the wake-up routine. Which of these seems to fit your pattern most appropriately?

You throw back the covers so she or he freezes—and wakes up.

You shake him or her and shout, "Okay, time to get up!"

You go into the bathroom and in a minute yell out, "Come on, you're going to be late."

You pass a steaming hot cup of coffee under his or her nose.

You invite your two-year-old in to play with daddy or mommy—and jar him or her awake.

You take him or her in your arms and whisper, "I love you," adding a kiss and . . . you name it.

You reset the alarm and place it three inches from his or her left ear.

You turn on the *1812 Overture* and let it do the job for you.

You stalk out of the room in disgust, slamming the door —*hard!*

You pull at him or her rather briskly, crying, "Can't you ever get up on time?"

You rub his or her back or neck and whisper, "Time to get up, darling."

Think about it: the method of awakening your spouse is very indicative of the quality of your relationship and your composite feelings. Do you use love, anger, humor, tenderness, thoughtlessness or indifference? Why not ask your spouse how he or she would *like* to be awakened? Such a query could pay off in long-range understanding and intimacy to rekindle the spark I hope you felt the first morning you ever woke up together.

THE SECOND FOUR MINUTES

The second contact point of the day, when a married couple is reunited, has equal impact on relationships and can be just as revealing. Most husbands seem to have traditional patterns. Typical are complaints about traffic, weather, the mess down at the office or just plain fatigue. A man may also come home with a cheery smile, whistling, and with a warm greeting for his wife and kids. However, the well-known stereotype—based unfortunately on reality—is the guy who returns in silence. Everyone is primed not to talk to daddy for thirty minutes until he has changed his clothes or had two martinis. On the other hand, a man may make the effort to comb his hair, wash before leaving work and apply aftershave lotion. The effect is obviously more conducive to the benefits of family life than the slob who comes in looking like the runner-up in an eight-day dance marathon.

Somehow in our culture the image of the alluring woman who has prepared herself to entice, or at least to be nice, when her man comes home, is a lot more prevalent than the counterpart concept for husbands. It seems rather unnecessary, therefore, to point out that the neatly groomed wife who has accented her femininity, though not necessarily in an obviously sexy way, will provoke a more positive contact from the tired and hungry breadwinner than the woman who looks, sounds and acts like she had been through the same dance marathon.

There is also a stereotype for wives who barely kiss but kind of grapple quickly, anxious to start complaining about the children's atrocities (which the husband *must* do something about immediately), the tiring chores of the day, or the frustrations she's had with *his* mother.

Interestingly, if a wife greets her husband with a smile and a kiss, the entire family usually catches the mood, and if she's irritated, the children are usually indifferent or aggravating. No matter how upbeat a man may be on homecoming, his attitude will be dampened by a curt "Hi" from his wife while the kids stay glued to the TV without acknowledging his presence. If he persists, he may be rebuffed with a "shhhhh!" which could make him feel he should have gone home with his secretary.

In short, these first four minutes of contact can shape and determine the course of an evening's interaction and communication between a man, his wife and all the members of the family. This evening contact is also a mirror of a marriage relationship. Happy or abrupt, the first four minutes affect how each individual feels about himself as a person, and about himself as a member of his or her family.

For example, Hazel and Don are both under thirty, have one child, have been married five years, and were once romantic lovers filled with fine fantasies of married life.

Dr. Z: Where are you usually and what do you do when Don comes in the door?

H: I'm usually in the kitchen or I'm with the baby who has just been fed.

Dr. Z: How does Don greet you?

H: He doesn't. I mean, he sometimes just comes over and starts to take off my robe. He's always been sex-oriented—that's his thing.

Dr. Z: Are you usually wearing a robe?

H: A robe, or a blouse if I've just come back from someplace and I don't know when to expect Don. I'm not trying to tempt him, and I might be in bra and panties. I'm never sure when he's going to pop in.

Dr. Z: What happens when he approaches you?

H: He starts making advances that I call stupid because they repulse me, so I wind up pushing him away and doing something else. Then he'll want to talk.

Dr. Z: What does he say?

H: "I wanna talk."

Dr. Z: And what do you usually say?

H: I don't! And he says, "We *must* talk," and I refuse, and he wants to know when I'll talk, and I say, "I don't know," and he may say, "How about tomorrow?" and I say, "Maybe." He'll push me to talk that night, and I usually don't want to, and that's the way it goes most of the time.

What went wrong with the dreams Hazel and Don had is not germane here, but the significance of their evening greeting might have been a springboard for them to stop, look and examine their relationship—if they were able.

There are all sorts of indicators in what they say and do during the evening contact, if you can sort them out and zero in on their meanings. Don and Hazel had lost touch with each other and with their past. He hoped to rely on physical contact, and she didn't wish to be seduced as a temporary substitute for settlement. Yet both of them were ambivalent; he wanted to talk if he couldn't sweep their differences under the sheets with lovemaking, and she wanted to make love, as witness her wearing a robe or underwear when he came home. Symbols. We need to spot them for the insights they may offer.

Just as morning backache can be real and treated with tender, loving hands spreading Ben-Gay, evening contact need not be based on pretense if an individual is troubled. "Be nice," I said at the opening of this chapter, and even be phony, but when there's trouble, a functional phoniness can set the mood for resolving problems. When a husband usually greets his wife warmly, and several evenings in a row he is grouchy, then is the time to contrive a sympathetic attitude if it doesn't come naturally. Here's a case when a couple shared troubled feelings in a constructive way:

He: I'm bushed. How do you feel?

She: Well, I'm completely exhausted, too.

He: What time is dinner?

She: It's all ready, but there's no hurry. Tell you what; I'll get the kids started and come right back.

He: Great. You don't mind if I lie down a while?

She: No problem. I'll be back in a minute.

When she returns, and though she is genuinely tired herself, she gently lifts his head and places it in her lap. She longs to tell him, as she often does, of her frustrations with the washing machine or the child's terrible report card, but she remembers the times when he has willingly absorbed her pain, and she restrains her urges in favor of being a loving blotter.

He: I'm really upset, you know. A very rough day. Joe called and he's ready to cut out if that contract isn't signed. Our man in Detroit was picked up on a drunk driving charge. I'm really up-tight. Think I'll go soak in the tub. I'd appreciate it very much if you'd wait and have dinner with me.

She: Lovely, darling. I'll see that the children get dessert, and I'm going to lie down here myself for an hour. We'll eat at seven, just the two of us. How does that sound?

He: You're a doll. I'm so damned nervous, and I have to talk about it, bath or no bath.

She: Okay, I'm listening. *(She's also running her hands around his face and forehead.)*

He talks and talks, unloading the large or trivial weights she knew he carried.

He: I guess you sensed I might be upset this morning when I left, didn't you? And that's why you called this afternoon, just to yak it up and help relieve a little tension. That was nice, baby; I love the way you pick up my vibes. You know, I feel like I've had a drink, and I haven't, but it's a helluva good idea. Will you join me?"

If that wife's way of relating was hypocritical, it was only momentary, and it happened to be typical of the way this couple had matured together, each seeking to meet the other's needs without forgetting their own. Just as the first four minutes in the evening can start with talons bared and hostile, the time can mirror a healthy, growing marriage as well, no matter what problems must be faced.

In the morning or on being reunited at the end of the day, a couple who realize the sense of *renewal* each opportunity offers also realize the most gratifying feelings being together. This particular couple expressed to me their conscious awareness of interaction morning and evening. The wife said it was like a scale on which his empathy yesterday could be balanced by her warmth and understanding today—on an indefinite, far-reaching schedule.

It's too easy to visualize the man who comes home, throws his jacket on a chair, sweeps through the kitchen to the liquor cabinet and calls out in resignation, "Sally, I'm home. Where's the mail? Did you call the TV repairman? Why are Julie's toys all over the living room? Where the hell are you?"

It's also not difficult to sympathize with the wife who is anxious about her husband's irritation, and who lies down to sleep twenty minutes before he's due. And there's the guy who really looks forward to seeing his bride (even of many years), but faces a barrage of verbal misery before he can get half a kiss. Here is part of a dialogue with Lorraine who became aware of Contact at a seminar I gave, and returned to a later one as a kind of progress test:

Dr. Z: You said you've changed; how so?

L: Well, I discovered that in the first four minutes when Al came home, I tried to tell him everything that happened during the day; it was awful. I found I could cover it all in two-and-a-half minutes if I rushed!

Dr. Z: Give me an example of what you said.

L: Oh, things like, "I'm tired! What an awful day I've had! My mother called and she's feeling lousy again. The kids are driving me nuts, and I can't stand it another minute." It's always been some variation of the pity-me theme.

Dr. Z: And now?

L: Well, it's different. I give him a hug and ask him if he'd like a drink. I'll usually ask him how *his* day went, and really mean it. And he'll give me the news, things that happened with people I may know. He almost never complains. When I stopped giving him a bad time in the evening, I once asked him how come he never blasted me with gloom and doom. He said he just thought it was a terrible way to run a family, to dump all that crap on me as soon as I opened the door. Besides, I was too busy dumping my neuroses on him! Now, I'm trying to show the children how to greet daddy better, and Al and I both notice a difference.

Earlier I mentioned that contact situations between husbands and wives, especially when one of them is upset, are usually preplanned. A problem, or an assortment of irritating incidents, is revolving in the troubled one's mind, like clothes tumbling in a dryer. The upset spouse can hardly wait until the evening contact so he or she can unload these irked feelings. As soon as the unburdening is over, he or she will fantasize that he or she feels better. Typically, the dumping begins during the first four minutes, and since this initial time affects the rest of the evening together, the dumper has set up a very unpleasant situation which is apt to backfire. Even two minutes of unrelieved verbal static is enough to turn someone off for hours, particularly when it is only the surface manifestation of deeper trouble.

As much as dos and don'ts can be encapsulated, here are some pointers for more rewarding contact at day's end:

1. Give your spouse your *total* attention for the first few minutes, or longer; you might think of it as mouth-to-mouth resuscitation to *prevent* drowning.

2. Don't be guilty of the "didya's!" Don't greet your spouse with "Didya pick up the cleaning?" "Didya take back the broken can opener?" Or didya do a hundred other things—queries which will wait.

3. If kissing isn't your style, do have some physical contact; hug each other, hold hands, fondle, whatever gives you a feeling of affection—and the wordplay is intended.

4. Don't be a dumper or chronic complainer. Don't dump all the complaints and anguish of your world on him or her before trying mouth-to-mouth resuscitation—and if that lasts a few minutes, the cares of your world may have met their antidote.

5. Try to arrange this time of your day with no other obligations such as immediate phone calls, tea parties you couldn't tear yourself away from or the neighbor whose life seems far more interesting than your husband's, at least in his view. If possible, have dinner prepared so you can sit down and relax.

6. Occasionally, for no special reason, plan a surprise, something different, whether it be soft music, pale pink lights or a new blouse cut down to there.

7. Try to look appealing when he comes home—or you get home. Your grooming says a lot about how you feel about him, yourself and vice versa.

8. Pretend you're not married. Take her flowers or a new book based on the secret writings of Joe Namath. Wear a new perfume and no bra, and put a flower in your hair, even if it's a geranium.

9. Have the house as neat as the kids will let you. A messy setting is no place for a sexy wife, and a messy wife is usually not sexy.

10. Give him time to relax before you put any pressures on him, and the same goes for you, sir; let her relax before you rush her to bed, or start the inquisition.

11. Look forward to *his* or *your* arrival—it can be a lovely occasion.

12. Do be nice.

The first four minutes of the morning, or when you and your spouse are together again after a busy day, is only indicative of the past and future minutes, hours, days and years of your lives. A total examination of your contact relationship might very well:

—help you both overcome stress from many sources.

—renew your sexual feelings to give them new intimacy rather than a sense of catharsis.

—replace guilt with love as a motivating influence.

—give you a new view of problems with the children, with money, with the whole array of mutual concerns you have.

—exchange anxiety, fear and frustration for mutual confidence, joyful anticipation and unexpected fulfillment.

—break down the walls of loneliness and tension to bring back the old feelings of warmth, esteem and closeness you once felt for each other.

11

CONTACT
WITH CHILDREN

The interests of our children and youth are basic to the interests of mankind. Child rearing is a most demanding occupation, replete with both rewards and frustrations. Most parents try hard, yet some meet with more frustrations than do others. How we interact with our school-age children will be explored in this chapter through three daily contact points. I view these points as critical to successful child rearing.

The three basic times when parents and school-age children interact regularly are: in the morning, after school and when the child needs "Band-Aids," which I call the minor injury syndrome.

MORNING CONTACT

Habit patterns vary widely, but one or both parents usually talk briefly with their children before the latter take off for school. During those first few minutes, whether a child or parent is still in bed, in the bathroom, at breakfast or at the front door, the mood for the day can be established. We can and should make conscious efforts to send children off to school (or day camp or play) in a cheerful and positive mood.

Unfortunately, in some homes the day begins negatively with a barrage of criticism such as, "You forgot your books; you're late already; you didn't button your jacket," or "Is *that* all the breakfast you're eating?" Such remarks are not exactly music to a child's ears, and have a tendency to initiate the day on a sour note. With a feeling of inadequacy, the youngster is unlikely to bounce off to school and absorb learning with any degree of enthusiasm.

None of us enjoy criticism, and though many children seem to demonstrate amazing techniques for sloughing it off, criticism leaves its mark. Though they hear it's "for your own good," it doesn't feel good, nor is it really their own. Even if the child seems by his morning behavior to be creating his own disasters, there are still supportive ways to handle your relationship with him. Hold criticism for a time when issues can be discussed, rather than come across with what may appear to be or actually be an attack. Instead of the critical statements above, you could try something helpful: "I saw your books on the piano; you might put them by the back door now, so you'll remember them." Or, "Let's both watch the clock; then neither of us will be late." Children respond more favorably if you share responsibility with them and also demonstrate your own responsible behavior. Children have more need of models than of critics.

"Did you read the weather report this morning? It's going to be chilly. I'm wearing my warm jacket. Are you wearing yours?"

"I'm not very hungry for breakfast either, but I can get a snack at the office. Would you like to take something to eat on the way?"

Discuss your observations about behavior and ask the child to suggest alternatives at a time other than during morning contact when there's tension. In a warm, friendly atmosphere, when feelings of anger have subsided, both of you can throw some light on problems—without the heat. Remember, your goal is to bring about a change in behavior without creating feelings of rejection, anger and obstinacy. You can prepare for positive morning contact in the afternoon or evening when perspectives are clearer and emotional upheaval might be avoided.

AFTERNOON CONTACT

In the first four minutes after a child comes home from school, the interaction, usually with mother, can determine if the child will "open up" or "clam up" about the day's activities. The mother who routinely asks, "How was it today?" is practically guaranteed an answer of "Fine" or "O.K." The child's superficial response may be a reflection of the mother's activity at the moment; if she continues to wash dishes or sweep the floor, her lack of involvement with the child is likely to breed a similar indifference in him. How does your child know you're glad to see him when he returns home? For example, do you have the door open, unlocked, step outdoors to greet him, etc.?

If a parent takes time to pay full attention to children, just for a few minutes, it pays off. Sitting at the table while the kids snack, or perching on the edge of a bed while clothes are changed, can reap a harvest of open communication about the day's events and the child's feelings. If pleasant circumstances don't inspire conversation, instead of questioning reflect on the child's emotion or demeanor. What can you see or deduce from nonverbal contact? Children are more likely to share their experiences and feelings with you if you appear "tuned in" to them. Observations such as, "You look tired today," or "You look discouraged, as though it wasn't one of your best days at school," are helpful. An empathetic statement tells the child you understand, you care and you want to be involved. You imply a willingness to help, even listen, without prying directly. "Stop, look and listen" applies here as well as when crossing the street.

When a child does come home complaining and angry, whether it pertains to schoolwork or peer relationships, it is better to be sympathetic and acknowledge that you noticed, rather than turn to a detective-type gathering of facts. Initial questions can seem like an inquisition, and if a child already feels guilty about something that happened, you'll only compound it.

I happened to be visiting an acquaintance one day when

her fourth-grade daughter arrived home in the afternoon. She was dragging her sweater and the pile of books under her arm was about to get away from her. The mother missed her child's apparent happiness to be home, that showed through her fatigue. "Get your hair out of your eyes," she barked. "And pick up your sweater before it looks like a rag."

My silent reaction was "Ouch!" I saw the gleam leave the child's eyes, and she slumped down in a kitchen chair as though she had been slapped in the face.

A positive opening to homecoming children often reaps a fruitful bounty. Mother remarks, "You look very cheerful. It must have been a good day." And the child responds, "Yes, it was. Jane asked me to her birthday party next Saturday, and I got an A on my spelling test." From that beginning, a child may reveal that he or she was upset or angry about something else that occurred. A contact that started on a positive note may continue into areas of disturbance which might not have been shared unless a receptive climate had been provided first.

Dr. Haim G. Ginott, in his book *Between Parent and Child,* (Macmillan, 1965) underlines the importance of going from the general to the specific: "When a child makes a statement about himself, it is often desirable to respond, not with agreement or disagreement, but with details that convey to the child an understanding beyond expectation." In illustration he offers a child who admits he is not good in arithmetic. It is not helpful to agree, nor to offer "cheap advice . . . which only hurts his self-respect . . . and decreases his confidence."

Dr. Ginott suggests replies such as, "Arithmetic is not an easy subject."

"Some of the problems are very hard to figure out."

"We have faith that you'll do your best."

Children in whom you show trust, in this case by easing into their problems or making positive conversation when they return home from school, will react to an instinctive urge not to disappoint you. If they are not threatened, they are not defensive.

Physical contact by hugging or kissing is also an affirmative way of greeting a child. Kids enjoy touching, and they'll be turned on, rather than turned off, by warm feelings invoked.

Consider the frequency of touching babies. Studies indicate that in extreme cases an infant who is not touched may lose his will to live. As children grow, learn to do things for themselves and physically need our attention less, we tend to forget or ignore the fact that emotionally our touch is still necessary to their growth and well-being. Touching your teenager will help show him you still care and love him as much in his move toward independence as when he was your dependent infant.

THE MINOR INJURY SYNDROME

A third contact point with children may occur any time during the day or evening, every day throughout the years children live at home. This encounter follows an accident, a wound or associated trauma which I categorize as the *minor injury syndrome.* How a parent handles the injured child can be a major influence in shaping character structure and personality, especially in the early developing years. As is true in all phases of contact, parents typically respond with consistent patterns, some of which may be supportive, and some undermining. Any of these responses repeated hundreds, if not thousands of times, wield a powerful influence.

As an example: An eight-year-old child, skating on the front sidewalk, falls and skins his knee. The parent, usually mother, hears his crying, rushes to his side, and she may come up with a variety of dubious phrases such as:

—"Oh, my poor darling! You've hurt your sweet little knee. Come into the house, lie down, and let Mommy fix it for you. Then rest for a while and I'll tell you a story."

—"You stupid, clumsy idiot! I told you you were too young for roller skates! Now get in here and take them off. I'll put them away until next year when you're smarter and older. Next time, listen to Mother." Perhaps the child *is* too young for skates, but the general sense of inadequacy he feels from that tirade will hardly encourage him to try new things.

—"Don't worry, honey, it's not your fault. It's those dumb skates and that stupid sidewalk with all the nasty cracks and bumps in it." She may embellish this obvious displacement by stomping on the sidewalk, crying, "Nasty old sidewalk! Don't you hurt my boy!"

Isolated incidents like these may seem insignificant, but when they are repeated many times, they can become a powerful influence in molding a child's orientation of himself in the world through a distorted view of reality. Particularly the parent who consistently blames people, things or forces in the outside world—the skates, the sidewalk, the weather or the teacher—regardless of what has happened to her "poor child," is setting up a pattern wherein the child learns to blame others or external forces for all of his misfortunes. Instead of developing a healthy sense of responsibility, the youngster feels it's not his fault, it's out there, it's "them." He may end up seeing himself at "the mercy" of others and his environment—a mere cork on the sea of life.

In its extreme form, this blame-somebody-else syndrome can develop what in some psychiatrists' jargon is referred to as a paranoid personality. This means living in a severe state of illusion and suspicion, which makes relating to the world of reality a painful experience.

As for the parent who always blames the child for all his difficulties, even those as simple as a splinter in a finger, such reactions can gradually riddle a young personality with self-defeating feelings of inadequacy, inferiority and depression, which may carry through to adulthood.

An appropriate response to the minor injury syndrome is to treat it on a realistic scale. If appropriate, make light of the injury, assuring the child, "It's just a scratch. Let me put a Band-Aid on it. We'll clean it up later when you have your bath. Go right on skating, because you're doing fine. Everyone takes a few spills when they're learning to skate. I fell down a lot more times than you have when I was learning. Pretty soon you'll be a fine skater, and won't fall nearly so often."

Keeping the trauma in perspective supports the child's ability, which increases with confidence instead of decreasing through fear. Such support is the most influential and helpful contribution a parent can make towards his child's growth and maturity. The warm realistic approach helps a youngster gain a well-balanced orientation towards life, with a feeling of responsibility for himself and his behavior, without putting himself down or blaming something or somebody "out there."

Symbolically speaking, if the song you sing is positive, and you are aware of the words, the tone, and the method of your delivery, especially, during frequent four-minute contacts, your child will sing the same tune. "Ac-cen-tu-ate the positive . . ." is the song he or she hears from aware parents who want their kids to develop secure, self-confident personalities, with an ability to love and a deep sense of self-respect and worth.

In our society, with the highest divorce rate in the world, delinquency, drug addiction, teenage pregnancies, runaway kids and child abuse are well-publicized manifestations of an extremely difficult career—namely, parenthood. Rarely in the news but often discussed by authorities in books, magazines and lectures, are the day-to-day enigmas concerned with raising children. We *should* know more today about interacting with offspring of all ages than our own parents did. The media have brought us the techniques, but the tensions of our times make it a formidable task to apply emotionally what we know intellectually. How can a father and mother who are anxious about their own affinity relate with calm understanding to youngsters trying to endure the childhood brand of anxiety?

One answer is that as we develop insights about ourselves, we are more ready to sense our children's needs. Another answer is togetherness, a term that has unfortunately been reduced to triteness of late. But it is still meaningful.

You have heard parents complain about how they "do everything" *for* their sons and daughters, and yet the children "don't appreciate it," and mutual warmth and understanding is lacking. One goal to keep in mind as much as possible would be to reorient your thinking as a parent. Change the word *for* to the word *with*—do *with* your children rather than *for* them. Sadly, few of these families spend much time really talking with their children, even four minutes a day. In contrast, I have heard adverse comments about the kibbutz system in Israel, where parents and children seem to be separated, and only certain adults are given parental responsibility in the communal type of living situation. Surprisingly, studies have shown that these Israeli children grow up to be stable, solid, self-confident individuals with positive self-images. Why is this so?

For one thing, the responsibility of parenthood is clear-cut. If a child wants to be with an adult in the middle of the night, the parent is called. More importantly, half an hour to several hours are set aside each evening during which families are reunited. According to observers I have queried, the family is really *together*. They are involved in talking and communicating their feelings. The mother is *not* at the sink, the father at his newspaper and the children playing, watching TV or doing homework, with only intermittent verbal exchange. On a kibbutz work is put aside; recreation and human contact are the order of the hour.

How many families in America spend fifteen minutes each day together as a unit, sharing on a feeling level, with few interruptions, with everyone there? In some homes this only happens when the father calls a family meeting to discuss problems and discipline, or it is "squeezed in" during supper. Without stress or crisis to require family reunion, togetherness for even fifteen minutes a day is probably rare in our society. However, when the kibbutz system of family gathering can be made a habit, it paves the way for the more harmonious opening contacts mentioned above, as well as giving unity to parents and kids who may otherwise feel they only share a roof. While we can't work out a kibbutz system here, I would also recommend that every parent plan for times alone with each of his or her children. The goal is simply for parent and child to learn to know one another as individuals.

12

A SENSE OF
IDENTITY

Even the most fleeting contact with someone entails some involvement. Involvement entails communication verbally and/or nonverbally, even if "just in passing." But in order to become meaningfully involved and make contact, one must have *an awareness of self*. Put another way, we must have our own *identity awareness,* preferably positive and well defined.

Reality Therapy, a new approach to psychiatry, is based on an understanding that the need for identity is the most important social need that individuals experience. Striving for identity, to know oneself, is universal. It is a need we live with from birth to death, and it begins to crystallize at the age of four or five. It is at about this age that we find the individual developing the social skills, verbal skills, the intellect and thinking ability which enable him to begin to define himself in terms of being a successful or unsuccessful person. Teachers of young children describe the budding of self-image in vivid terms. They see youngsters beginning to develop a concept of themselves as either successful or unsuccessful in both social contacts and miniature accomplishments.

Often, not always below the level of awareness, some kindergarteners are saying to themselves, "I'm a pretty good person, I'm worthwhile, I'm a success, I'm okay." These children beginning with a success identity seek out and play with other youngsters who share a similar self-image. They do not intellectualize or analyze the motivation for choice of playmates. They just choose to play with those with whom they feel most comfortable.

Children developing a failure identity tend to associate with one another. Teachers observe that the two groups grow increasingly divergent as the years pass. This observation about early childhood is very dramatic in underlining the concept that a sense of a positive identity is basic to the development of a healthy personality, able to cope with the myriad problems of life and growth. Just as children segregate themselves into groups who share upbeat or downbeat feelings of their own worth, so do adults—and sometimes with equal lack of awareness, they become mentally pigeonholed as successes or failures.

No other person on earth looks, feels, acts, hopes or thinks exactly as you do. You are unique—each of us is. It is this reality that allows us to develop individual identity.

We all have a deep investment in our own identity. It begins in infancy and continues throughout life. Like a savings account, we can make deposits (in the form of positive experiences or increased awareness that boost our self-image), or we can make withdrawals (which means we change, sometimes thinking less of ourselves, according to "fate," choice of alternatives, or reversal of "fortune"). Every human being appears to regard himself as either a success or failure in life. Of course, people with success identities, experience temporary failure, and vice versa. But each individual's self-concept is reflected in the sum total of the success or failure column, whether strongly or weakly, know or unknown. I am referring to a total self-concept based on the sum of all your feelings and thoughts about yourself as an individual, including your physical and intellectual self-evaluation, your success or failure at hundreds of present and past tasks, your own psychological impressions, and your relationships with others.

It should be no surprise that an individual's self-concept can be a very powerful force in motivating or restricting him. Generally, the more positive is one's identity—within realistic limits—the greater his motivation to get involved with others and the less his fear of being rejected. A healthy self-image helps generate energy to do things, whether they be work, study, concentration or play.

In the field of mental health, as well as in education, there has been an increasing awareness of identity as a pivotal force. Improvement of self-image enables one to cope with the formerly insurmountable and proves a kind of mirror to assess one's progress. There is a definite relationship between an individual's feelings about his own identity and both his achievements and his interpersonal adjustments.

From this brief survey and from what you already know about the importance of a positive self-image, it follows that in making contact with a stranger or friend, knowing how you rate yourself has great significance. In general, the ability to make another human being feel better about himself in the first four minutes of communication is synonymous with the ability to make that person feel good about you.

Boring in a little deeper, if you hope to enhance another's self-image, you must be honest, and you must concentrate on traits or characteristics that are unique to that person according to your observation or instinct. Though we are all quite complex mentally and physically, it is usually easy to discover *something* of a positive nature about another person in the first four minutes of contact. The aptitude you develop to discover these traits, to comment on them appropriately and sincerely, and to imply your positive feelings so they have meaning for others is a very important aspect of successful contact.

How do we see ourselves? Perhaps we can learn something from studies of animals to reinforce how we, Homo sapiens, form self-images. It has been proven that animals, even fish, have a need for each other. Gordon G. Gallup, Jr., in his studies on the self-concept of chimpanzees, clearly demonstrated the ability of the chimpanzee to gain a self-image through exposure to mirrors. Baby chickens alone in a box will chirp 100 times per minute and flutter around looking for escape. However, if another baby chick or a mirror is placed in the box, the distress chirps and fluttering dwindle to almost zero. The chick is unable to distinguish his own self-image and responds to a mirror as if it were another chick. That imagined presence reduces distress. Female pigeons lay fewer eggs in isolation and will lay more in a box with a mirror or in the company of other pigeons. I have heard that a parakeet will look at a mirror four times as long as it will look at another parakeet. This I suppose, is also true for some human beings!

As far back as 1912, sociologist C. H. Cooley proposed that the concept of self arises from social interaction, and that the way we learn to perceive ourselves results from watching how others respond to us. Some people have a blurred or distorted self-image that springs from the need to protect their own self-worth, and yet it is often difficult and sometimes impossible to hide their real self-concept from others. The way we walk, talk, interact, dress, etc., are all indicative of how we feel about ourselves. We often reflect our own self-image to others, whether we want to or not. Yes, you can fool some of the people some of the time, and so on, but if a contact proceeds beyond four minutes, the likelihood that a satisfactory relationship can be enjoyed without divulging the way we really feel about ourselves is minimal.

Remember some of the things mentioned in Chapter 2 regarding assumptions we make—or others make—in everyday interaction? How can we be sure that we are seeing the "real" somebody? In fact, how can we successfully display or hide our own feelings of worth? For one thing, we should avoid formula stereotypes. For instance, a homely man or woman can enjoy a very positive self-concept, while in contrast a handsome man or beautiful woman may suffer from a poor self-image. One reason for the latter paradox is that some very attractive people often receive such recognition and praise for their surface appeal that they develop little motivation to build a sense of worth from their experiences.

To a large extent, "we are what we do." Regardless of how we think and feel, how we agonize over changing and improving, losing weight or learning Chinese, the ultimate and effective reality is *doing it*. We are all endowed with three attributes: thinking, feeling and behavior. We have limited control over the first two, but we have maximum control over behavior. Behavior is doing, and it is this aspect of our lives over which we can exert most control. Dr. Norman Barr, in his forthcoming book *"I Power,"* identifies behavior as the road to the conscious mind. He views a person's potential to utilize creative consciousness in choosing his behavior patterns as a largely untapped, intrinsic human power— I Power. We may be anxious about making new friends or accomplishing goals, and we may think and feel ourselves into a frenzy or a state of numbness, but these mental activities won't help if they don't lead us into action. Through using I Power by trying, risking, venturing, and talking, we manifest behavior that can help wipe out depression, whip the stuffings out of inertia, and blast cerebral dreams and illusions into visceral activity.

A sense of worth or a positive self-image is a product of getting out there and taking chances—feeling and thinking, of course, that you *can* succeed. Thinking failure can help to breed it, just as a success syndrome is necessary to making chances pay off in pleasure or any other measure of profit you may use. Success or failure in contact experiences, where you get involved with other human beings even for short periods, is instrumental in the growth of a healthy self-image.

A healthy, positive self-image is imperative to accomplishing the social goals we each have, either with new acquaintances or in ongoing relationships. The subject of identity, how we see ourselves and the esteem in which we hold ourselves, is obviously integral to making effective contact. It is also an aspect of total personality that blurs easily. We know what happens in laboratory conditions, for example, when people experience psychoses under the influence of LSD. They may begin to feel their physical identity is blending and shading into the environment. This causes fear or panic in some people.

We also know how the image of one's identity shifts under the influence of alcohol. Some people drink too much because they are dissatisfied with their self-image. If they can blot out their self-image temporarily, they can imagine themselves far more adept in the social whirl; or with seemingly increased confidence they can face the problems that have not been solved while sober. Intoxication, unfortunately, usually compounds the existing mess people are in or imagine themselves in. Identity *seems* to be improved but ends up even more muddled when sobriety returns along with a hangover.

Only in rational behavior that seeks to take advantage of new opportunities can we hope to improve self-esteem. One way of approaching reality is through psychotherapy, of which there are many schools, methods and theories. We can project our image to a therapist, or in group therapy, and hopefully the reflection we get back will be closer to truth than we are able to see ourselves. In therapy we take time to look inward carefully, to understand mysteries, to extend our awareness of self and society. Many people with problems try to blame others, such as over-indulgent parents, rejecting lovers, or hostile employers, but primarily most people's problems stem from the results of their own poor choices.

I would like to summarize some of the main ideas, from my vantage point, of Reality Therapy, which pertain to behavior—the one aspect of life over which we have control. This digest, gleaned from numerous lectures and workshops I have given on the subject, resolves around the search for a success identity:

1. To achieve success, a person must develop self-confidence.

2. The self-image of an unsure person is enhanced through *doing* things that result in feelings of success.

3. Confidence that you will succeed improves the probability of success; *if you expect failure, chances are it will result!*

4. When one is self-confident, one can tolerate rejection more easily, whether one is offering love, friendship, assistance, or innocuous contact.

5. Eeach of us must discover his or her basic identity; each of us is *someone* distinct from others, and that someone is worthwhile.

6. A feeling of love, affection or friendship exchanged with others is both a cause and effect on the path to a positive personal self-image.

7. There are two kinds of failure: failure to love and failure to achieve self-worth. Without love and/or realistic self-worth, one develops a failure identity, causing withdrawal from reality.

8. Failure should not be blamed on circumstances or other people. This precludes a feeling of *personal responsibility* for failure. Success is potentially open to everyone.

9. People must also take the responsibility for their own actions. Just as making excuses and looking elsewhere to place the blame is unrealistic, we cannot disguise the fact that people are responsible for *fulfilling their own needs*. Others may help or encourage, but no one can do it for you.

10. People must also take the responsibility for modifying their own actions and behavior if they have not been successful. Someone may prompt you or urge you on, but *you* must *do* it. Your own self-image must help motivate you, for it is your identity that is being improved. It's as though your self-image were a motor that became more

powerful and ran more effectively as it was used to move you forward in time, space and life.

11. The feeling of "resignation" is an insidious cloud of stifling smog; it stems from the erroneous idea that one has very little chance to succeed to be happy in this world.

12. A person who senses failure must learn to evaluate what he is doing to contribute to his own failure. After realizing his own contribution, he must discover what he can *do* to change his *behavior*—and thereby turn the negative into a positive situation.

13. One must learn to give love as well as receive it. Giving makes you feel good about yourself as you respond with joy to others. Receiving love without reciprocating is a prelude to certain failure.

A book called *Contact* may help you distinguish your identity in this supersonic world of idea and activity, but it can't *do* something for you, other than perhaps point out what you can *do for yourself*. When being responsible for your own behavior becomes a creative joy, making friends and keeping loved ones will be a welcome challenge. You'll know and feel that success is yours for the *doing*.

13.

THE
WINDOWS OF
SELF-ASSESSMENT

The concept of Contact can serve as a mirror in which you can see yourself and your encounters with others reflected distinctly, perhaps for the first time. Making thought and theory, feeling and behavior symbolically serve as mirrors is not an unusual endeavor. Whenever we illuminate with awareness an activity or phenomenon which has previously been habitual, automatic, or merely taken for granted, we give ourselves the opportunity to replace *overlooking* with *looking at*. For example, just by realizing that most of our contacts with others open with a four-minute prelude, during which connections are made either successfully or not so successfully—just by realizing that fact we begin to *see it happen*. In the fresh light of this new awareness, we can perceive our behavior with others as we interact, a mental process not unlike the reflected view of ourselves offered by a mirror.

In this chapter I want to introduce some supplementary tools of perception, in this case useful for looking *into* ourselves—as through windows—for the purpose of self-assessment. All of us have the potential sensitivity for making more accurate self-assessments; in some of us it needs to be nourished, encouraged, or even discovered. While it is obviously impossible to be totally self-objective, we can, given the proper openings for introspection, achieve some of the insight others have into us. It is exceedingly important to our self-awareness and confidence to have someone—either another person or ourselves—take a long, balanced, and above all, friendly look at our strengths and weaknesses.

Over the years, in lectures and workshops, I have often voiced disappointment and disapproval of the traditional psychotherapist's report that is classified as a "case history." Almost every case history I've read, well-written or not, is 90 to 95 percent a compendium of the traumas, failures, inadequacies, problems and shortcomings of someone. The amount of time and space given to a discussion of an individual's attributes and potentials is sadly minimal. After the usual inventory of problems and anxieties, it also seems traditional to end a case history with a statement that goes something like: "With appropriate therapy and counseling, this individual has made constructive progress and, I believe, will achieve additional positive gains in the future." Sometimes this is the only affirmative note in an entire case history, which may run to twenty pages.

Lecture and workshop participants usually ask me, in effect: "If you don't like, don't approve of, and don't use the usual case history form, how do you assess a person? How *do* you handle the information you glean from someone in therapy? If you don't make a written survey of his problems, what sort of study do you prefer to sort out and record a patient's history and psychological status?"

For several years, I've been compiling ideas and testing techniques for assessing people according to their changing values and improving recognition of their own assets. A modification of this same approach can also be utilized by individuals to assess themselves.

Self-assessment in a therapeutic sense means in part discovering what you have going for you. The plus side of the character ledger is emphasized; there is a realistically balanced look at the debit side, which you will understand as you read on. A long list of hangups and negativisms can be just a block of cement into which your feet are set. An examination of yourself, as seen through an assortment of windows I'll describe and you will explore can help you become *more in touch with yourself*. Who you are, what in life has meaning for you, what emotions you call upon to deal with life, what your expectations are for yourself—these are all a part of your positive profile. As I unfold my ideas about assessment, I will encourage you to reflect on them with deliberation. You may find it worthwhile to do this with a friend or an intimate; such an interchange can reveal your feelings and values more sharply than a silent mental survey.

None of the assessment topics stress failure, short-comings or inadequacies. None concern specific incidents in the past which you might choose to forget or ignore. Rather, the focus is on the here and now, on present self-awareness from a positive and constructive viewpoint. On this basis, self-assessment is made through a clean window and onto a ledger that has many columns —primarily on the plus side.

Because of the frustrations that often plague us, life can sometimes feel like a closed-up, shuttered room with a locked door, from which exit seems momentarily difficult or impossible. In such a situation it is self-defeating to concentrate on the barriers, on our inadequacies to the task of setting out and moving on. It is self-defeating to be crashing against the locked door or the wall in frustration, when drawing on our resources and talents may lead us to something as simple and successful as opening the shutters for light, the window for fresh air.

Self-Esteem

In the last chapter we examined the roots of identity: each of us has a collective self-image. In elementary terms, color it successful or unsuccessful. These words do not refer to specific ventures, physical attributes or emotional characteristics but, rather, our *total* identity assessment. In this reckoning are all the ways you feel about yourself emotionally and physically, all the activities in which you are involved, everything you have accomplished with satisfaction, merit or love, and all the feelings you have of how others see you. Sit back, close your eyes, do a little probing. Is yours a success or failure identity?

The panorama of your identity, in terms of self-esteem, should be viewed in respect to yourself, as well as in terms of how you feel about other people. Dr. Thomas A. Harris wrote a book called *I'm O.K.— You're O.K.* (Harper & Row, 1967) in which he describes four possible relationships of ourselves to others:

1. I'm O.K.—You're O.K.: Obviously the ideal identity stance which portrays someone who has positive self-esteem, likes and accepts people, and is inclined favorably about humanity.

2. I'm O.K.—You're not O.K.: Essentially the position of one who has a good self-concept, but generally finds "people are no damned good." This individual may like a handful of friends, relatives and intimates, but generally he perceives humanity in an unfriendly way.

3. I'm not O.K.—You're O.K.: Here's a failure identity, coupled with the impression that the rest of humanity is successful and happy.

4. I'm not O.K.—You're not O.K.: These individuals feel nobody is worth a damn, including themselves.

Into which of these four categories do you place yourself? This is a critical component of self-assessment. The better you feel about yourself, the better you feel about other people. It follows that if most individuals appear superior to you, your chances of becoming involved are dimmed.

Is your self-esteem healthy and balanced so that you can approach everybody "out there" on equal footing as a fellow human being?

Responsibility—To Yourself and Others

I also mentioned in the last chapter that how we relate to lovers and strangers is highly influenced by the degree to which we see ourselves responsible for our own behavior. When you acknowledge and accept that *you alone* have the power, control and guidance for the vehicle of your own being, there is a far greater possibility that you will fill your needs, reach your goals, satisfy your desires and find fulfillment during your decades on earth.

The more one perceives his behavior and fate as dominated by friends, business associates, wives, husbands, children, mothers-in-law, mysterious vibrations from outer space, or "circumstances beyond control," the greater the chance for disappointment and misfortune.

Who is the master of your fate? Are you reading this book because it is an assignment? Because someone told you to? Or because you want to? Is it your choice? How about the circumstances or events that made you happiest lately? Did you instigate or initiate them? Even when we are faced with making necessary decisions that may all lead to something temporarily undesirable ("choice between two evils" is the cliché), the course we choose must be our own. Even in psychotherapy, no progress can occur until an individual acknowledges and accepts that he is responsible for his own behavior.

Do you acknowledge and accept the fact that you are responsible for your own behavior?

Anger

Learning to recognize, understand and deal with emotions such as anger, irritability, frustration and hostility are primary problems of mankind today. How do you deal with anger? The ability to respond appropriately to anger from others and the ability to express your own feelings of anger are important to your well-being and your relationship with others.

When you become angry, do you withdraw?

When someone is angry with you, do you impulsively lash back with your own feelings of anger?

Do you try to understand, to reason, to stay with the issues? Do you strive for less heat and more light on problems in dispute?

Do you have difficulty expressing anger until it explodes like buckshot all over everyone?

Do you bury your anger until its psychosomatic manifestations appear as ulcers, backaches, muscle tension, or headaches?

Do you recognize anger that is realistically directed toward you, and can you deal with it fairly?

Can you express anger directly, without explosive behavior, when the time seems appropriate?

We know anger is a basic human emotion in ourselves and in others, and if we cope with it effectively, our chances are improved for loving and being loved, for caring and being cared about.

Do you acknowledge that anger is a normal experience? Are you willing to give and receive it appropriately?

Love

It's a sticky word, bandied about easily, sworn casually, retracted hastily, and perhaps felt with depth too infrequently in one lifetime. Love is also an expression of affection, tenderness, sacrifice and personal dedication. Reaching out to make contact symbolically offers and asks for love. Love, to some, may be "never having to say you're sorry," but it's a lot more synonymous with *caring*. If you care and you feel regret, you'll find a way to express it.

Love and tenderness, admiration and affection can be bottled up. Are you able to express these feelings to others? Are you able to comfortably experience all the ramifications of caring?

How is your receptivity to revelations or demonstrations of love and caring? Do you back away? Are you comfortable with touching, kissing, fondling and embracing? Do honest expressions of goodwill, warmth and generosity make you want to respond in similar terms?

Are you able to say—and accept—"I really like you" in words and behavior?

What part does hypocrisy play in your responses to love and caring? Do you become flustered, do you feign nonchalance, or do you pretend something else that is partly a pose?

Love is a sexual exchange to some, an intense career, a mythical distant dream, a firm foundation of realistic give-and-take. What is it to you?

Are you comfortable giving and receiving expressions of love?

Values

In actuality, self-esteem, responsibility, anger, love, and most points of personal assessment considered here depend on the system of values an individual develops from childhood to the grave. Suppose you had to write an essay on *your own* values, not values you hold for others or humanity in general—what would your inventory include? Are equality, freedom, honesty, sincerity, trust or fidelity important parts of your value system and life style? Does religion have separate requirements in your life or is it part of your personal value system? In other words, what primary concepts and beliefs have meaning and importance in your life?

Some of the assessment headings below echo this one. Most people rarely stop to appraise the values which determine the direction of their lives, the doctrines which ideally make us be good to ourselves and to others.

What are five important values you live by?

To Laugh and to Cry

One of my children eloquently responds to irony in Laurel and Hardy tones by saying, "That's *not* funny." Sometimes it really isn't, but one man's humor may be another man's tragedy. Laughter is a response that develops within us, though crying is instinctive. Babies are born wailing—a healthy sign, and they smile before they laugh. Though laughter is a lubricant to social contact, it could be the prelude to hysteria. Crying, on the other hand, may also instigate contact since it is brought about by both sadness and happiness.

In the assessment frame of reference, the ability to laugh at one's self, to see one's foibles, follies and incongruities, is an important criterion of mental health. This is not something that an acutely disturbed individual is able to feel or express. For such a person, to be laughed at is demeaning and threatening. Various types of conformists regulate their habits, dress and behavior so that no one will laugh at them. In some ways, when viewed on a broad social level, their mass urge to drift with the tide is sad, and we end up crying for them instead.

In making contact, the ability to provoke laughter or get a chuckle from others is a talent. However, it should not be at your own expense or at the expense of others, by putting others down. Acting like a clown or a boor is quite different from being witty and amusing.

Are you objective and mature enough to laugh at yourself when the occasion arises?

Do you realize the value of satire or irony in gaining perspective on realistic, sometimes unwelcome events or interchange?

Can you recognize a nervous laugh that springs from insecurity and offer words or gestures that show you care for someone in mild and temporary anguish?

Where does crying fit into your value system? Do you equate it with weakness, emotional instability, pain, manipulation or bereavement? Objectively, crying can be associated with each of those forms of behavior. In a stable person, the ability to shed tears can be a necessity, and it exhibits trust in self as well as others. In our culture, it is much more acceptable for women to cry than for men, but in tragedy or exceptional pain, the man who weeps is demonstrating a human tendency that transcends gender.

Chlidren cry easily and often to express their frustrations or pain. Perhaps adults seldom cry because there is a childish connotation.

It is unlikely that you first meet people while you or they are crying, but this condition is more likely in ongoing relationships. How do you feel and respond when a companion, male or female, cries at a sad movie?

How freely do you laugh and cry and accept those emotions from others?

Changing Roles

Do you realize how many roles you play in relation to various situations and individuals in your life on a daily basis? Here's just a partial "cast of characters" one man and one woman might represent from the time the alarm rings until the late show signs off: mother, father, student, employer, employee, driver, pedestrian, friend, neighbor, confidant, nurse, housekeeper, repairman, bon vivant, babysitter, barber. In self-assessment, give yourself high grades for the ability to shift suitably and rapidly from one situation to another, neatly picking up the cues which accompany them.

For example, you react and interact with a friend using certain personal characteristics that differ from those you exhibit with someone who shares your bed. At a party, you may respond gaily to members of the opposite sex, but in the office you could have a "position of authority" to uphold—which means you play another role. In a traffic jam you may scream bloody murder at the stupid driver ahead of you—who can't hear the brilliant advice you're offering—but at home you are a patient counselor to a son or daughter who has made a dumb decision.

Role shiftability is a dominant trait of figures in fiction who fascinate us by the predictable, as well as the unexpected. But in real life, the battlefield sergeant who is courageous and admired by his men had better temper his qualities of leadership as a husband and father, or his domestic life is headed for shambles. In my practice, I hear people complain their families don't understand them, in statements such as: "My wife just can't get it into her head that I'm an engineer, and that's the way I think." In my opinion, this is a smokescreen for someone's lack of effort or ability to shift roles as settings and circumstances change.

The person who can move freely and appropriately from one role to another has contact flexibility. In familiar situations or in meeting the unknown, he can be at ease, calling upon the various facets of personality which are most adaptable to time and place. *His value system remains stable,* for it is the firm armature in the animated human psyche. I do not subscribe to the notion that we should act as we please, according to a literal translation of "be yourself." On a widespread basis, such behavior could only lead to mass hostility and chaos, with no social traffic regulations for selfish, antisocial activity. To "do your own thing" may be a philosophical positive but it can be, in extremes, a real-life "nothing," calculated to set one in th role of being an out-of-place stranger in his own land.

Patients occasionally ask if I "act the same way at home as you do in the office." To which I answer of course I don't. If I "acted like a psychiatrist" at home, my wife and children would find me intolerable and probably throw me out. I'm a husband and father at home, and I bring with me principles and experience gained from training and practice, but my family are not my patients. Physicians rarely treat members of their own families, incidentally, because close personal entanglement can cloud sound judgment and treatment.

What roles do you play? On what stage? In what order of importance? Would you rather switch than fight? Good—because behavioral versatility is tantamount to a fluid personality that can adapt in four minutes almost anywhere, outside of a Saudi Arabian harem or an election campaign in Vermont.

Do you shift roles appropriately and suitably as situations change?

Interpersonal Relationships

This is a nice clinical term for how you get along with people, which is only the topic of this whole book; but at this point I want to zoom in on a specific: What kind of friends do you have? What is the depth of your relationship with them? With whom do you feel comfortable sharing your sorrows, joys and routine trivia? Are there enough people in this category to suit your needs—outside of your family, I mean? Is the sharing mutual; do they come to you as well? Do you have one *intimate* friend whose trust is equal to, or exceeds that which you have with a blood relative?

To some readers, these may sound like simplistic questions. Others will discover they really don't have *one* really close friend. At a recent workshop during a self-assessment session, a mature man of forty-eight, married and the father of three children, told us he was startled to find there was no one except his wife to whom he could confide his deepest feelings. "She was in the hospital for a few weeks," he said, "with problems both emotional and physical. I could talk to my kids, but our interchange was limited to their awareness level. I wanted to spill my guts, to simply tell somebody how disturbing it was to have my wife away and sick, but there was nobody. My close 'friends' would have listened, but they were not clued in to me well enough; I wouldn't have felt safe in revealing myself. I finally got it all out on paper. Just sat and wrote what was in my head and heart, and I felt relieved; but there was no feedback. It's funny, because I was sure I had lots of friends I could turn to in an emergency."

A friendship may start in four minutes, but it has to be cultivated like a plant. You water it with attention, fertilize it with mutual interchange, prune it with awareness; and its roots go deep. Real friendship flowers when you need it most; you have given it the best you have, and it's ready—when you are—to reciprocate, absorb, please or console.

Who are your friends and how much do you mean to each other?

Sexual Adjustment

Whether you enjoy sexual intimacy with one or more partners is less important than realizing *how* you relate sex to your life. Is it the cause or the result of intimacy? Healthy, fulfilling sex should be both.

Questions about your sexual values are very approximate. For instance, do you consider yourself a passive recipient or an active aggressor? Are you really sensitive to your partner's moods, movements or ministrations? Is communication open and free before, during and after sexual contact? Have you hangups or inhibitions which seem quite justified, but have been challenged by individuals or through changing customs?

Only recently I tuned into a late-night talk show and watched a former madam discuss the house of prostitution she ran for forty years in Kentucky. The woman had written a book of her experiences, and among other things, she said, "We had all sorts of men as clients over the years. Married men and older men, young fellows, big shots—and somehow they were all kind of lonely. Some of them just wanted variety and some had ego hangups, but many just didn't know how to get out in bars or places and make contact."

The discussion about prostitutes and their regimentation in this woman's house was frank and far less clinical than it might have been a decade ago, before the sexual revolution had revolved as far as it has. Sex was depicted not as something dirty to titter about but as a natural human activity, subject to a wide variety of tastes and gratifications. Is sex still under the covers in your home or your system of values? It may still be a manipulation game for many people who are searching for real intimacy, but sex is "out front" with many young people today. Promiscuity is as hard to define as Einstein's theory of relativity. "We love each other—or we dig each other—and we make it together." That's the position of some healthy, active people, young and old, that I hear.

How tolerant are you of sexual values unlike your own? Do you feel that everyone should be sexually monogamous? Is "sleeping around" *ever* justified? Are swingers, wife-swappers or participants at orgies all sick, or could they have a sexual orientation you just don't understand?

What are your sexual prejudices, values and orientation? And how do they affect your contacts, new or familiar?

Leisure Is a Good-Time Thing

Many people are so preoccupied with filling their time constructively and conscientiously that they become guilty about making time for leisure activities. The drive for success, identity and material improvement can be a curse that gives leisure fun the wrong connotation.

In the last decade, I feel that the enjoyment of leisure has become a more honorable and desirable goal for rich and poor. Our national parks are so crowded in summer that you have to make reservations to drive into some. Bowling alleys and beaches are jammed—and they are only symbols of popular recreation. What's your orientation to pleasure and leisure? What do you do for fun, and how varied are your activities? Do you plan recreation, or wait for someone else to propose it?

What is really fun to you anyway? Golf, hiking, reading, painting, getting high, or a dozen other things? When was the last time you *really* had a good time? Was it a compulsive activity or easy? When other people are having fun, are you able to join them or are you usually on the periphery? What would you do if you had a month of no responsibilities or obligations and money was no problem? If that sounds like a snap to answer, it isn't for some people who don't know what to do with their leisure time. They are not jaded but simply not motivated by getting away, doing something different, seeing new places, meeting new people, or exposing themselves to adventure.

Many people have a fantasy of springing free from routine responsibility and "taking off." Those who are successful in everyday contacts are most likely to find leisure, faraway places and new experiences fulfilling. A surprising number of people have difficulty adapting to time off.

In contrast, do you long for leisure so avidly that all routine is a bore? Do people enjoy you as a "fun person," but find it hard to talk seriously with you? Or would you consider yourself a drudge who thinks of play as a waste of time?

It takes effort and positive direction to make leisure a good-time thing. Most healthy people feel they earn time off and plan it with pleasure. The ability to enjoy leisure time is not something we all burn with, but is a learned process.

Have you learned to enjoy your leisure time?

Work is a Four-Letter Word

The enjoyment of work—a job, a profession, homemaking, or acquiring a formal education—is a more difficult accomplishment for some people than acclimating to leisure. How many men, women and children merely tolerate work in return for a necessary paycheck or goal? At the other end of the scale are those who don't have to work but volunteer their time and efforts for organizations that pay off in recognition, gratitude and appreciation for worthy public service.

In any case, whatever you do, whether you're completely satisfied or not, do you do a good job? Do you gain as much satisfaction as possible?

My experience in psychiatry has shown that some people have a special characteristic—and they're not born with it—that enables them to find satisfaction and feel good about tasks. Developing this trait is not easy, but it is feasible and inevitably worthwhile. While many individuals move from job to job, chasing a rainbow they may never reach, others learn to assess themselves to discover the best elements of a job which can be gratifying. They pinpoint the personal characteristics which help them adapt, and they amplify these, without delusion, to make a springboard of their assets. When new opportunities arise, they are better prepared, either with the same firm in the same town or with something different but better.

Are you one of the people I've just described, or do you shift from job to job, city to city, finding new work and settings as disappointing as the old ones were? Perhaps it's not the job nor the town, but you. Stories of men and women who started in jobs they hated but looked ahead and moved to the beat of opportunity are legion. Don't attribute other people's accomplishments to luck, for "luck" occurs when preparation meets opportunity.

If work is a dirty word and play is the nicest four-letter word you know, self-assessment should help you realize better the true meaning of both. If you're muttering "Pollyanna" under your breath, I can't hear you because I *want* to go back to work.

Is work a chore, a hardship and something you endure for eight or more hours a day as a necessary evil, or do you make it pleasant and enjoyable?

Whom Do You Attract?

Most of us are aware of the kind of people that turn us on, give us good vibrations, and are interesting or fascinating. However, when we reflect about the kind of people who are attracted to *us*, it can be startling and revealing. How many times have you heard somebody say, "I don't know why, but the wrong kind of men (or women) are always attracted to me"? Most individuals rarely stop and analyze what qualities and characteristics the *right* kind of person might have.

At workshops when I ask single women for a general appraisal of the men who find them interesting, they may reply with a declaration that "Most of them are tall, dark, poor and average looking," or "They're usually too short, rather demanding and overly dependent." When a summary evinces such disappointment, I point out the significance of recognizing that the guys (or girls) who are attracted to them are not the kind they find most appealing. The same might be said for couples who seem to attract other couples that leave something to be desired as ongoing friends.

What's the hangup? It could be various things. Perhaps you are not honestly projecting your real image and, by masking some of your more appealing qualities, are failing to magnetize others more preferable to you. Maybe you aren't reaching high enough—your mental equivalent needs to be elevated—because you underrate your own ability or what you deserve.

What sort of people *do* you attract? Do they tend to complement your needs? Do the same kind of people gravitate toward you today as did five or ten years ago? What do your answers say about you?

Do you attract the kind of people you are attracted to?

Who Attracts You?

Read the last section again in reverse. In this case, what are *your* criteria, your requirements, your desires? Are the girls always sexy (and often unobtainable) and are the men always handsome, or slim, or wealthy, or dependent? Are the physical and personality characteristics you look for realistic? Fiction is full of chambermaids pining away for dukes and princes, but there are few eligible heroes who ally themselves with the plain, uneducated, or unrefined. Eliza Doolittle might be an exception, but she had a helluva lot on the ball as Bernard Shaw envisioned her, or Professor Higgins could not have done so well with his fair lady.

It's easy to make a catalog of idealized qualities you want in a mate or a friend, but they can become a barrier between you and almost everyone you meet. If sights are high, your hunting grounds had better be diverse.

You may have heard the story of the man who spent thirty years looking for the ideal woman for him to marry. One day he mentioned to a friend that he had finally found her; he was rhapsodic at first, and then glum. "What's the matter?" asked his friend, "aren't you going to marry her?"

"Not actually," replied the seeker. "You see she's looking for the ideal man."

What kind of people are you attracted to?

The Yes vs. the No of It

There are optimists and there are pessimists, and we know both. I'm *not* going to ask you to assess yourself in this regard, but, rather, I want to focus on the analogous positive vs. negative orientation which everyone has. In evaluating others—and yourself, as well—which has priority to you?

When you see a movie, read a book, visit a town, or meet somebody new, do you think first of their attributes or liabilities? If you came upon a dining room scene where twelve people had left the table, would you describe it like this: "It's a mess, with lots of dirty dishes, wrinkled napkins, scraps of food, stains on the tablecloth, and chairs turned every which way." Or would you be more likely to say, "The people who left here must have had a sumptuous dinner for the decor and the silver are elegant, the flowers are beautiful, and the wine bottles indicate the vintage was first class."

Each of us has a predominant orientation to people, places and things that springs from a positive or negative attitude. Some people look first into the shadows, and others are first impressed with the highlights. Of course, the well-balanced person looks at both sides and integrates positive and negative into all of his appraisals.

When you hear somebody describing a new acquaintance with a list of his shortcomings first, their evaluation might be quite accurate; but it may be that their orientation is negative because they see life unfolding mostly under big, black clouds. Often in my office I'll ask a patient to describe the room to me, from which I get an introduction to some of his positive/negative priorities. In my experience, as I listen to people describe situations, other individuals and life experiences, I find there are four basic orientations:

1. Those who see only the negative.

2. Those who see only the positive.

3. Those who see both and look for the negative first.

4. Those who see both and look for the positive first.

Those exemplified by category four, who see both positive and negative and typically look for and describe the positive first, are clearly healthier emotionally, happier, and most pleasant to be with.

In initial contact, the connection is clear. Does the world more or less glow for you, or does it have a dull and ugly patina? Do new acquaintances always seem to have drawbacks, are they on unreachable pedestals, or do you seem to hook in neatly when so inspired? If you are continually disappointed, you may be avoiding the potential of intimacy because it scares you for some reason. It's a negative mechanism to feel that "nobody turns you on," for you don't have to pursue a relationship, nor are you challenged. You set yourself up to reject—maybe before you feel you'll be rejected.

Perhaps none of the gloom-and-doom framework fits you. That's obviously healthy because you don't want to be seen through dismally smoke-colored glasses yourself.

Do you see the positive and the negative and typically accentuate the positive?

How Do Others See You?

Imagine half a dozen or more of your closest friends (not relatives) in a comfortable living room, with you as the topic of discussion. Each in turn is asked to say

frankly the two or three things they like best about you.
What do you imagine, or assume, they might mention?
Of course, you can't know for sure, but perhaps you can
make an educated guess. Are you able to assess your outstanding personality characteristics which friends might
list?

During workshops, there are those who find this exercise easy, but some are embarrassed and surprised at their
own struggle to pinpoint the qualities their friends might
name quickly.

In the same room with the same friends, imagine asking
them to name two or three things you might either change
about yourself or improve in a way that would make you
even more desirable as a friend than you are now. What
would they be likely to tell you? When you have projected
the points they may raise, would you agree with them all?
If so, how are you stopping yourself from making such
changes right now?

*What three characteristics do your friends like best
about you? What three characteristics could you improve
or acquire to make you a better person and friend?*

Character-Building Experiences

In the lives of all of us there have been episodes that
helped build or strengthen our character. List about ten
of these occurrences and decide how they influenced your
personality and behavior in ways that you appreciate or
still exhibit today. For example, there might be the time
you were elected vice-president of your class, or won a
blue ribbon for baking biscuits. Other experiences to consider may be the first week of military service, the day you
mastered horseback riding or water skiing, the day you
were married, having your first child, buying a home, or
flying off to Europe on your own. How did doing these
things make you feel? How have they influenced your
behavior and self-image since?

We've all met with many consequential situations over
the years, but we rarely stop to think of how we may have

changed because of them—nor do we assess the positive assets we had (and have) which made it possible to achieve, endure or triumph. We are more apt to think of such experiences as disturbing problems, rather than opportunities for success. It is those successes which I consider character-building experiences to include in this self-assessment program.

List ten positive character-building experiences and relate them to your current personality and behavior.

What Do You Have Going for You?

The key words here are: attributes, strengths and potentials. What are your most positive physical and emotional characteristics? Are you aware enough of your body and keeping it in shape? Do you respond with a cool head to emergencies? Have you a keen sense of organization that benefits yourself and others but is not compulsive? How is your patience, your talent in the kitchen, in bed, or with hobbies?

What potentials do you see for your own further development? Have you set goals in keeping with those potentials? These may lie in the areas of job, home, travel, appearance, or social activity. What's ahead that you can and will achieve?

What are your strengths and how do they have value in your life? For instance, are you handy with tools and do you like to build things at home? Do you have social graces that help you make contact easily, and do other people enjoy your company for this, among other reasons? Most individuals can recite a litany of their problems and inadequacies but rarely add up the strengths which can be definite advantages in the social and business worlds.

What are ten of your strongest positive qualities and characteristics?

Positive/Negative Habits

You can relate ordinary habits to strengths and attributes, as well as to how others may see you. Desirable habits are those which are fulfilling to you, such as being considerate of others, regular personal hygiene, or keeping promises. Undesirable habits could be drinking too much, driving too fast, biting your nails, or saying "you know" in every phrase of conversation. Your manner of eye contact is a habit, too. Do you look down or off into the distance as you talk to people, or directly at their eyes?

It is uncomfortable to examine our habit patterns, for some of them seem to be closely integrated into a lifestyle and easily rationalized as acceptable. However, if self-assessment exposes habits we like, they become assets in our ledger, while habits we dislike, once we can recognize them more distinctively, can be revised or eliminated.

List five of your "good" and five of your "bad" habits.

Religious Beliefs

Do you know what your religious beliefs actually are? What are your feelings or convictions about God? About death? It is amazing to me that most therapists don't ask their patients what they believe will happen to them after their mortal life on earth ceases. What an individual feels and believes about death and afterlife helps to shape in a significant way the kind of life he chooses to lead—even in day-to-day behavior.

I recall an old book called *An American Exodus* by Dorothea Lange and Paul Taylor (Reynal & Hitchcock, 1939) which touchingly documented the migration of Okies to the West. There is a full-page photograph of a gaunt woman with one hand on her forehead and the other on her neck, taken in the Texas Panhandle in 1938. The caption reads, "If you die, you're dead—that's all." The stark pathos of this statement has stayed with me; the woman had little hope for happiness on earth, and death registered as a blank to her, a parallel of her life.

What do you believe will happen to you, or to your soul, after you die? Do you know the feelings of your spouse or your closest friend? Have you ever asked them? Do they know what you believe? Married couples seen together in my office often become uncomfortable when I pose this question to each of them. They either don't know or have not discussed it in years.

In my opinion, it is important to analyze your own convictions about death, about dying, and about what might be in store afterwards. Whether your emotions have a religious origin or not, it is important to give consideration to death. I believe that those who do not face their feelings, fears and beliefs about death and dying have difficulty enjoying life.

What do you believe about God? About death and dying?

What Illusions?

We all entertain certain illusions about ourselves—believing that we are more clever than we really are, or even more prompt—but only the mentally ill are predominantly guided by fantasies and self-inflicted distortions of reality. Are there things that you pretend about yourself? Are you sustaining illusions about your health, your appearance, your weight, or how informed you may be? Do you pretend to others that you are more informed, more secure, more independent, less conservative, less sensitive, etc.? Are you waiting for your "ship to come in," either financially or in the form of an opportunity which you imagine will appear inevitably? Do you imagine that somebody is in love with you when it's just wishful thinking?

Illusions are like balloons which we float in the air and enjoy, but that we must puncture regularly in order to stay sensibly earthbound ourselves. By first becoming aware of the things we pretend to others, we can then deal with them internally, after which it will not be necessary to delude others. The more we pretend to be something we're not, the greater the chance of believing fancy to be fact. The reality of self-assessment is relative, but we must set our own limits of illusion and pull in the balloons before they carry us away. Some pretenses create anxieties

—a fear that we may be discovered, which undermines self-esteem and hardly makes living more comfortable.

In what areas are your illusions? What characteristics or abilities have you been pretending about on a regular basis? It may be an illusion to answer that you have none!

Material Gifts and Giving

Sometimes, to express our love, affection or gratitude for others, we give a material gift or service. As you receive gifts, you should become aware of what you are feeling. What is the gift-giver trying to express to you? What are the most significant two or three gifts (things given to you or done for you) you've received in your life? What meaning did those gifts have? Was it a painting, a book, a greeting card which profoundly influenced your feelings about yourself and the giver? What led to the giving? Often the monetary value of the gift has little relationship to its meaning.

Which is easier for you—giving or receiving? What are the two or three most significant gifts you have given? Were they perceived by the recipient with the intensity of feelings you experienced in giving? I find that most people are more comfortable with giving than receiving. In my opinion, the ability to receive a gift with grace, dignity and appreciation is also "giving."

How we give and receive, how we express joy or appreciation, are important qualities and meaningful symbols for self-assessment and for evaluating our relationships with others.

What are the three most important gifts you've given and the three most important gifts you've received in your life?

Who and What Would You Die For?

I often ask patients at some point in therapy, "Who would you die for?" Since most people have never seriously pondered this question, it serves to put them in touch with many of their deeper feelings about those they love. However, it also reveals that some individuals believe they would risk death for others who are not related legally or by blood, which points up the close affinity of love and friendship. Whom do *you* love? The answer may be surprising.

There are many ifs, ands, or buts to these propositions. You may ask "Under what circumstances?" and the qualifier is valid; but who comes to mind—and who is not included? Is there anyone you believe would die for you?

A related twist to the hypothetical "die for" proposition includes also the *values* or principles which we hold dear enough to defend, even to the death. In World War II men were willing to die for their country because it had been attacked and the peril of fascism was real. Issues in the Korean War were not as clearcut but certainly less controversial than those raised by Vietnam. Is there any circumstance in which you feel dying for your country is still valid?

When I asked a group of fifteen professional women in Puerto Rico what they would die for, three of them said they would die to preserve their virginity. In ways this is an anachronism to many of us, since virginity is no longer held in such unique esteem in the States. However, to those women and to others like them elsewhere, virginity has deep-seated value.

Would you die to protect your property or possessions? To preserve your freedom or the freedom of others? To stand up for religious beliefs? If there is no one or no value you feel worth dying for, what does that indicate about you? There's no universal answer. In the consideration of your feelings, however, you will learn something about your commitment to certain values and to people whose lives are most important to you. I'm not suggesting that you die—but that you be involved to the degree that enormous sacrifice can be seriously considered.

For whom would you die and for what values? Who would die for you?

Past Present and Future

Each of us has an orientation to the past, the present and the future, but which direction our lives, thoughts and behavior are focused on is important in shaping lifestyle, attitudes and adjustment. Which direction of time seems to dominate your activities and thoughts?

Depressed, elderly people may spend 80 percent or more of their time thinking and talking about past events, while typically, children spend the majority of their moments in the present and talking about the immediate future. A healthy mental outlook blends liberal amounts of here-and-now with suitable portions of past and future. Priorities shift as needs change; one looks back or ahead with feet firmly planted in present time.

However, I believe the population in our society has been influenced to adopt a future time perspective. People begin thinking and talking in terms of the future; and, when it's upon them, they are already thinking ahead again, planning for the next tomorrow. As our daughter once asked when she was awakened early in the morning, in anxious anticipation of the day we were to leave on our vacation, "Is this the right tomorrow?" For some there is never a right tomorrow; when the future arrives, rather than experience and enjoy it, they are hung up on anticipating a "better tomorrow" than the one they are experiencing. As an example, there is the typical traveler who makes elaborate plans for a trip. But when he's into it, he's concentrating on shooting color slides, collecting brochures and ferreting out historical details, anything but savoring the experiences he's having. Later, while giving a slide show, he's full of facts and is actively planning his next trip, which will be longer and to places more exotic than those he just visited, so that his future slide show will be even better.

In contrast, during the "hippie" movement of the sixties, the emphasis on "being in the now" rather overwhelmed and dismayed many adults. The tendency to live in the "now" was so intense that if one asked, "What are you doing tonight?" the typical "hippie" response might be: "That's two hours away, man. Who knows what will happen? I'll take care of it when it gets here." Tomorrow was the distant future, and planning for next week was ridiculous and very "square."

From my experience, I feel that well-adjusted people with a healthy time balance spend approximately 60 to 70 percent of their thinking and talking time in the present. Perhaps 15 percent is past-oriented and another 15 percent devoted to the future.

Can you "guesstimate" your time profile? Is it similar to, or much different from that of your spouse, for instance? When you meet new people, are you able to tune into the here-and-now with ease, or do you find yourself thinking ahead or referring in great detail to the past?

In a time sense, are you a dreamer? Do people and experience sometimes seem disappointing because you're preoccupied with other faces and places you *might* encounter in the future or have enjoyed in the past? Are your job, or a party, or a leisure activity less than fun because you usually compare them to the past or anticipate better in the future?

Whether a watch or a calendar seem to influence you more, does your orientation to the present seem satisfactory to you? This particular assessment may be viewed more closely during an interchange about it with someone close to you.

How much time do you spend thinking, talking and living in the past—the present—the future?

Push-Pull, Click-Click

What specific feelings, ambitions or activities seem to motivate you? There are strong influences from the past which push us and future goals which pull us toward doing things. Many of the motivations that seem to push us were planted there by people (particularly parents) who were once and perhaps still are important figures in our lives. Leftover expectations for ourselves may be fantasies, which could stem from previous emotional conflicts we have not resolved. Many of us have some echo of the past pushing us towards goals, desires or accomplishments that seem worth fulfilling. Can you sort yours out, save the realistic ones, and abandon the fantasies? What do you hope will actually click into place to improve your knowledge, experience, or emotional stature? Those expectations that push us are generally less reality-based than those of our own choosing that pull us like magnets toward our goals.

What are your goals? Are you pushed towards them or pulled?

What Makes You Feel Important?

Think of all the activities in which you're involved that give you a sense of self-esteem and importance. Everything we do cannot be so categorized, but each of us needs to know what builds our self-image. Is it your work? Your hobbies? The number of invitations you get to parties? Your pleasure as a sexual partner? That people compliment you about clothes and grooming? The home or apartment you live in and have been redecorating? The car you drive? The clubs to which you belong? The charitable activities in which you're involved? Or perhaps a habit you've broken (such as smoking) or become comfortable with (such as spending Sunday afternoons with your children).

The sources of your feelings of importance say a lot about you, because it is toward these things you direct your energy. From accomplishments in these things come constant reinforcement of your self-esteem.

In assessing where your feelings of importance originate, you will discover more about your values and priorities. Perhaps material possessions are overly dominant, or your need to be needed improves your self-image—whatever it is that makes you feel most worthy. Therein lies a revelation about yourself.

What things, people or activities give you your sense of importance?

Current Problems

What seem to be the current problems you face today and will face in the near future? Is money, or earning enough money, a special annoyance? Is the main enigma of your life loneliness and making contact with people whose association will have real meaning for you? Are your problems centered around education, child rearing, health, relatives, political climate, reorientation after divorce or death, finding leisure time, or having unfulfilled ambitions for a career? We all have issues which trouble us; laying them out on a mental table helps us focus on them more clearly and perhaps will prevent these problems from becoming barriers in our contacts with others.

Define three current problems you face. How are you dealing with them?

Dealing with Success and Failure

An important part of being well-adjusted and happy involves knowing how to deal with both success and failure, major and minor, in various areas of life. Your self-esteem and emotional stability are improved and stabilized by success, but how do you deal with a negative situation, with rejection or failure?

Life has its ups and downs on a regular basis, whether we recognize them or not. When we successfully overcome obstacles or problems, and reach certain goals, life seems rosy. But it is not simply problems that make people anxious or unhappy; it is the way they *deal* with reverses that determines an optimistic or pessimistic outlook. Life without problems would be a weird distortion of the reality we live, for dealing with adversity helps one gain maturity. A vital interest in our own and other's fates, our curiosities, motivations and desires are all linked to the way we approach problems. Without emotional or physical hills to climb, there would be no joy in reaching the peaks where happiness adds meaning to life.

Basically, there is no way to avoid some disappointment, frustration or failure. However, in discovering how to deal with various unpleasantries, or even tragedies, we can become more aware of our own capacities of interacting with others; we learn and we grow.

Some people face and accept failure with elasticity. They bounce back to try again, to improve their efforts or behavior and to gain knowledge from mistakes. Others overreact to compensate for reversals in life. For example, a housewife may cook a lovely dinner in which every dish has gourmet distinction, but perhaps she has accidentally burned the potatoes. It is not uncommon for a woman in such a plight to condemn herself, express disgust with the dinner and with her ability to cook, all because one item was not perfect. Unfortunately, many people follow this pattern, allowing one failure to overshadow a hundred successes.

We experience the same imbalance in work situations. Someone may breeze through the day handling a job with dispatch, but if he mishandles one aspect, causing even mild criticism from a superior, he may consider the day a total failure. "Nothing went well," he may feel, forgetting how capably everything was handled, with that one exception.

Failure in matters of the heart, in love affairs, in marriage, between intimates or close relatives, can be one of the most upsetting occurrences in life. Several failures in a row to achieve a satisfying rapport in love, because of sexual misunderstanding, ignorance or differences in values, can be even more traumatic. At such times we need strong convictions about our inner resources, and we need faith deep without ourselves that we *can* recover and find happiness with others, though rejection or amatory misfortune is still fresh in memory. It is rare that a first love or first sexual experience leads to a lifelong affinity between two people. That which you learn from what seems like failure gives you momentum to move on, to venture, to succeed in the future.

No one is born knowing how to deal with failure—or success—effectively. We learn through living, by trial and error. Learning is not automatic, or spontaneous, or inherited. It is not a gift but an achievement, one that must be continuously pursued and perceived.

It is usually easy to sustain interest, enthusiasm and motivation, as long as success is consistent in most things we do. But how much of a roadblock is failure? Do you discard your dreams, hopes and ambitions because of a small or moderate reversal in love, finances, school, work, hobbies or other activities? Or do you take misfortune in stride, and step around it and move forward again?

I've heard it said that many millionaires have either filed bankruptcy or experienced several business fiascoes, only to dig out of the shambles and begin anew on the road to success. These men actively demonstrate that taking risks is inevitable on the road toward accomplishment. To take a risk, we must loosen the reins on security, which are often so comforting, but which can also be shackles and chains that prevent us from attempting the new, the unknown and the exciting.

What place has failure in your life? Does it seem to overwhelm you? Are you able to ignore it and learn from the experience? Do you realize how to put adversity in proper perspective? Do you have the courage to examine the causes of failure and admit mistakes that can be avoided in the future or rectified now? Do failures dominate your life or lifestyle, or do you become master of the failure situation? When you stumble, blunder or meet with disaster, do you react by depreciating yourself, and walk around like a beggar asking for sympathy and understanding? Or do you try to pretend that nothing at all happened, rather than breeching the storm squarely in the center?

This reminds me of a poem Natalie wrote on the drive home together the day I completed my two years of military service:

We are all comparable
to flowers blowing in the wind.
Our strength lies in our ability to bend;
Our existence depends on it!

All of us must assess our abilities to confront failure, even those who attempt no risks and make few efforts to change, grow or endeavor. These latter characteristics are a kind of failure in themselves, which lead to emotional atrophy.

Keats said, "Failure is, in a sense, the highway to success, inasmuch as every discovery of what is false leads to seek earnestly after what is true, and every fresh experience points out some form of error which we shall afterwards carefully avoid."

How we handle *success* in both major and minor accomplishments is far too often taken for granted. We need the ability not only to enjoy, but to appreciate success. We must tune in to it as it occurs, rather than just look at it retrospectively, in order that success be truly the foundation for future achievement. Many people strive for prosperity and triumph, only to move quickly ahead towards other goals without really enjoying those just fulfilled. This kind of "tunnel vision" inhibits one from relishing accomplishment, gives priority to running, when you should be standing still momentarily.

Some people have serious difficulty coping—yes, actually coping—with the phenomenon of their own success. In fact, they can turn it into a symbolic failure by feeling guilty about it or unworthy of it. Others become uneasy or depressed when "things are going well," feeling they don't deserve good fortune, or that catastrophe is just around the corner, so they may as well mourn in advance.

You also know individuals who ride on a significant prior success until it's worn out and stale. They don't realize that success is a dynamic and transient phenomenon, or perhaps a pleasant resting place—but not the end of the line.

How do you assimilate success? Can you keep *it* in perspective as capably as you do failure, feeling comfortable about it within, and in your contact with others? Do you tend to be overly modest to your own self-detriment? Or do you overemphasize and brag about accomplishment to the embarrassment or boredom of your family and friends?

How about success that others achieve? Are you noticeably envious with a tendency to undermine it even subtly, or can you share their happiness, basking in reflected glory? If you feel you must put down the attainments or good fortune of others, you are at the same time reproaching yourself, even unconsciously, for not keeping pace. But if someone you know gets a new and better job, makes a "killing" in the stock market, has half a dozen paintings sold in the first hour of an exhibition, or otherwise attains a temporary pinnacle, your sharing of the moment with pleasure and compliments is a tribute to your own healthy self-image. Love, creative accomplishments, financial security, or simply the triumph of a few hour's work are more likely to be yours as well, when the blessings others receive seem to spread your way.

Do you keep adversity and failure in their proper perspective? Do you assimilate and enjoy success?

Life-Goals

Are your hopes and desires for the future clear in your mind, or rather vague and irritating because they are still unfulfilled? Do you know what you would like to accomplish, and how soon? How detailed are your plans and expectations? Do you ever anticipate how old you may be when you die? Are you bogged down in wishful thinking, or are your goals consistent with your abilities, circumstances and needs? Or do you tend to overplan your life and miss the joys that spontaneity affords?

People with emotional and physical stability should have a balanced perspective about the rest of their lives. Most of us are directed toward systematic change and improvement of lifestyles and standards. In what direction are *you* going? Are your goals realistic? Do you hope to retire, travel, write a book, marry again, build a house, study philosophy, buy a farm, or visit the moon? Personally, I want to study contact techniques in many cities and countries. What would you like to find in your crystal ball?

What are five realistic, important goals you plan to achieve?

Idealistic Goals for Others

What are your idealistic goals for others? They are very different from realistic life-goals. In your daydreams, do you imagine participating in achieving world peace? Elimination of poverty? Dissolution of racial and religious prejudice? An end to pollution of the earth?

In determining your idealistic goals, keep in mind that some of them are indeed achievable. Some of mine include:

1.—Establishing scholarships, in universities and colleges, for the *most average* student. Although most of us are average, the average student is neglected. It seems that money and effort are basically directed at the highly intelligent, the wealthy, the poor, and intellectually limited people.

2.—I would like to be instrumental in organizing a living chain of people holding hands simultaneously, from coast to coast, in a gesture of brotherhood and peace.

3.—I would like to see our culture adopt the tradition of a "decade party," which, beginning at age ten and once every ten years thereafter, one's friends and relatives gather together and literally shower the celebrant with hours of reflecting, verbalizing, and realistic praising for all his accomplishments and personal attributes.

What are three of your idealistic goals for others in which you would like to participate?

In summary, self-assessment can offer you greater awareness of where you are, were, and will be. Are you developing more realistic value judgments about activities and characteristics you wish to change or enhance or retain? Understanding ourselves more completely and with greater clarity is a gratifying process that assures continued growth and happiness. Were you surprised to discover the large number of alternatives available to you? *Never underrate the power of your personal freedom.*

14.

ON
REJECTION

So far the primary theme of this book has been centered on the initial phases of communication where *goodwill* exists, or is intended, between people. However, there are also encounters of four minutes or less when the feeling engendered is *rejection*.

People vary a great deal in their ability to cope with rejection—to put a single rejection in proper perspective, and even, if applicable, reject the rejection.

The ability to cope with rejection has its origin in childhood. For normal psychological development to occur, a child must feel loved and accepted by his parents or whoever is his main source of security. Without a base of acceptance of self from "important others," the ability to cope with problems, disappointments and *rejections* is seriously impaired. Since every child's self concept primarily evolves from the way he feels "significant others" react to him and his actions, parental rejection can produce a massively devalued self concept. No individual child or adult can remain "normal" if he discovers that he is rejected by the overwhelming majority of the individuals with whom he makes contact in his environment.

In spite of the importance of self-acceptance, I do not believe it can survive without validation and agreement from others. Therefore, we might even say that acceptance from others is a need, not a choice or a desire.

Reports of American prisoners of war held by the Communists during the Korean conflict indicate the Communists knew this well. One of the methods utilized to accomplish dissolution of prisoner camaraderie and acceptance of the enemy preyed on the individual's need for acceptance. Mistrust among one's fellow prisoners was created by a variety of tactics. For example, the enemy would suddenly reward an unknowing prisoner among fellow POWs for his "information." In spite of his denials to his friends that he "said nothing to anyone about anything," he became, at least, a subject of suspicion. Use of tactics such as this created mutual rejection, fear of association and distrust of other POWs. In the height of the prisoner's depression, dejection, and self-imposed isolation, the enemy then offered him acceptance. Many took it—someone cared, and at that point the prisoner didn't care who. Of course, many heroically did not respond to the enemy's psychological tactics, but perhaps their faith and insight were greater.

Active rejection is more acceptable to most of us than passive rejection. To be ignored—treated as a nonentity—is far more psychologically devastating than to receive anger or insults. That is why many rejected, lonely children react with negative attention-gaining behavior. Hostility received as a result is better than nothing.

A solid base of self-acceptance evolved from and through acceptance by others provides us with the cushion we need to cope with inevitable, periodic rejection—something that, in reality, we all encounter from time to time.

The subject of rejection is highly complex and has many other ramifications, but this chapter deals with three specific dimensions of rejection related to our contact theme: positive phoniness, criticism, and some specific ways to handle rejection.

POSITIVE PHONINESS

If a waitress feels irritable, angry or upset about something in her personal life which has nothing to do with you, would you prefer she mask it, be phony, and serve you in a pleasant, cheerful manner, or slam the dishes down and express her annoyance openly?

There is a place for positive phoniness in our culture; there are certain times when "be nice—even if you have to be phony"—applies. We appreciate this empathetic effort from others, and we should expect it from ourselves as well.

In my judgment, a segment of our society has gone overboard in asking people to be direct and honest at all levels, all the time. When we understand the relationship of behavior and feelings, perhaps we can better subscribe to my conjecture that being *phony is not necessarily being insincere*. The waitress who comes on pleasantly, subduing her anxiety or irritability while she helps make a mealtime enjoyable for you, is being quite sincerely phony. Call it functional fraud or appropriate deception, the truth is there's a distinct social grace in not expressing anger or criticism at times and kind words may also help alleviate your own wrath.

There is a kind of cultural proposition today that open expressions of hostility, criticism, or just bad feelings are desirable because they are genuine. Certainly, facing our own emotions honestly is healthy, but turning disturbing feelings on an unwary public or even culpable intimates is an overextension of the be-direct theory.

In a *Life* magazine article (March 10, 1972) about Marlon Brando, there is a beautiful quotation from this actor that underlines my thesis about positive phoniness. Brando was saying that, in effect, people are acting all the time. "You can't *live* and not act," he added. "If you expressed everything you thought, nobody could live with you. Say your daughter comes in wearing the ugliest dress you've ever seen—spangles here, and a big brown butterfly in the armpit. She made it in school, and she says, 'Mom, isn't it gorgeous?' Well, you can't say, 'Jesus, sweetheart, it really is horrible.' You can't do it! You've *got* to pretend."

Interviewer Shana Alexander responded, "But, Marlon, most people have trouble not in disguising their feelings but in expressing them."

He gave her "the patient-guru look," and replied, "The

biggest gap is not expressing what you feel but knowing what you feel. Most people don't know." That could be an extension of the point, but sincere "pretending" is obviously an accepted form of behavior, if that word rings a more familiar bell than "being phony."

In the chapter on marriage, I touched on the topic of phoniness. In essence, it is equally important to be nice, even if it's phony, in the first few minutes when you greet a stranger or casual friend. Don't "dump" your hostility, complaints and setbacks on anyone who expects a more affable encounter. This is asking no more than common courtesy, the same as one expects from a waitress who must disguise a bad mood or a harassed airline ticket clerk who must retain at least some civility. Although, at times, courtesy takes a certain amount of effort, keep in mind it requires less energy and psychological drain than most verbal combat.

While there are appropriate times to be nice and hide your irritation or even fatigue—at a party, with your boss, dealing with an employee or relating to your spouse—of course we must be flexible. To express anger or dissatisfaction tactfully is realistic, and at times it is ridiculous and self-defeating to hide it. However, in terms of contact in the first four minutes, there is no doubt that people get along with greater satisfaction and achieve easier rapport when everyone attempts to "be nice."

"Dreamer" you may be saying to yourself. Not actually, because I'm talking about people of mature judgment who understand how to control their behavior and the positive benefits of doing so. The most interesting result of being phony in the sense I've described is that frequently when someone is irritated but makes the effort to come on pleasantly, there is a shift of mood and the troubled one begins feeling better. Affability has its own rewards.

There are probably masses of people who will not acknowledge that they are sometimes phony. For these people, it may help to realize that there are analogous social and emotional reservations that encourage us to reserve natural functions for private places, or restrain hunger and sex urges for appropriate times and locations. It is not incongruous for us to recognize that being phony is a sincere effort to empathize with other people, and that it has its place in the spectrum of human relations.

CRITICISM

In Chapter 1 are listed "the four C's": confidence, creativity, caring and consideration. Perhaps a "fifth C" might be: criticize not, unless it is specifically requested of you. And then be judgmental with tact and discretion. Although minor criticism may be done merely in terms of an evaluation rather than fault-finding, the word criticism carries connotations of disapproval or unfavorable comment about someone or something.

I do not believe criticism helps relationships on a person-to-person basis, except in highly unusual and infrequent situations. It can work well between tuned-in people, on a mutually agreeable basis, when aimed at enhancing interpersonal relations. Yet it's not news that criticism is all around us. Most of us receive it on a regular basis and usually reciprocate it, or we offer it voluntarily to friends and loved ones.

I do believe in the words of John Ruskin, who said: "The question is not what a man can scorn, or disparage, or find fault with, but what he can love, value and appreciate."

During a child's first year or two, it appears that parents —particularly mothers—seem to spontaneously understand the validity of "criticize not." This probably does not originate with the advice of authorities on child rearing, but rather from instinctive knowledge. When an infant is learning to walk, most parents employ what I feel is the best method of assistance: they praise the steps and ignore the falls. They do not criticize nor shout every time the toddler falters, but they reinforce the positive by saying, "It's okay," or "That's a good boy—you can do it." They rarely make any adverse comment when the baby stumbles. They simply pick him up and help him start again . . . and again . . . and again.

For reasons that are difficult to analyze, the parental approach begins to change after one-and-a-half or two years. Figuratively, stumbles beget criticism, and praise is often omitted.

I have used this same "praise-without-criticism" technique as an effective tool in psychotherapy with parents who have difficult children. One of the many tools I have found useful is to request, without rendering judgments on child or adult behavior, that the mother maintain two lists for a period of two weeks. One list is a record of each time she criticizes her child, including the time of day, date, and a summary statement of her critique. On the other list, she notes each time she praises the child, again with time and a digest of the positive comment.

Parents who are willing to do this conscientiously soon become aware of the typically massive amount of criticism and minimum praise they give their child. Usually, without specific advice from me, they begin to taper off criticism and increase praise, primarily, I think, because they don't want to be embarrassed when they show the list to me! Whatever the motive, mothers who stick to their lists guide themselves into accentuating the positive and reducing the negative. To their amazement, they find that this shift in viewpoint usually results in a marked improvement in parent-child relationships, and disruptive behavior in the child is reduced.

I use a variation of the same system in counseling couples in a troubled marriage. While they are both present, I ask each partner to maintain a list. On this list are criticisms received (not given), detailed briefly in a notebook not available to the spouse. Date, time of day and circumstances should be noted or remembered and recorded later at a convenient time. Couples are asked to be conscientious about their lists for two weeks.

Again, those who have followed my suggestions discover a dramatic decrease in the criticism they receive (and conversely, dish out), which becomes a giant step in improving a marital situation. Of course, this is only one aspect of therapy; but, combined with other techniques, it can be meaningful and constructive. Perhaps you have heard the line from a poem called *If*, which applies to youngsters and parents alike: "If a child lives with criticism, he learns to condemn." Later comes the converse: "If a child lives with approval, he learns to like himself."

While civilized cultures are attempting to improve interpersonal communications through many means, consider the Babemba tribes of southern Africa, where the social structure includes only an elementary criminal code. Apparently, the lack of fixed rules to enforce justice stems from close community living, which never made such laws necessary. Brian Sharpe, our red-bearded friend, and director of the William Roper Hull Progressive Education Center, Calgary, Canada, was reared by the Babemba for the first nine years of his life. He passed the following information on to us, along with the tribal method of handling antisocial, delinquent, or criminal behavior, which were exceedingly infrequent.

When a person acts irresponsibly or unjustly, he is placed in the center of the village, alone and unfettered. All work ceases, and every man, woman and child in the village gathers in a large circle around the accused individual. Then each person in the tribe, regardless of age, begins to talk out loud to the accused, one at a time, about all the good things the person in the center of the circle has done in his lifetime. Every incident, every experience that can be recalled with any detail and accuracy is recounted. All his positive attributes, good deeds, strengths and kindnesses are recited carefully and at length. No one is permitted to fabricate, exaggerate or be facetious about his accomplishments or the positive aspect of his personality.

The tribal ceremony often lasts several days and does not cease until everyone is drained of every positive comment he can muster about the person in question. At the end, the tribal circle is broken, a joyous celebration takes place, and the person symbolically and literally is welcomed back into the tribe. I repeat, not a word of criticism about him or his irresponsible, antisocial deed is allowed. The person in the center, we can only suppose, experiences a variety of feelings about his misdeed, having been flooded with the charitable warmth of his acquaintances, friends and loved ones. Perhaps this overwhelming positive bombardment not only strengthens his positive self-image, but also helps him choose to live up to the "expectations" of his tribe.

My friend said the necessity for these ceremonies was quite rare. His account should make us ponder whether so-called primitive societies might not teach valuable lessons to influence our highly organized eye-for-an-eye social and legal traditions. If you had broken a law and experienced such a ceremony within your own circle of friends and relatives, can you imagine the effect it might have on you?

I've since wondered how this type of positive bombardment might work in miniature as part of a family ritual. Aside from the obvious feelings of guilt that would be provoked, I believe an accused individual would be reinforced in his awareness of who he was in a positive way, what people appreciated about him, and what he had to offer in life. Suppose our prison systems were reorganized along the Babemba line. Would rehabilitation be more effective? Would lawbreakers better understand how irresponsible and destructive acts could be replaced by constructive social behavior? Would fewer men and women be returned to prison after serving time and gaining release, only to return to antisocial patterns?

In *How to Win Friends and Influence People*, Dale Carnegie emphasized the self-defeating nature of criticism. Here are some pertinent excerpts from that 35-year-old book:

Let's realize that criticisms are like homing pigeons. They always return home. Let's realize that the person we are going to correct and condemn will probably justify himself, and condemn us in return; or, like the gentle Taft, he will say, "I don't see how I could have done any differently from what I have. . . ."

When dealing with people, let us remember we are not dealing with creatures of logic. We are dealing with creatures of emotion, creatures bristling with prejudices and motivated by pride and vanity. And criticism is a dangerous spark—a spark that is liable to cause an explosion in the powder magazine of pride—an explosion that sometimes hastens death. . . .

Any fool can criticize, condemn and complain—and most fools do.

Carnegie felt criticism was futile because "it puts the man on the defensive and usually makes him strive to justify himself. Criticism is dangerous because it wounds a man's precious pride, hurts his sense of importance, and arouses his resentment." He felt there ought to be a law requiring complaints to be filed, only after a period of waiting, by "whiny parents and nagging wives and scolding employers and the whole, obnoxious parade of faultfinders."

Criticism among friends and intimates, as I have said, can be useful when phrased with tact and courtesy in the clear implication that your intent is to help or understand. This seems to work best when initiated or requested by another individual. Courtesy, of course, has a deciding influence in this area, and I am reminded of Kenneth Clark's statement that "courtesy is the ritual by which we avoid hurting other people's feelings in order to satisfy our own egos."

Criticism usually seems like a form of rejection, a close relative of hostility in the first four minutes of contact. Avoid it. It is almost certain to shatter the potential for a satisfying relationship.

DEALING WITH REJECTION

There are several manifestations of rejection which may occur in initial contact. Here's how some of them may be handled.

1. To the person who continually relates by taking objection or contradicting you, even tactfully, it may be futile to waste your time and logic. Listen briefly to whatever frictional dialogue he or she offers, then, if you choose, exit diplomatically, remarking that it was obvious he has given those matters a lot of thought and it was interesting to hear his views.

2. When someone sprinkles conversation with gossip you don't like, you are a passive participant unless you try to stop it. Change the subject with a positive tone and a comment such as, "I've always liked Hal, and I'm sure we're all sorry he's having problems. Let's change the subject. By the way, who do you think is taking off for Japan next week?" There is also the classic line when someone is running down a mutual friend, mentioned by Barbara Walters in *How to Talk with Practically Anybody about Practically Anything* (Doubleday, 1970) "You look amazed and say, 'Funny, she always speaks well of you.' "

3. It can be difficult to respond when a person comes up to you and says, "I'm certain you won't remember me, and there's no reason why you should—but do you?" Or the opening line may be, "You don't remember me." You may be tempted to agree directly, but a better reply may be, "Your face *is* familiar" (if it is); or, "I'm not sure I do, but I promise I will the next time we meet"; or, "No, but perhaps you have me confused with someone else," and give your name. Don't worry about your own embarrassment if you actually have forgotten—it happens! Another response I like is: "No, I don't. Would you help me remember?"

Dr. Leo Madow, in his book, *Anger* (Charles Scribner's Sons, 1972), states: "The most 'mature' man is the one who has the best control of his emotions." Though one of "man's most powerful drives is his need for love," there is another emotion, says Dr. Madow, which is only now being widely examined—the feeling of anger. He adds, "This 'energy' probably has a greater influence on a human being's behavior and mental and physical health than the drive for love."

Dr. Madow concludes that individuals with the healthiest egos are least inclined to be distressed by adversity into open display of anger. In my context, the release of anger resulting in rejection by a stranger or friend can be handled calmly by all of us whose heads are on straight, turning a nasty situation into a satisfactory interaction.

4. My approach here is within a narrow frame of reference—a specific technique for dealing with hostile service personnel. In fact, the approach might be abbreviated to, "Would you please tell me your name?"

A specific incident illustrates how rejection can be handled smoothly, to allay anger and achieve immediate goals. As I parked in my driveway one day, I noticed a giant drilling apparatus boring a six-inch hole deep into the ground on the line between my property and my neighbor's. The machine was perched on its side, but several men were gathered around it, and two were operating from my side of the property line.

I was interested, but I was even more concerned. What was this drilling about? As I approached the men and asked who was in charge, one man stood up from a squat and glared at me. I said in a friendly way, pointing to my residence, "I live in this house; what's happening?"

Apparently the man facing me was the foreman, and his reply was cryptic: "We're drilling a hole." His tone suggested that I was a blind incompetent whose only motive was to annoy the hell out of him. He abruptly returned to a squatting position with his back toward me.

I restrained my feelings of anger and continued, with a knowledge based on experience, that the man would be changing his tune shortly. Calmly I asked him to his back, and loudly enough to be heard over the machine, "What is your name?"

He ignored me. I made the request again, "May I have your name, please?" This time I pulled a small note pad and pen from my pocket. He now turned and stood up, slightly uneasy but still defiant. "What do you want to know that for?" he asked.

Without answering, I asked, "I would like your name, please, the name of your company, and the name of either the president or your general manager."

"What are you going to do with all that?" he responded defensively. I merely repeated my request, detail by detail, and my pen was poised awaiting his answer.

The foreman was perceptibly becoming less hostile and more attentive. With a slightly more friendly shift of tone, he replied, "I'm not going to tell you."

"Would you say that again, so I won't misquote you?" I asked, scribbling on my pad. He was silent, so I repeated, " 'I'm not going to tell you.' Is that precisely what you said?"

At this point the man's agitation and my steady grilling disarmed him. In slow succession he gave me his name, the company, and the name of its president. With some hesitation, he concluded, "What are you going to do with it?"

He obviously knew what I intended to do. Very deliberately, I closed my note pad, slipped it inside my coat pocket, and then in as friendly a tone as possible, I told him, "I'm certain that the president of your company would appreciate knowing how one of his foremen handles himself professionally on a job. And I'm certain that he wishes to be advised when three of his men, while trespassing on private property . . ."

I left the inference about his behavior unfinished and continued, "Wouldn't you want to know about an incident such as this if you were president of the company?"

The man was now obviously embarrassed and began to fidget. Then he blurted, "Please don't write the president. It's just that I have trouble with people. I don't know why I'm so irritable and angry and I don't have a lot of friends. In fact, my wife divorced me because I was so hard to get along with. It wasn't you, sir. It's just my way, and I've got to learn to be nicer with strangers."

Slowly I took out my note pad, tore off the top page, and ripped it into pieces. "Thanks for the explanation," I said. "Now what are you drilling the hole for?" He gave me a full account about the soil survey my neighbor was having made, ending with thank-yous and apologies for his behavior.

These techniques for handling momentary rejections were learned by trial and error over a long period. I have found this response very successful; but I am somewhat concerned about including it here because it may become used so often that its impact may be diluted. However, I feel that readers will try their own variations and the spontaneity will not be dulled. I've used this approach with rude sales personnel in stores, rude telephone operators, snippy waiters or waitresses, and abrupt airline and other service personnel.

The technique, as you see, is simple; and here are the important guidelines for making it work:

1. You *must* remain calm. Even if the person rejecting you becomes vehement, you'll be cool and on top of whatever takes place.

2. Speak with a mild-to-moderate tone of authority, whether you feel it within you or not.

3. Never answer the other person's questions before obtaining his name, his superior's name, and any other data you want. It is inevitable—and fascinating—that people very well know why you want their name.

4. Don't make threats—it's all a matter of inference.

5. Give importance and credibility to your inquiry by writing down the names you ask for; if you don't have pen and paper, ask for them as you are talking.

6. After writing the names or having the person write them, carefully and conspicuously tuck the pad or paper into your pocket, wallet or purse.

7. If a person refuses to give you his name and other

information, appear undaunted and undismayed. Jot down a few notes, repeat his refusal—to get his exact words, and take heart that your systematic calm will probably rattle the rejector. I haven't ever had to go one step past this point, but if necessary, I would conclude with "Thank you very much," and go to anyone nearby and begin talking. I'd try to get the same information and point to the person I just left. I would not seem angry, nor would I state why I wanted the names until I had them. If a second employee refused, I would ask for the manager or supervisor, depending on circumstances.

Here's another story where "please tell me your name" paid off. At a Midwestern air terminal, I arrived on one flight with the intention of connecting with another airline almost immediately. In moments I discovered I'd missed my next plane by 20 minutes because the departure time on my ticket was incorrect. With a certain amount of dejection, at the counter of the second airline I explained to the agent that, because one of his colleagues in another city had made a clerical error on my ticket, I was stranded.

He laughed and glibly stated, "Well, that's the way it goes. We all make mistakes, you know, but there's another flight out in a couple of hours. We'll get you on it."

He talked without making real eye contact with me, and his lack of genuine concern or remorse seemed a clear put-down. I went through my "Please give me your name" procedure, at the end of which the agent apologized, changed his tone, advised me that another airline had a flight in less than an hour, and arranged dinner for me in the interim—compliments of the airline.

With some regret, I must say that incidents like these happen more frequently than most of us would imagine. Since rejection is usually unavoidable in the commercial world, at least one gets a certain satisfaction from turning the contact away from personal rejection while accomplishing his specific goals. Although my intent is not altruistic, I do believe this technique may have made these personnel "think twice" before rudely rejecting others.

I want to add that I use somewhat the same technique

when I am *pleased* with service or the attitude of someone who makes an extra effort to help me. I ask for names, and people are usually eager to accommodate me for they realize that I'll be offering recognition, which most people deserve more often than they receive. I do follow through with an appropriate report to a supervisor. I do the same on the telephone with an operator, for instance. If friendly contacts in the world of commerce were pointed out and commended more frequently, perhaps there would be less hostility and inefficiency—even if the pleasant way someone handles you is positive phoniness.

15

CONTACT
BY TELEPHONE

Alexander Graham Bell could never have imagined the vast resources he was to open for humanity when he invented the telephone. It is likely that everyone who reads this book has a phone, or access to one, since it is our number-one medium to live communication when distance is involved. People who have never seen one another carry on business together, others get help in emergencies, shop from Sears catalogues, and begin potential love affairs over wires and microwave lines that connect wherever you are to just about everywhere else. Yet telephone conversation is taken for granted by most people who may not realize the importance of the contact impressions they leave with strangers in four minutes or less.

Each of us has a telephone personality which, while it is a digested version of our total self, has qualities that emerge because we are *not* face to face with the other party. Probably the blind-date form of communication illustrates this principle best. The couple may open with an exchange of personal information, then search together for pathways to more meaningful rapport. Their modes are limited to voice inflection, tone and choice of words. People typically reveal themselves with caution during premeeting phone calls. They *assume* the personality details will be verified later—or discounted.

One of the most delightful blind-date stories I know came from a man who said he met a young woman through mutual friends who felt they would be a good match. The friends invited both to dinner, and though the evening was pleasant, the man didn't find the woman especially appealing. He took her home and promptly forgot about her. Several weeks later he received a phone call which opened with a female voice asking, "How do you feel about being pursued?"

"It depends on who's pursuing me," he answered. "Who's this?"

The caller chatted amusingly and somewhat provocatively for a few minutes, until the man realized it was the lady he'd met at dinner and decided to forget. Now he was intrigued. On the phone she gave quite a different impression than she had in person. Later she explained that she was concerned about coming on "too strong" when they met, and she deliberately took a conservative approach towards him. In the interim she had thought about him seriously, and decided to try a different, perhaps more forward approach.

As a result of her telephone pursuit, he asked her out to dinner, they became involved and later married. The man told me he can still remember, years later, the pleasing sound of her voice when she called him, a contact that paid off when in-person interchange had failed.

On the telephone, friends already have a basis for understanding which strangers must achieve. Some parents try to teach their children telephone techniques as a matter of manners as well as in the interest of family communications. Opening greetings may range from "Hi" or "Hello" to "This is the Smith residence." Formality or informality of a household or a person may be assumed by the manner with which they answer a telephone.

There are many correct ways for a family to open telephone calls, but parents should instruct their children to use the words they find most appropriate. Important messages get through with more ease and routine information is not sidetracked when you or a child asks, "Who is calling, please?"

The business world is where the largest volume of

verbal communication between persons unseen happens, and often the success or failure of a particular exchange depends on how well one or both parties express facts and feelings via telephone. The simplest exchange occurs when you call and leave a message for someone. In my own case I try to pronounce my name clearly, but people seem to interpret it in unusual ways, from "Zoon" to "Zoomin." The response I like best came from a secretary who asked simply, "Will you help me to spell your name, Doctor?" Her request to share the responsibility for accuracy struck a pleasing note that I feel sets an example for many telephone message-takers.

Business firms usually give a great deal of consideration to instructing secretaries regarding telephone manners and protocol. However, there are many variations, some of which seem to create better impressions than others. Large firms almost always use their own name to identify themselves to callers; the only difficulty occurs when receptionists or operators have pronounced the name for so long that it becomes a blur when they pronounce it. Executives of such companies should make a habit of phoning their offices regularly to check the impression that clients or customers get in the first few seconds of a call.

When a secretary or operator answers the phone by repeating the telephone number you have just dialed, it creates a question in my mind sometimes about the business's need for anonymity. This practice may be appropriate when several firms or individuals have the same number, as in the case of five graphic designers I know who share the same offices. But the image of a company that does not wish to announce its name, and seems to hide behind seven digits, should be considered. In just a few seconds the caller may instinctively wonder if the company knows who they are!

Tone and cordiality of a secretary's or operator's voice are obviously influential in initial telephone contact. Telephone company operators usually learn how to make their voices effective, since the word "operator" or "number please" can convey a wide range of feelings, from "Good morning" to "Why the hell are you bothering me?" Short courses in telephone contact are part of the basic training a phone company operator receives, and for good reason.

Answering services, while they should use the same friendly telephone techniques as secretaries or phone company operators, sometimes fall into ruts that may be unique to this work. While secretaries and operators do represent a company and create distinct contact impressions, an answering service is usually the end of the line. By that I mean, the person you're calling is not available at that moment, and you somehow want to be handled with special consideration. As a physician who has had answering services for many years, I suppose I'm particularly sensitive to this situation. My service should be an appropriate extension of me; though I may be away or in consultation, a patient or caller must hang up his phone with the feeling that I'll return his call as soon as it is feasible, and my service must take and give messages with tact and understanding. If the caller's voice indicates that he is irritated or upset in the first place, the answering service must respond sensitively so that his anxiety is not worsened. When a service operator is abrupt, makes errors, or keeps a caller waiting too long, the reflection is partially on me and anyone else represented by that operator. It is not unusual for physicians, dentists and other professional people to change services because of the ennui or lack of involvement that answering-service personnel show their callers.

In the last dozen years, reasonably priced electronic telephone-answering machines have been perfected that have become very popular with both business firms and individuals for home use. It's no trick to install a machine that answers the phone in your own voice after the first ring and records the names and messages of callers. The trick seems to be to word your response in such a way that it varies occasionally, and so that it prompts the caller to talk rather than scare him away. It's surprising how many people who use phone machines tell me that frequently callers hang up rather than talk their messages into a tape machine.

Here is a situation in which the first four *seconds* of your recorded reply must be carefully considered. Rather than the formal, traditional, "This is Pete Jones. I'm out of the office (or the house) and will return at about seven; at the sound of the tone, please leave your name and message," you may need a more original and creative opening to increase your harvest of answers. A public relations man who works out of an office at home uses this verbal device: "Hello, I'm an electronic answering machine. My master, John White, is away at the moment, and left me as his genie to greet you. In a few seconds you'll hear a beep tone, which is my way of indicating it's your turn to talk. Help me serve my master by leaving your name and message, and I will deliver it to him as soon as he returns. Thank you."

Another acquaintance gave me this opener: "Hi, I'm Walter's answering machine, a mechanical instrument with a soul. Walter asked me to take his messages since he's away until this evening. Please tell me who's calling and leave a message when I give the beep signal. This will make Walter happy and keep me warm and friendly, unlike most machines, you know. Thanks a lot."

Telephone answering machines offer you delightful opportunities to personalize your tapes so callers will be drawn to reply without trepidation. A word of caution: Your opening words may tend to become stale in a few weeks or a month (depending on how frequent your calls are), and if you hope, to maintain the effectiveness, change the message at regular intervals. Friends and business associates may begin to note your verbal variations, which will not only hold their interest, but give you a certain distinction as an individual. A mere machine can become a contact tool that serves beyond its primary function.

Many firms use the telephone to solicit business from extensive lists of potential clients. I've found that usually the solicitor is a girl with an attractive voice who gives a pitch that almost invariably sounds as though she is reading it or has memorized it and is somewhat bored by having to repeat it again and again. Most of us listen to ten seconds of a solicitation and are turned off. "What is she selling?" is the immediate silent response, and I often ask politely if the caller will get to the point. I don't believe that giving the correct answer to "Who is buried in Grant's tomb?" is really my special entrée to a hundred dollar's worth of free dancing lessons, nor am I interested in being persuaded to drive or fly 500 miles for a free lunch and a tour of "Distant Acres" or whatever land development is being pitched to me. Actually, it is difficult to give an individual feeling to such calls in order to keep a disinterested listener on the phone long enough to intrigue him. It *can* be done by the most skilled of telephone solicitors whose choice of words is interesting and whose delivery is sincere without sounding recorded.

Sincerity is probably the most important characteristic of a business telephone contact between people who have never met, just as sincerity scores points in face-to-face meetings. Executives, sales personnel, purchasing agents, policemen, secretaries, and the whole gamut of people who run businesses and services locally or nationally depend to a great extent on information they can project and gather, sometimes at a dollar a minute on person-to-person cross-country calls. To be convincing quickly, to extract or impart facts and figures clearly, to obtain orders or cooperation easily, takes practice on the phone. All the principles of verbal contact are involved to make your mission successful. You and your mother-in-law can dilly-dally about trivia until your ears ache, but in the commercial world a little humor, brief inquiries about health, weather and personal conditions go a long way toward gaining the interest of someone—someone who may end up offering more than you were going to ask because of your warmth, and because you got to the point as soon as possible.

I know a woman who answers the phone with a certain enthusiasm, but who invariably lets her voice trail off to a note of apathy when she says goodbye. I've never asked her about this quirk, but I wonder if in telephone conversations with people from whom she has requested service or cooperation whether there may finally be some doubt about her total sincerity after the call is completed. Certainly, if your call requires a pose of interest and honesty to achieve a goal or respond to a message, don't raise doubts in the goodbye phase by your inflection, or lack of inflection.

There is one other phase of telephone contact which I hope occurs infrequently, but which requires the most concise organization of thought and verbal communication. That phase is an *emergency*. When you phone a doctor, an ambulance, the fire or police department, or even a relative to come to your rescue quickly, get to the point without panic. Or at least with as little agitation as possible so that the receiver of your call gets pertinent facts fast and can give advice or make decisions without the static of your anxiety muddling the contact. The tone of your voice will help you hook in as you describe your situation. Then be prepared to listen attentively, make notes if you wish, and get off the phone to deal with the emergency as soon as possible. The person or service you call may be quite familiar with your problem, and if your verbal delivery is cool, assistance or advice can be given you without delay.

Many metropolitan centers have "hot lines" and suicide prevention centers where people, often not medical professionals, are trained to make the initial few minutes of telephone calls meaningful. In time of crisis, the recipient of a potential suicide call is in an important position to help in situations that may offer a choice between life and death. They are prepared to ask for names, phone numbers, etc., trying to establish immediate rapport despite the minimal involvement possible, so that the caller will feel accepted. Suicide prevention respondents know that by being warm, calm, interested and honest they can help build confidence in callers, even though they are strangers. They avoid a rigid authoritarian approach and try not to be judgmental, as they draw out the caller to create the thread of trust necessary, however thin, to provide any immediate assistance. The same techniques and manner apply to you as an individual if the occasion should arise when someone you know expresses a feeling of deep trouble during a phone conversation. Listen, absorb, reflect the emotion of the caller, and offer advice or asssistance gradually and carefully. In an emergency your intuition can help stabilize initial contact to a far greater degree than during ordinary conversations.

It is easy to hook a tape recorder to a telephone and make a sound record of your own and another's voice for the purpose of playback later. As an exercise, this might be helpful if you wonder how you come across in telephone contacts. Listen to yourself critically. If a change of inflection, words or mood might help improve your reception by unknown individuals on the other end of the line, practice on tape until you like your own sound better. Don't take telephone contact for granted, because there may be business, friendship or love at stake.

16

CONTACT
BY LETTER

Secretarial courses, English classes and many, many
books are devoted to letter-writing techniques, so the
"how-to" of self-expression by pen and typewriter would
seem easy to come by. However, just as making contact
with a stranger or friend in person requires a basic understanding of how you look and sound, contact by letter has
its special requisites. On the telephone you have the per-
suasion of voice to project personality, but on paper your
choice of words and the mood you create are all you have
to evoke response, empathy, action, or whatever your
goals. Because of these literary limitations, it is all the
more important to be aware of making the first minutes
or lines of your letters positive and effective.

Most of us write to exchange news and views with
friends and relatives who realize we're not writers, and
who are happy to get regular communications in almost
any readable form. In business and in love, however, letter
writing may have a more important influence than we are
aware. Sales and services amounting to thousands of dol-
lars are arranged via the mail between people who have
never met and probably never will meet. Business letters
must be polite, considerate and clear. Short letters are
usually more effective than long ones, and tact can accomplish things that salesmanship may not.

Let me quote from a letter received recently, written by
the president of a large telephone company to a new sub-
scriber. It opens: "Your telephone conversations are a

very important part of your personal life. And, your telephone company provides a very personal service."

The letter, on the gentleman's personal stationery, continues, "When you pick up your phone, your telephone company's function is to perform efficiently and in a manner satisfactory to you. There are exceptions when delays and other inconveniences have resulted in a very personal kind of irritation. These failures are both human and mechanical. Some are avoidable, some are not. However, when they occur, we become very sensitive to them and try to take the necessary steps to avoid their reoccurrence.

"Ours is fundamentally a people-to-people business and our operating philosophy is designed to produce that kind of customer-company relationship." The president adds that the company is instituting a new one-to-one program to improve service, and mentions an office where problems that warrant his personal attention can be taken *"for positive action."* (The italics are his.) He ends the letter asking for comments about his thoughts, and with the hope that the "care and concern" his company has will be mutually beneficial.

This unsolicited letter struck a very positive note in me, and though the company has had a somewhat spotty reputation for service, the words and attention offered by the chief executive office improved the initial contact I had with his firm. Though his letter was a form (but individually typed and signed), it was successfully composed to create goodwill at the beginning of my relationship with a public utility that plays a prominent role in my life. (Actually, the company was unaware of *how* important telephone service is to me as a physician, because they addressed the letter to "Mr." Zunin.)

There are many ways of being persuasive on paper, ways which should be matched to individual personalities as well as to the reasons for the letter in the first place. A personal note preceding the transaction of the business in a business letter is often a pleasant opening. It says, "You are special," or "I think of you as an individual," and it engages the reader into whatever follows. Letters are written *on* machines, but they should not sound as if they were written *by* machines. Contemporary ways of exciting attention, even in form letters attempting to sell things in which you have no interest, are cleverly handled these days. I've received several solicitations from book publishers offering the first volume of a series free, with letters that started with openers like this one: "I've given it a lot of thought, and I can't decide why *everyone* doesn't accept our offer for a free book, with no strings attached. Yet some people ignore a potential gift, perhaps because they believe there *is* a catch. Let me assure you, there is not. We want you to have Volume One complete without obligation because it is the best way we know to help you realize how marvelous our series is, and how it will be an asset to you, your children and your library." I have a number of free books now because I couldn't resist that initial contact, though I have gone ahead and bought only one series of volumes and canceled the others.

Here's another example of an ingeniously engaging letter, sent me by a man who attended a Contact Workshop:

"As one of the nameless 600 faces who sat spellbound before you at UCLA last Saturday, let me express my fascination and appreciation both of your thesis and delivery." *There* is an irresistible beginning that would arouse the interest of a sourpuss hermit. He continued by saying the day ended too quickly, and gave some reasons why he had attended the workshop. In the third paragraph he states, "Successful life insurance men develop certain markets in which they operate most comfortably, efficiently and profitably. Mine is successful business and professional men . . . with a sense of responsibility . . . and if I get an extra bonus . . . of humor."

He mentioned his age, the fact that I probably already have insurance, some of the values of life insurance, and the fact that he has some unique approaches which I would be certain to find different. He also made the opportunity to compliment my wife when he expressed the hope he could meet with us to discuss his services after "examining and diagnosing" our needs. Near the end he says, "I see that I have used a number of your verbal modes, even though addressing you in writing. Perhaps I might try one more: You remind me of our Temple's Assistant Rabbi!"

Flattery is a potent mode of reaching somebody, especially if it is realistic in scale. Phony flattery usually falls flat, except for the blatant egotist for whom it might be inadequate. This insurance salesman's praise was offered directly in his effort to show me that his workshop day had added to his business acumen. In a postscript he told me how he had enjoyed one of the nonverbal exercises because of what seemed like his ESP at work in making correct assumptions about his woman partner, a complete stranger to him. He was proud of his own sensitivity, and in sharing it, he put a little icing on his skillful self-introduction.

I did call and thank him for a memorable letter, which reflected very favorably on his potential for pleasing a client, as well as on the company he represented. Certainly, letters can invoke a variety of assumptions on the part of the reader.

Personal letters between friends or lovers are subject to even more dramatic interpretation, depending on the people and messages involved. Love letters, particularly, are sometimes in a class with political promises in the kind of dreamy contact they represent between people who eagerly desire to communicate their emotions across the void of distance. A young man once told me of a passionate correspondence he had with his girlfriend during a summer when they were separated. "When I returned home," he explained, "there was an explosion of love and passion our letters had been kindling for two months. The promises we had made and the fantasies we shared for togetherness had been powerful on paper, so strong, unfortunately, that no reality could fulfill the dream. In two weeks we had drifted apart in disillusion, and later I thought how nice it would have been to simply write to her for years on end, and never meet again!"

If love makes the world go 'round, love letters are tickets to a joyride that can circumnavigate the globe. There is nothing I can say in a book that will help anyone substitute realism (which is relative anyway) for fantasy (which is erotic and exotic), but it's a pleasure to touch on the subject briefly.

The well-written letter of bereavement falls into a special category where love or concern is expressed. During the time I directed "Operation Second Life" for widows of servicemen killed in Vietnam, I collected a large number of such letters which are being prepared for a book to be titled, *When You Help to Say Goodbye*. As I note in that manuscript, trying to write a condolence letter often gives people a feeling of helplessness because they don't know how to start, nor how to phrase their feelings of sympathy, to comfort friends or relatives who have faced a death in the family.

A paragraph or two need not be considered an awkward contact if you realize that the very act of communicating helps bring solace to the bereaved. Following are some pointers to guide you in this situation:

—Letters may be short and succinct. The message is important, not the length or style. Your sincerity and brevity will be appreciated.

—It is preferable not to refer to death as a blessing, if there has been a long illness; rather call it a "release." Instead of sympathizing with the tragedy of the departed, it is usually better to praise his or her courage.

—The spirit, strength and patience of the bereaved may also be mentioned, but one should not make martyrs of those in mourning.

—Say something about what the deceased meant to you personally, and how you will miss him or her, particularly if your relationship was close.

—References to your own previous personal losses should be made carefully, if at all.

—Letters of condolence are generally addressed to one person, the individual closest to the deceased. An exception would be if *you* are closer to another member of the departed's family.

—Try to avoid *long* discussions on religion, or your own philosophy of life, but comments from deep personal belief may well be integrated into your letter naturally.

—In addition to letters, you may make contact with mourners in the form of sympathy cards with or without a personal note, flowers, a telegram or a meaningful book.

Though death is inevitable, there still seems to be a reluctance to face it frankly. A letter of condolence sent or received soon after a death offers a feeling of sharing appreciated by sensitive people in any walk of life.

Where you, your credibility, your sincerity or your requests are to be evaluated through letters, the skill with which you can express yourself to attain your goals can be developed by an awareness of all the principles of contact discussed in this book. Some of the most convincing letters ever written have been ungrammatical and poorly constructed according to rules of composition. They were moving because they were direct and without guile. Four minutes of honest communication—entreaty, explanation, request for aid or whatever—may constitute a letter strong enough to accomplish many purposes.

17

IN CLASSROOM
AND OFFICE

Essentially, the first four minutes a teacher, secretary, businessman, physician, dentist, social worker, clergyman, etc. spends with students, clients, customers or patients should be governed by the same principles discussed in previous chapters. Contact is both verbal and nonverbal; the goal is mutual understanding, rapport and an atmosphere in which to serve (in a broad, generic sense) or be served. Identity, self-esteem, role-playing, assumptions, the use (not abuse) of contact and every other point of encounter applied to social situations must be considered in education, business and professional life. In this chapter I will deal with a few specific areas that lend themselves well to our theme of contact in the first four minutes.

THE SUBSTITUTE TEACHER
(And the "Regular" Teacher)

In his or her regular role, the aware teacher makes the initial contact in the classroom and modifies or adjusts his modes of contact to fit specific classroom situations.

A substitute teacher is in a special situation. He (meaning "he" or "she" in this context) is "on the spot," and the first few minutes can be critical. In this time the teacher must rapidly "size up" the class, as he is being evaluated by the students. A sense of self-confidence and positive direction makes a good impression, while an air of indecision and groping can "turn a class off." Students will sense almost immediately if the substitute can keep order and follow through with proper instruction, or whether he is merely "baby sitting."

In my lectures and workshops on education, as well as in private practice, the unique problems of the substitute teacher are frequently brought up. Among the more interesting generalizations that have come out of these sessions is the following list of self-defeating personality-behavior types, here characterized in brief word-pictures:

The *commander* comes on barking orders, relying on his peculiar brand of rigidity. He rarely smiles, announces the "rules," and expects to handle the class like a Marine drill instructor. Except in a totalitarian country (or school district), these efforts are doomed. No class, from elementary to college level, will tolerate the impression given by the commander that they are robots and initiative is illegal. Almost nothing is taught, and almost nothing is learned.

The *milksop* enters the classroom, trailing loose ends, and gives the instant impression that he is "wishy-washy." He may apologize for being there unprepared and admit that substituting is a difficult job, implying that he isn't up to it. Unless students are extraordinarily mature and self-sustaining, their response will be apathetic, if not outright defiant or unruly. They feel they deserve better—and they do.

The *trivia chatterbox* introduces himself with a barrage of extraneous facts or wanders about the subject under discussion like a verbal drunkard. He may tell stories of past experiences to fill time and attempt rapport, but his manner soon becomes soporific.

The *lovebird,* usually a female, is a real sweetheart who tries to make everyone in class love her in the first thirty seconds by saying how glad she is to be there and how lovely and charming everyone in the room must be. This type is most prevalent in the lower grades where children are more likely to be conned on a temporary basis. The lovebird is as transparent as the misfits described above, and usually is seen quickly to be a hypocrite.

The *pal* is buddy-buddy, the male version of the love-bird. He masquerades as a long-lost friend, but his presumptuous declarations usually fall on deaf ears. Students realize that friendship cannot be applied like a coat of paint.

On the plus side, substitutes who have favorable experiences in the classroom enjoy their work and its challenge. They share these qualities:

1. They like children.

2. They like teaching and see substitute teaching as a challenge, not a chore.

3. They are prepared either for the course at hand or with supplemental materials that can be used after or instead of the regular teacher's course outline.

4. They anticipate many of the verbal pranks and distractions innate in students and head them off in less than four minutes by offering the impression of calm, knowledgeable authority.

5. They take initiative, rather than expecting directions from the class. They consider the feelings and needs of students, and they also confer with the class about topics to be taught, but they don't offer the steering wheel to anyone who requests it. They stay in control, no matter how many twists there are in the road.

6. They state the ground rules and keep the list short. Students feel most comfortable knowing the limits of behavior beyond which they may not depart. The substitute is in command but as a civilian, not a "chicken colonel."

7. They stick with lesson plans whenever possible, offer ideas and stimuli that are related, share talking and listening, are friendly and smile genuinely, and they do not demean either students or the regular teacher by direct criticism or inference.

Regular teachers who schedule informal individual discussions with students often discover that these brief contacts are a welcome surprise to young people, who may customarily equate the teacher-conference with being disciplined. A teacher who regularly chats with students individually, for even a moment or two before or after class, can detect and help improve a student's self-image and motivate him through this special attention. Negative assumptions by both teacher and students go down the drain as they get to know one another and discover themselves to be allies in the educational arena.

Studies have shown that effective teachers have three things in common, all applicable to success in almost any work or profession:

1. They perceive themselves as reasonably secure and adequate to their tasks.

2. They perceive their pupils, counselors, colleagues and administrators as generally able and worthy of respect.

3. They perceive their jobs primarily in terms of freeing and developing potentialities, rather than of controlling behavior or simply pouring knowledge into human containers.

Teachers have an emotional interaction with pupils analogous to that which office managers have with employees or marketing directors have with salesmen. Their initial and long-range goal is not only to teach "the three Rs" but also to build self-esteem and inspire achievement through a warm, supportive attitude.

IN THE OFFICE

The first four minutes at work have different ramifications for the boss, the secretary, the salesman, the assistant manager or the service station attendant. These are symbolic job classifications, and the points to be made are general reminders to renew your awareness. The items below are meant to apply generally to most employer-employee relationships; some may fit your circumstances better than others:

1. Distinguish between *showing* authority and *accepting* authority, at least until the lines of demarcation be-

come more distinct through experience. If you're new on a job, you're expected to listen; if you're a veteran, you're expected to inform and explain. There's a street term that sums it all up: "Nobody likes a smartass."

2. In personal terms, the key words are "acceptance" and "effectiveness." The first word refers to handling yourself and relating in ways which will find approval, *without* feeling like a doormat. In accordance with a positive self-image, you can achieve a balance. The second word involves assuming responsibility, following directions with imagination, and taking initiative without being excessively aggressive.

3. *"Tune-in,"* ask questions, and make the most of your patience. Yours may be "to reason why," but tactfully at first, until your self-esteem is more closely matched by the esteem co-workers hold you in.

4. *Initiate,* to express how aptly you are prepared for the job, without giving the appearance of "taking over." If your position is managerial and actually requires taking over, you may listen appropriately to suggestions of others who have been there longer and can be of help to you, until you "know the ropes."

5. *Absorb* as much of the atmosphere and feeling-tone of the office, store, or wherever. Once you have knowledge of the facts, your intuition, when dealing with customers, clients, etc., is better prepared to function.

6. *Support* the existing policies until you know enough to be able to appropriately make suggestions for change. Initial contact in an office means you are going to be part of a structure to which you respond, at first, in a status quo way. Later you'll be better able to make changes which may, if offered prematurely, be threatening to fellow employees.

7. *Operate* from a base of your own assets: technical know-how, honest curiosity, genuine interest in other people, and a firm belief that you *can* do it. The latter develops when you launch it in the right direction by a positive mental equivalent.

IN THE PROFESSIONS

The basic concepts of contact also apply to the professional physician, therapist, dentist, social worker, architect, attorney or clergyman, with their patients, clients or parishioners. Aware professionals learn how, figuratively speaking, to leave their personal problems at home or in a desk drawer in order to deal with people, many of whom are apprehensive about physical or emotional pain, money problems, time, bereavement, family crises, or budgeting for the future. The first few minutes in a professional's office may have a great influence on the confidence a layman will have in his advice, plans, or treatment.

A professional learns to observe both verbal and nonverbal signs that indicate a person's mental and physical condition. He should know how to seek information while putting someone at ease, how to probe around delicate subjects, and how to focus his positive attitude and interest directly on someone in need. If patients or clients have been kept waiting very long before an appointment, the professional tries to alleviate anxiety or anger in the first minutes to demonstrate his empathy (assuming the delay was not intentional).

All professionals are "evaluated" in initial contact, no matter how well recommended they might have been, no matter what their skill and experience. Most successful professionals make a point of personal contact and receptivity that aims at making someone comfortable.

James E. Rota, D.D.S., a dentist friend of mine, states in his forthcoming book *To Your Mouth with Love:* "The manner with which the patient is contacted (usually by the dental assistant), in the initial few minutes before treatment is begun, is of primary importance. In those moments anxieties and fears may be increased, decreased or unaffected." Naturally, Dr. Rota explains, "having a *relaxed* patient in the chair is conducive to efficient and effective treatment."

In the world of the professional, the ability to make contact effectively is a highly significant factor, affecting not only interpersonal relationships but also job satisfaction and personal fulfillment.

18.

CONTACT
EXERCISES

In a fast word-association game, you might connect the word "exercise" with "muscles," since we associate "exercise" with keeping trim. There is a parallel here in that the exercises that follow help to develop what might be called contact *tone* by building awareness. Under somewhat controlled circumstances conducted by individuals for themselves, or by a group leader, these exercises are designed to be an aid in focusing on many of the facets of interpersonal relationships.

In my practice of psychiatry, while working with groups, and while lecturing and conducting Contact workshops, I've seen how eager most people are to participate in awareness exercises. These exercises afford the opportunity to explore personality characteristics in a structured environment. They also enhance awareness of ideas and theories that have been absorbed intellectually, and they make it easier to integrate new behavior patterns.

Most of these exercises require a minimum of half a dozen or more people; they have been successfully utilized in workshop groups as large as a thousand. They have been developed to provide first-hand contact experience, verbal and nonverbal, for groups to whom I've lectured.

Contact awareness can be accelerated when the pleasure and problems of human communication are experienced through structured exercises with known boundaries. Hold a stranger's hand, look into the eyes of a new acquaintance, tell him how he looks and sounds; an exercise is a catalyst to a new awareness. At least, that is the consensus of those whose participation helped me develop and improve the sight-and-sound exercises in contact which follow.

EXERCISE 1: HELLO-GOODBYE

This format works best with a fairly large group and may be conducted in an auditorium or meeting room with immobile or movable chairs.

Each member of the group is asked to find a partner of either sex. This may be done at random or, in large groups, by counting off "one" and "two" in sequence. Ones and twos then seek opposites as partners.

At a signal, each set of partners begins a "conversation," but number ones may say only "hello," while number twos are limited to "goodbye." No other verbal interchange is allowed.

Participants are directed to be as innovative and creative as possible, within the range of voice, modulation, tone, inflection and intensity, and to use any variations of physical position that seem appropriate. It is explained that partners should attempt to communicate as many moods and feelings as possible, using only the one word they have been assigned.

A time limit of two or three minutes usually halts the exercise at a peak. Partners are then requested to shift words, and interact again for two or three minutes.

After time is called, partners explore together the reactions and feelings each had in saying and hearing the two words. What did each word seem to mean in its varying contexts of voice, stance, etc.? During this time, they should also discuss which of the words felt more comfortable in use and why, and why the other word felt less comfortable.

Individuals will discover, and, hopefully, learn that "hello" can mean "goodbye," and vice versa, depending on how the words were spoken with their nonverbal accompaniment. For example, one person may stand on a chair shouting "goodbye" at his partner, who is sitting on the floor, meekly squeaking "hello." Or "hello" may be expressed in a pleading tone opposite "goodbye" said with forceful finality. One partner may turn his back and walk away saying "goodbye," as his partner tries to get "hello" in edgewise. Two partners may hold hands, skipping together, chanting the words or singing a duet. "Goodbye" may come out with tenderness and warmth. A cold, aloof "hello" may be uttered without involvement. The simplicity of the exercise creates a surprising complexity of reaction and interchange to reveal individual awareness and sensitivity to verbal and nonverbal expressions of greeting and departure.

Exercise 1A:

This is an extension of the above. After partners have switched words for several minutes, everyone is instructed to meander through the group for two or three minutes, using their most recent word ("hello" or "goodbye") on others at random. They should continue to vary the style of their one-word delivery.

Following this, each participant should find his original partner and then discuss how they felt using their words, and also describe their reactions when meeting other people who were using the same word. How does it feel being with a group of people all saying "hello" together? If your word is "goodbye" and you continue to meet others echoing the same word, does its meaning change?

This variation can be successful with ten or with hundreds of participants, for it provides an opportunity for nonthreatening total group interaction. I've discovered that those saying "hello" will often band together in small groups and stand, with interlocking arms, smiling and pronouncing their greeting to one another. However, those assigned "goodbye" will generally not cluster together but will maintain their one-to-one format. The opening "hello" of contact develops unity while its termination, "goodbye," seems not to. In contrast, when a group has shared an intensive experience over a period of many hours or several days and warmth and closeness between them has been established, saying goodbyes together is an extension of those good feelings.

At workshops I point out that there are several languages in which the word or phrase for "hello" and "goodbye" are identical. In Israeli it is "shalom," and in most languages where the words are interchangable, the meaning is "peace be with you." As a greeting, it is distinguished from an expression of parting purely by nonverbal gesture as well as inflection. In our culture, there is a hybrid of this phrase, used by young people especially, who greet one another with "peace," accompanied by the old Winston Churchill two-finger "V," and goodbye is expressed in the same manner.

EXERCISE 2: NAME-CALLING

This is not a "nasty-name drill," but rather a verbal experiment in the use of proper names. Most of us are aware of the way in which we like hearing our names pronounced, and in Chapter 4 I discussed the importance of using the name of a new acquaintance during the first four minutes following an introduction. However, we are usually not conscious of the strong emotional investment most people have in hearing their own names. What are the verbal variations and how do we react to them? During this exercise, participants can discover more about their personal response to names than might have been possible in all the years they have lived previously.

The group divides into couples who are strangers, and they sit facing each other. Pairs decide who will be first to begin saying the first name of the partner. They are instructed to say only that name, directly to the other person, as inventively as possible, varying voice and stance to be friendly, hostile, soft, harsh, detached, seductive, interested, indifferent, etc. The listener remains seated, but the name-caller is urged to stand, bow, change distance, and vary nonverbal as well as verbal delivery.

After each pronunciation of his name, the seated

participant nods "yes" or "no," without speaking, to indicate whether he likes or dislikes being addressed in that specific tone and attitude. Rapid nodding or head-shaking may be used to show the degree of approval or denial of the mode. It should be emphasized that there is no need to be pleasantly positive in either saying or reacting to this name-calling exercise.

When the first person's name has been said or shouted between ten and fifteen times, the caller sits down, and the partners discuss the listener's feelings about the variety of first-name delivery. It is suggested that they particularly compare their reactions to those they have when their name is called by important friends or relatives. After several minutes of interchange, roles are reversed, and the former caller is seated, listening to his partner's repertoire of name variations. The second time around, a caller usually benefits by limited familiarity with his partner, as well as more cognizance of his own ability to run the scale of emotion from pathetic to furious.

It is important to stress that only first names be verbalized, and only nonverbal answers be given in this exercise. This restriction enables the listener to better analyze his emotional responses as he hears his name pronounced in wide diversity.

During workshop discussions after this exercise, I am often amazed to find how many married couples have never investigated their mutual tastes about how they like their names said. Names, nicknames, words such as "darling" or "honey," usually imply a great deal that is informative in an exchange between people, especially intimates. Just the pronunciation of a familiar name can help set the tone of a contact through irritation, desire, approval, anger, supplication, or pure joy. For example, a man who calls his wife "Sandy" when things are relaxed between them, may say "Sandra" when there's tension or he wants to make a point strongly. Listen to the way strangers pronounce your name, for it can indicate something about how they feel about you.

EXERCISE 3: I LIKE MYSELF BECAUSE . . .

This one makes a worthy warm-up to a group experience or an experimental workshop format because it lubricates the wheels of friendship.

The group is divided into pairs, with each person opposite a stranger. Partners decide whether they will be "one" or "two." Number ones tell number twos all the things they like best about themselves for sixty seconds. At that time, the situation is reversed, and number twos declare their most affirmative points to the ones. After sixty seconds, the ones are "on" again with the same theme, after which the twos have a second go-round.

At the next signal, number ones relate all the things they enjoy doing in life, followed by the number twos making the same disclosures. In the following minute, the number ones then tell about their recent successes, no matter how small, followed by the number twos reciting their recent successes.

The power of positive portrayal links strangers together as it helps boost self-images. Most people tend toward modesty as they recount their best points and accomplishments. What better way is there to begin an interaction than enjoying a dossier of upbeat information about a person and getting to reciprocate in kind? In a way, this is a do-it-yourself version of the Babemba tribe's ceremonial for anti-social behavior, except that its goal is to begin a contact on a positive note in a structured situation.

EXERCISE 4: ASSUMPTIONS VS. FACTS

This is another good warm-up experience for groups of any size. Participants are asked to find partners with a minimum of conversational prelude. Couples are seated facing each other, observing but not talking, for about a minute. To begin, one of the pair completes the following phrase: *"Right now it is obvious to me that . . ."* with a statement of fact about his partner. As soon as the statement is made, the partner chimes in with an observation of *fact* (not an assumption), beginning with the same opening words. No replies are made, but the pair continues to alternate, using the given phrase with a variety of observations about each other for one to two minutes.

Participants are directed to stay in the here-and-now with their observations, which should all be factual and related to the present environment or partner. In addition, one may share *his own* feelings. (Statements regarding your thoughts about your partner's feelings are to be avoided.) Sample statements include: ". . . I feel anxious and tense"; ". . . you are wearing a red blouse"; or ". . . the walls are green." Assumptions are not allowed, but internal and external feelings of awareness about yourself and your partner are required.

In the next stage, partners continue to alternate completing a sentence, this time based on assumptions. They complete this phrase: *"Right now I assume that . . ."* For instance, either might say, ". . . that you're a pretty intelligent lady," or ". . . that you must be a college graduate," or ". . . that you must be hungry by now." Reasons or explanations for these assumptions are not included; but after about ten alternate exchanges, the pair stops and checks the accuracy of those statements which were most provocative or call for investigation.

A third stage follows, alternating the completion of: *"Right now it is obvious to me that . . .; therefore, I assume that . . ."* Examples: "Right now it is obvious to me that you are smiling and leaning toward me; therefore, I assume that you are an outgoing, friendly person." Or, "Right now it is obvious to me that you are wearing a wedding ring; therefore, I assume you are married." Again, notes are not exchanged on the accuracy of assumptions until about ten statements have been made by each partner.

There are several variations or extensions of this exercise which may be used when it seems appropriate:

Exercise 4A:

Make a statement about what you assume your partner detects *about you*, or has noticed during your previous interchange but has *not* mentioned. Your partner makes his own set of assumptions in the same vein, following which you compare reactions and offer facts to supplant fancy.

Exercise 4B:

Tell each other alternately what you assume the other feels about you but is hesitant to say. Then discuss these new statements.

Exercise 4C:

State to each other what you *hoped* might have been noticed about you, and examine these thoughts.

Exercise 4D:

Exchange statements to indicate what you hoped your partner would *feel* about you, and follow with verbal investigation.

This exercise is an aid to discovering the difference between facts and assumptions, as well as enabling participants to better discern facts from which assumptions are projected. In addition, it gives us an opportunity to air thoughts and feelings we want noticed or sensed about us especially during the first few minutes of contact. Are you aware of how you want your face, body, clothes, personality and emotions to be noticed by others? If so, are you able to handle your verbal and nonverbal encounters in such a way that you project those specific characteristics clearly and in the positive manner you prefer?

EXERCISE 5: LIVING PSYCHOSTATIC SCULPTURE

This interaction works best after people know each other to some extent, e.g., following Exercise 3 and/or 4 or after a few hours together in a group. Again there are partners, and the number ones are assigned to sculpt the number twos into a position that symbolizes how he sees the partner, using whatever has been learned in their time together. The sculptors are directed to think of their creation for a park or museum, and the living statue can be standing, sitting, lying, etc. In addition, the number ones must announce the media, e.g., wood, stone or papier-mâché. The sculpture is to be a summary statement of the subject's personality, desires, goals, and self-image.

Living sculpture may be timed for two or three minutes, after which each pair settles down to discussion. In groups of convenient size, it is preferable to set up one sculpture at a time so everyone can watch and subsequent comments will be pertinent. With very large groups, participants might be divided into groups of ten or twelve, watching one sculptor at a time in their midst. As an adjunct in smaller groups, if the leader were to make a Polaroid photograph of each final living statue, it would be a helpful reference during discussion.

Once each sculpture is dissolved, the sculptor describes why he chose to mold his partner in the pose used, which, of course, reflects his view of number two, based upon what person number two has communicated and, of course, his own assumptions about his partner. Former "statues" then join the conversation, with their feelings of how accurate the "artist" was in molding them. Self-images often differ considerably from impressions others receive, and the divergence may be dramatically disclosed. A number two may now demonstrate what he thinks would have been a more accurate statement of his personality by taking a new pose, if he wishes. Members of the group join the discussion, pro or con, and the time limit should be flexible, depending on the number of people involved.

Once the number ones have all had their turn as sculptors, the numbers twos take over the same roles, benefitting by the enlightenment of the verbal communication that preceded. Another group examination of the proceedings follows.

It is sometimes amazing how accurately individuals can depict the salient personality features of their partners, based on limited previous experience together. The choice of media can be insightful and thought-provoking. Consider the connotations of antique bronze, marble, deep-grained oak, wire, ceramic, jade, clay, ice or cotton. Sculpture poses can convey predominant personality traits and interests, such as a woman symbolically holding a child in her arms, a man poised to start sprinting, or someone in a hostile or passive stance. Hands may be thrust forward as though to keep others away, or positioned against the body sensuously.

I have coined the phrase "living psychostatic sculpture" to indicate that the sculpture utilizes a living person, represents their partner's impression of their psychological status, and is "static" in the sense that it is a temporarily immobile sculpture.

Many people are surprised to discover how much others can deduce about them in a short time, regardless of the facades they attempt to present. This exercise is beautiful in the basic understanding it offers people about the assumptive world we all encounter in initial contact with strangers.

Exercise 5A: Self-Sculpture

This is an extension of the above exercise. After a person has been set in a sculpture pose, he or she is given the opportunity to change his pose and correct it according to how he sees himself, in contrast to how his partner saw him. He may form a new sculpture, depicting himself *as he would want to be or hopes to be.* He may also change media if he wishes, after which he should explain to the group the reasons for his new pose and media, and these new revelations are then discussed.

EXERCISE 6: SHAKE HANDS

This one works well in groups numbering ten to several hundred and is designed to offer honest feedback on individual ways of shaking hands—an evaluation I've found is rarely experienced by adults today. Since the handshake is simple and universal, it is taken for granted. Valuable awareness can develop through this exercise.

Large groups should be divided into segments of four, six, or eight, depending on the total number of participants. Each small group is then directed to discuss their feelings about handshaking, according to types, pressure, male-female, etc. Since the handshake is going through cultural changes, I often pose this question for consideration: Assume your group was invited by a government agency to recommend a handshake which would be established as a standard for men to women and women to men. Participants explore this among themselves for five to ten minutes; it may be optional in small groups to compare various recommendations.

Other questions that groups might probe include: 1. How and on what basis do women prefer to shake hands? 2. Should a man or woman offer a hand first on meeting? 3. Should there be any protocol about women shaking hands with other women?

At this point, small groups are disbanded and the entire assembly is instructed to begin wandering and shaking hands at random. It is explained that handshakes will be graded on the basis of *handshake and eye contact*, on a scale of one through five, with "one" indicating the weakest or least effective shake, and "five" the best. Individuals grade each other on the basis of the feel of the grip, facial expression, and eye contact. Participants should understand that they are rating handshakes according to how they feel *personally* about the tactile impression and eye contact of their momentary partner.

As people intermingle, shaking hands with as many others as possible, each person announces after each contact the grade he's giving, i.e., "That's a four," or "Yours is a three." Briefly they discuss the reasons for the grade given, adding suggestions for making the handshake more meaningful. The focus is on *how to improve* shaking hands, rather than making criticisms.

After participants have had the opportunity to shake hands with ten or more strangers, time is called and everyone returns to his original small group to discuss the feedback they received. It is not uncommon to hear comments such as, "You know, I always thought I had a good handshake, but after this experience, I found many people suggested my grip should be firmer. I was able to improve my shake as I went along." Someone else may add: "I've often wondered whether my handshake was too firm or too gentle, too soft or too aggresive, but everyone I met gave me a four or a five. It's nice to know people reacted favorably."

Others may find, for the first time, that it is best to vary your handshake for different people, young or old, male or female. They discover that good handshake contact includes immediate "sizing up" of someone and acting on assumptions in regard to the kind of handshake they might appreciate most. In this exercise, awareness of both variety and flexibility grows quickly and may easily be applied to everyday contact.

Corollary discussions often involve such things as the feel of the hands themselves, with comments about sweaty palms, cold hands or size and texture of hands. People are usually relieved to find that these anatomical features which made them so apprehensive don't particularly bother others.

EXERCISE 7: FROM HAND TO MOUTH

This outgrowth of the handshaking exercise is intended to help people increase the variety and intensity of their greeting techniques, using a number of options appropriate for strangers, friends or lovers. Groups numbering ten or more intermingle for timed intervals, and the following steps or stages are announced by a leader. Some of these may be changed, eliminated or substitutes added, according to the nature of the group. I've numbered the stages approximately as I sequence them.

1. Participants are asked to greet one another nonverbally, using eye contact or body language, i.e., gestures.

2. Shake hands at random and silently, though facial expression should be included.

3. Shake hands and say "hello" to each new contact.

4. Shake hands, say "hello" and chat for a moment.

5. Shake with left hands only and say "hello."

6. Other variations to suggest include touching elbows, shaking wrists, rubbing noses, touching cheeks, ears, hips, knees, etc.

7. Improvise greetings, such as those above, trying to be in touch with how you react and feel about the different styles of making contact. In a large group, this stage should be structured by change signals at short intervals given by the leader.

8. After experimenting with a number of greeting techniques, choose and use the one you like best that also seems most appropriate for your momentary partner.

This exchange will vary in its intensity and the modes of contact. It can serve not only to loosen up a group through non-threatening, pleasant interplay, but also demonstrate the gamut of greetings suitable for strangers, friends and intimates. Inhibited individuals have the opportunity, in the discussion that follows, to touch on the difficulty they may have in experiencing warmth in initial contacts. They begin to understand, through example and experiment, how some of their hangups can be eliminated.

EXERCISE 8: GETTING ACQUAINTED

Groups of eight strangers are formed. One pair volunteers to begin talking for four minutes to get acquainted. I've found it is preferable *not* to pretend an artificial situation, such as an airport waiting room, but to approach contact in the framework of its here-and-now reality.

Of the remaining six participants, three are assigned to observe one of the partners, and three observe the other. Each of the observers has a copy of Form A (reproduced at the end of this exercise) to fill out, according to their own impressions during and after the four-minute interchange. Either the overall group leader or one member of the eight keeps track of the time, notifying the communicating pair at three-and-a-half minutes and stopping the conversation at four. Observers remain silent to concentrate and not distract.

Form A may be completed in whatever sequence the observer chooses, with the provision that each point that can be evaluated is scored or checked. When in doubt, evaluation should be delayed in favor of efficiently filling in areas that seem most readily answerable. Examine Form A to get a preliminary idea of the contact modes included. At Contact workshops, participants receive these forms ahead of time so they may be partially familiar with them, though I do not explain each section in detail until we are into this exercise.

At the top of the form, each observer notes a small amount of data about himself or herself. Under verbal contact, each mode used by the conversing pair is circled during their interchange, and the degree of use of each mode is checked in the appropriate column after time is called. Nonverbal contact is also rated according to how body language is involved by each of the participants. Minor nonverbal items are checked but not evaluated. Comments on grooming should be brief and pointed. Suggestions for improvement in nonverbal contact should also be concise and specific.

After the forms are completed by all six observers, the whole group discusses various evaluations and comments about the two conversationalists, including suggestions for improvements. Reasons for ratings will evolve during this time, which should take from ten to fifteen minutes, after which a new pair of strangers move to the center of the group and make their four-minute interchange. New forms are filled out, and the procedure continues until four sets of partners have talked and been evaluated.

Workshop experience has shown that some people may begin this exercise feeling it is quite artificial but soon realize they are involved in a process which transcends the contrived. Couples in conversation often find they have used traditional and habitual modes of interaction rooted in their personalities. This may be explained by the fact that the stress of the situation does not always allow for creativity, and individuals often fall back on patterns stemming from experience.

This getting-acquainted exercise has proven to be very beneficial to those who can appreciate having their methods of making contact evaluated by a group of impartial and objective observers. In turn, participants gain insights about their own behavior while grading and scoring others. People begin to better understand the importance of flexibility, of techniques of making contact or ways to break the ice with a reluctant partner. After one has been observed and played observer to other pairs, awareness of their contactability is amplified. Adaptation of improved communication skills to social and business situations is, of course, the next step.

EXERCISE 9: VOICE GUESSING

This one originates with a little game I sometimes play after talking on the telephone for the first time with someone I've never met. After the conversation, I spend a few moments imagining and making assumptions about how that person looks, in terms of face, figure, and height. I've found that, over the years, my ratio of accuracy has improved, but there are always surprises. Some people just don't look like they sound!

Participants circulate silently and choose a total stranger as partner. Without verbalizing, the pair stand facing each other, observing from head to toe, but not touching. After a minute or so, partners close their eyes and imagine what the *voice* of the other will sound like. In another minute, everyone may open his eyes and talk. After a short interval, partners share their voice-guessing assumptions and compare them to what they hear in actuality.

As an adjunct, participants should talk about their own voices, offering self-perceptions that confirm or augment impressions given by their partners. Quality of sound, tone, inflection, flow and intensity are all topics of comment. How voices seem to match appearances, stature, or general aura are all feelings to be shared about your own and someone else's voice in this exercise.

An experiment such as this emphasizes the way you sound in any contact, and the feedback from a stranger not emotionally involved can be a valuable asset in considering self-improvements. The satisfaction you feel about your voice has a direct bearing on your self-image. A flat, expressionless voice, or an annoying accent can be enriched or refined through speech therapy, if the need seems important enough to you.

This exercise should be done several times to compare variations in feedback from diverse partners.

Form A:
VERBAL CONTACT

Person completing form	Participant
Male___Female___1st name_____	Male___Female___1st name_____
Age: 20+___30+___40+___50+___60+___	Age: 20+___30+___40+___50+___60+___
Willingness to participate:	Willingness to participate:
Little___Moderate___Much___	Little___Moderate___Much___

At the end of the interaction place checks in appropriate columns on right-hand side of only modes utilized. Higher numbers indicate greatest use of mode.

Modes

	1	2	3	4	5
1. Asking questions re identifying data					
2. Existential views, personality and feelings					
3. Spontaneously volunteering information about self					
4. Giving compliments					
5. Talking about here-and-now environment					
6. Search for mutual acquaintances					
7. Creative insult					
8. Humor					
9. Party hobbies and games					
10. Would you tell me . . . Help me . . .					
11. Extending invitations					
12. Verbalizing awareness of individual's nonverbal communication					
13. You remind me of . . .					
14. Apologizing for oneself					
15. Asking questions about employment					
16. Volunteering information about employment					
17. Other					

Speech

___Forthright ___Vague ___Imaginative ___Trite
___Hesitant ___Verbose ___Eloquent ___Monotonous
___Clear ___Rambling ___Spontaneous ___Paced

Sincerity and genuineness in verbal communication:
___"fly chat" ___"sparrow chat" ___"canary chat" ___"no-chat"

Form A
NONVERBAL CONTACT

Major Body Language	Poor (uninviting or repelling)	Satisfactory (acceptable)	Excellent (inviting and receptive)
1. Eye contact			
2. Facial expression			
3. Use of hands and arms			
4. Use of legs			
5. Posture-positioning			
6. Sexuality			
7. Overall			

Comments and/or suggestions for improvements

Surface Language
1. Dress:
___Casual   ___Conservative   ___Messy
___Meticulous   ___Seductive   ___Unremarkable
___Noticeable   ___Mod   ___Appropriate for age
___Reserved   ___Elegant   ___Inappropriate for age

Comments and/or suggestions for improvements

2. Grooming: Comment on such qualities as:
   a. Hair

   b. Fragrances

   c. Cleanliness

   d. Make-up (women)

   e. Other

Overall approach of communicative behaviors
   % Fact-seeking
      Involvement-seeking
   100 Total %

EXERCISE 10: NONVERBAL CUES

This is another exercise that was developed in Contact workshops to demonstrate how accurate—or inaccurate —we can be in assuming a number of things about strangers according to the many cues they give us. It is directly related to contact situations in the first four minutes and can be used with groups of ten or more.

Participants are requested to *silently* find a partner who is a stranger and sit together without speaking. *Each* of the partners has Form B (see end of this exercise), which they fill out, based on visual observation, intuition and assumption. About ten minutes is sufficient for this, during which time partners are urged not to attempt any nonverbal signals.

The success of this experiment depends, to a considerable degree, on the willingness of each person to probe the depths of their awareness, with a minimum of anxiety, and take chances about "guesstimates," without fear of later contradiction. Again, in my workshops there is an opportunity to study the forms beforehand, though their use is not explained until the exercise begins.

When Form B has been completed about the other person, each participant fills out another Form B *about himself*. In this case, without verbal communication having begun, individuals try to "guesstimate" what their partners have written about them. They are instructed not to necessarily use actual facts about age, marital status, etc., but to simply guess what, through appearance and nonverbal cues, someone else may be assuming about them.

After both partners have completed two forms, conversation begins, as they exchange, compare and discuss the "guesstimates" made about each other and themselves. Before I first tried this exercise, I assumed that there would be a preponderance of wild guesses and erroneous assumptions among workshop participants. After all, the only things two strangers seemed to have in common as a basis for judgment was perhaps their sex, body language, type of dress and grooming, and the fact that both were in the same place together. However, I have been amazed, as have participants, at the uncanny accuracy possible within some areas of the assumptive world. Where observations have been correct, self-esteem is often boosted for both the guesser and the guessee. Where estimates were off, impressions gained on this unemotional, non-threatening level lent new insights to many people whose self-image may have been positive enough but somewhat blurred.

The feelings of awareness that this structured nonverbal contact can instill often enhance one's ability to meet new people in an effective manner. In effect, each partner is looking into a human mirror with the computing skill of all the senses operating in a positive atmosphere. Images are often reflected in this way that have never been experienced before. Identity is viewed in a new light.

It is most important that this exercise be given at least twice during a workshop session, so that each participant may interact with at least two separate strangers. This is suggested because it is important to get feedback from more than one human mirror to make averaging possible. In addition, one may also have another opportunity to test one's own sensitivity to nonverbal cues, based on what has been learned previously.

Contact—Form B
NONVERBAL EXERCISE

Instructions:

1. Silently find a partner who is a total stranger and sit together but do not speak ... or whisper.
2. Silently complete Form B answering the questions strictly by your observation of your partner. Do not attempt to deliberately signal nonverbal answers in any way.
3. Silently complete another Form B about yourself, estimating what you suppose *your partner has written about you* (not the actual facts about yourself).
4. When both forms have been completed by both partners, you may now speak. Discuss and review the sheets with each other.
5. Check one: This sheet to be utilized for
    ·Nonverbal observation of partner
    Nonverbal estimate of partner's observation of you.

	None	Little	Moderate	Much
Willingness to participate sincerely in this exercise				
Degree of anxiety about participating in this exercise				

Estimated age_____Place of birth_____Month of birth_____

Marital status:

Married_____Separated_____Divorced_____Single_____Widowed_____

Children: Yes___No___Est. no._____

Est. max. education _____

Nationality_____

Generation: 1st_____ 2nd_____ 3rd_____

Occupation: First guess_____Second guess_____

Economic status: lower___ low middle___ middle___ upper middle___ upper___

Interests:

___ dancing
___ civic activities
___ spectator sports
___ participant sports
___ music, type
___ movies, type
___ reading, type
___ artistic & creative, type
___ gourmet foods & drinks

___ participation in membership
      organizations
___ TV
___ writing
___ camping, hiking
___ travel
___ politics
___ gambling
___ sewing, cooking
___ other

Comments

	None	Little	Moderate	Much
Flexibility				
Receptivity to change				
Degree of personal warmth				
Degree of openness about self				
Generosity				
Self-confidence				
Sense of humor				
Ability to receive				
Concern for others				
Openness to consider new ideas				
Ease of establishing friendships				

Religious belief:

First guess_____Second guess_____

Practice:

   strong___ moderate___ little___ none___

___ Leader   ___ Follower   ___ Impatient   ___ Insightful
___ Aggressive ___ Assertive   ___ Rigid   ___ Extrovert
___ Passive   ___ Patient   ___ Shy   ___ Introvert

Is this the kind of person with whom you would like to establish an ongoing relationship? Yes___ No___ Explain answer:_____

EXERCISE 11: A POTPOURRI

In Chapter 3 are a series of verbal contact modes, many of which may be the subject of experiment in this exercise. Since people repetitively use only a few methods of initiating verbal exchange during the contact phase of conversation, new and different ways can be tried in a comfortable, nonthreatening group numbering a dozen or more. The strange or difficult can become more familiar in this kind of laboratory setting.

The leader directs everyone in the group to walk around the room, interacting via each contact mode he suggests. Each technique is given four minutes, after which the leader claps or signals its conclusion, and several minutes are devoted to discussing what happened between partners. Participants find new partners as the modes are changed, for variety of response and feedback are basic to the exercise.

To begin, for example, the leader may state, "Everyone open a conversation with a stranger nearby, using identifying data such as name, residence, kind of work you do, etc. Stay with identifying data as long as it is comfortable for the four-minute period." In the discussion that follows between partners, how they *felt* about using that mode and how it fits into their contact experience should be the principal topics.

The group then meanders again, finding new opposites in another mode chosen by the leader. You might check Chapter 3 to review these modes: they include existential and personality subjects, compliments, here-and-now surroundings, mutual interests or acquaintances, "you remind me of . . . ," humorous gibes, hobbies and fads, or a provocative hook-in. In a typical workshop, I usually use six or seven categories.

This exercise is valuable because it gives individuals an opportunity to experiment and improve in a variety of contact modes which they may not have tried before. In therapy I sometimes use a variation of this by assigning contact homework. For example, in one phase patients are instructed to begin a conversation with at least three strangers in a week, opening with compliments. Later in my office, we discuss how they felt using that type of hook-in and what sort of reaction they received from the strangers. In following weeks, I change the mode. The exercise is particularly useful to those who have been reticent or unsure of their contact capabilities. By trying and taking a few chances, almost everyone discovers hidden talents that become part of a natural repertoire.

SUMMARY

Exercises in this chapter are a sampling of those used in either workshops, intensive experimental weekend groups, or both. Locations have ranged from the Los Angeles area to northern Canada, and the variation of response by various audiences to exercises as simple as "hello-goodbye" have been fascinating.

Setting makes a difference. The same exercises have a different quality and vitality in a church, an auditorium, a warm, tastefully decorated living room, or out-of-doors. The level of sophistication of the groups also influences the outcome of exercises, although they are adaptable to a wide variety of people.

These exercises are included here as a sampler to improve contact effectiveness by increasing one's awareness of modes of interacting with strangers or friends. Even if these exercises affect only the psychic surface, they are still a useful beginning.

19.

A CONTACT
QUESTIONNAIRE

What is your personality profile? How does it affect contact with your children, your boss, your spouse, beautiful women, attractive men, librarians, neighbors, others? How are your values different from other people's approach to life, time and space? When you meet someone new, are you able to tune in on a here-and-now basis to enjoy an interchange, or is your orientation predominantly in the past or future? Do you hold the attention of individuals who *matter* to you, for whatever reason?

These are a few of the questions you may ask yourself, in different words, using the questionnaire at the end of this chapter. Perhaps you have answered most of them to your own satisfaction at this point. If so, scan the list of statements anyway, for they may help you focus on facets of your personality that you've neglected.

Dr. Fritz Perls once wrote that "good habits are life supported." He meant that we *live* them or, as the late clergyman Emmett Fox put it, we *demonstrate* them. Fox had a theory of *mental equivalent*. In practice of his thesis, if one forms a positive mental equivalent of something he wishes to accomplish (Fox disdained using his theory to achieve material things directly), one is then guided to demonstrate, or achieve, the goal by action and attitudes that support it.

Dr. Perls' analogy of learning to type illustrates how new behavior patterns are incorporated into your lifestyle. In this analogy, "Your manipulation of the keys will change from strangeness to familiarity, from an unending stream of discovery and rediscovery to certainty—that is, to knowledge. Less and less time and concentration are required until this skill becomes automatic, becomes a part of self. . . . In other words, good habits are part of the growth process, the actualization of a potential skill." Making effective contact in all walks of life is a product of a positive image about yourself and others, about your ability to "hook in," and of *doing* it with as little trepidation as possible until, like typing, it's a "good habit."

IMPROVING YOUR CONTACT APPROACHES

Even if you feel I've said it all before, stay with me because I haven't.

1. *Observe* contact between others—between friendly, outgoing people. Study how they relate eye-to-eye; look at their nonverbal gestures, their grooming and dress. Watch their expressions of cordiality.

2. *Relate* to effective contact in others by analyzing your own methods. As you define what they are doing, how they talk, how they express tenderness, gratitude, affection, admiration, interest or respect, evaluate your own approaches and behavior in their place. Human warmth is exchanged between real, live people, but you can also observe it in movies, on TV, in the news or even in books. Listen and identify with people whose manner of relating to others seems admirable. You can imitate their ways that seem most useful and natural to you without anyone realizing the source of your change.

3. *Observe* those who seem to make contact poorly, as well, in life or in the media. Try to decide how they might improve their conversation and nonverbal modes. Think about what you would say if they asked you how they could improve their contact.

4. *Practice* ways of contact which may seem slightly foreign to you, slowly and deliberately. It is somewhat parallel to learning to type. Practice may seem artificial at first, but everything we learn seems applied before it becomes ingrained. Just because you are conscious of chang-

ing your contact techniques does not mean they will seem insincere to others. They may appear as spontaneous the first time as they will feel to you after they become an integral part of your lifestyle.

5. *Change* nonverbal methods of communicating, too. Look more directly at people, stand closer (or more distant, as the case may be), touch more even if it scares you. The interchange of warmth by touching can have a dynamic effect on people, yourself included, who may have thought you cool or distant.

6. *Experiment* with people you know well, for they will enjoy new closeness as much as acquaintances and strangers will respond to a more outgoing attitude from you. There may be humorous incidents with intimates or family, but laugh them off. Progress involves risk, and laughter blurs embarrassment in a happy fog.

7. *Go out of your way* to engage in new contact situations regularly that you might have avoided before you became aware that you could enhance your ways of communicating. At meetings or in any casual encounter, feel the joy of fleeting, partial intimacy, with no ulterior motives other than momentary self-expression. Comments to a lecturer, compliments to a sales person, or a relaxing chat with a child help you demonstrate your positive feelings about others. Being expressive is not being phony. A warm comment in an appropriate situation may help you over the hump of inhibition when future contact will have more significance.

8. Don't just sit there and make vague promises to yourself. *Do it*.

There are probably many examples in life of occasions when conscious change brought about gratifying consequences. In a *Cosmopolitan* (October, 1971) article, Suzanne Levine wrote of her feelings in "Confessions of a (Formerly) Fat Girl," and she describes how she observed other women as she was trying to "thin down my psyche:"

Surreptitiously, I eyed attractive women in restaurants, watched how they moved their hands and ate slowly, and how, when they excused themselves to freshen up, they did, in fact, look fresher when they returned. I eavesdropped on their conversations and tried to figure out how they managed to become serious without being leaden, gay without being giddy. Like some kind of nutty sleuth, I followed women down the street, measuring my stride to their graceful walk. . . .

That meant, to start with, that no matter how casual the situation, a chance meeting with a man in a museum, for example, I came on like a one-girl variety show, jokes, confessions, probing intensity. More often than not the sheer force of my single "interest" would send my audience screaming for the men's room. . . . Things got worse when I got the slightest feedback. Instead of relaxing and letting the gentle petals of intimacy open gracefully, I brought on the heavy machinery, and began blasting for lines of communication the size of a trans-Atlantic cable.

God knows, I had a lot to say—all those years of solitary philosophizing, understanding friendship and bouncing back from rejection had made me ready, willing (and how!) and panting to bring a downright gargantuan wealth of sensitivity, supportiveness and warmth to a relationship. But until I learned to control my tongue, I repeatedly over-analyzed, over-probed and lovingly smothered many a budding love affair.

Does any of that sound familiar—even if obesity was not your hangup, even if you experienced only analogous frustration in making contact as self-discovery was budding? The formerly fat girl was looking for love, as we are all looking for love; and, once we find it, the effort turns to holding it and making it increasingly fulfilling. *First we must like ourselves,* as I have said before, and then we can love others and be rewarded when it is returned. And contact, especially the first four minutes of interchange, is the beginning we create over and over again to make communication more than just a word.

CONTACT QUESTIONNAIRE

As the radio announcer says, this is only a test; it's not the real thing. It's less than a test since it's more an examination of your own feelings and understanding. There are no multiple choice answers, though if there were, they would be in a sequence such as "Always," "Occasionally," and "Rarely." Some of the statements can be answered "True" or "False," but only in relation to your own personal reactions.

Read the questionnaire point by point and mentally decide what fits you. Not your replies on paper if you wish to remember them or compare them with someone else's, or with your own at a later date. There is no provision for keeping score or making a total. Rating "100" on a self-imposed examination is somewhat akin to believing in fortune cookies. The questionnaire is meant to provoke thought. If you are warm, aware, mature and self-confident, you'll feel at ease with the statements. If you are somewhat hesitant and ill at ease about contact with others, you may squirm a bit. And if you are a rank contact amateur, you had better go back and read some more—except that a low rating will be quite your own and you may already know where it is, and what you want to improve along the path to more congenial relations with anyone and everyone. Take your time. Enjoy. If you can't fully enjoy, you're growing.

GROUP A

Needs Improvement
(in attitude or contactability)

1. During a conversation with a stranger, I notice he or she backs away and wants to stop talking fairly soon.

2. People often ask, "What did you say?" when I'm talking.

3. People often mention that I talk too loudly—or too softly.

4. After initial contact with a stranger, I know that I have many prejudices that influence the encounter.

5. I am never willing to consider advice from others.

6. I am preoccupied with the impression I'm making on others, and it is probably apparent.

7. People frequently say things on initial contact which annoy me, and I feel I must point this out.

8. Most of the new acquaintances I make seem to have something about them I can criticize later—and usually do it.

9. I usually feel uneasy when conversation with someone unfamiliar turns to sexual subjects.

10. Most people are so long-winded that I have to interrupt them to get a word in edgewise.

11. I can never accept compliments without embarrassment.

12. When I first kiss somebody of the opposite sex, I usually lose my composure.

13. I find it difficult to become interested in unfamiliar subjects other people talk about.

14. I am usually disappointed in people after I get to know them.

15. More than half the things I assume about strangers are usually misleading.

16. I think it uncouth for a new acquaintance to ask personal questions about me, such as my age or if I am in love.

17. If people really knew how understanding I am, I'd have more friends.

18. The jokes most people tell are either stale or vulgar.

19. When people disagree with me, I would rather terminate the conversation than get into even a friendly debate.

20. People should always say what they feel, even if they may sound a little bizarre.

21. Strangers usually seem cool and disinterested in me, and I usually feel it's their problem.

22. I often hurt somebody's feelings because most people are too sensitive.

23. I should never be judged by my physical appearance.

24. I never touch anyone unless they touch me first.

25. I should never make mistakes.

GROUP B

Good Contactability

1. I am in touch with my own feelings enough to know that contact with others is really not my hangup.

2. I can talk easily with others, strangers as well.

3. I'm active enough to hold my own in social activities.

4. I like to look at people when I talk to them.

5. I'm attentive to the physical appearance of others when we meet.

6. I show as much courtesy and consideration to others I meet as I expect them to offer me.

7. 1 listen carefully to the opinions of others, though I may intend to take exception to something in my turn.

8. I treat other people as equals when we meet.

9. I expect that everyone has something to say—and I listen.

10. I want other people to have a good opinion of me.

11. I generally have and communicate an optimistic outlook on life.

12. I believe we all should be willing to make certain compromises when communicating with people we love.

13. People usually find me easy to understand and get along with.

14. When I'm talking to a stranger, I try to convey the feeling that he or she has some special qualities.

15. People often consider me a strong personality, which is a pleasing thing to hear.

16. I look forward to meeting new people at parties or as business contacts.

17. Soon after being introduced to a stranger, I try to get him or her to talk about themselves.

18. I have no difficulty sitting or standing without fidgeting for a ten-minute conversation.

19. I can ask questions of other people in a way that does not make them feel imposed upon or "cornered."

20. When I am appreciative, it's easy to express it in a friendly way which sounds sincere.

21. When someone of the opposite sex holds my hand unexpectedly, I consider it a lovely gesture and try to show my enjoyment of the contact.

22. I can laugh at myself in appropriate circumstances.

23. In new contacts I make an effort to have people trust me by being aware of what I say and how I act.

24. I sometimes enjoy having somebody flirt with me, and I enjoy flirting with others, too.

25. *People are pretty damned good, myself included.*

PARTING
WORDS

Since I have had your attention to this page, I assume that we have made favorable contact. I hope your understanding of initial encounter and future involvement in friendship, love or business is enlarged. This book is only a guide. *The First Four Minutes* is a practical concept, not a universal truth. With *your* freedom of choice, your activities, your environment, emotions, thoughts and behavior, *you* are responsible for what happens next.

I hope that you and *Contact* have had a good relationship that inspires you to risk more toward attaining the delights of good contact with others; and, toward attaining the joys of being yourself with other individuals, accepting them in turn for their love or association, for the benefits to them and to your own self-esteem.

Above all, as you really learn to know yourself without masks or pretending, as you appreciate the dynamic state of human interchange both verbally and nonverbally, and as you discard stereotyped judgments, rigid values and stale assumptions, you will reach out to others with grace, and you too will be reached for.

SELECTED READINGS

Bach, George R. and Wyden, Peter. *The Intimate Enemy*. New York: William Morrow, 1969.

Bach, George R. and Deutsch, Ronald M. *Pairing*. New York: Peter H. Wyden, Inc., 1970.

Bergen, Polly. *The Book of Beauty, Fashion and Charm.* Englewood Cliffs, N.J.: Prentice-Hall, Inc., 1962.

Berne, Erich. *Games People Play*. New York: Grove Press, 1964.

Berne, Erich. *What Do You Say After You Say Hello?* New York: Grove Press, 1972.

Birren, Faber. *Color In Your World*. New York: Crowell-Collier Publishing Co., 1962.

Brelje, Terry B. and Irvine, Lynn M., Editors. *Law, Psychiatry, and the Mentally Disordered Offender* (Chapter 11, "Reality Therapy and Campus Prisons"). C.C. Thomas, Ft. Lauderdale.

Carnegie, Dale. *How To Win Friends and Influence People*. New York: Pocket Books, 1936.

Chartham, Robert. *The Sensuous Couple*. New York: Ballantine Books, Inc., 1971.

Corsini, Raymond J., Editor. *Current Psychotherapies* (Chapter on "Reality Therapy"). F.E. Peacock, Itasca, Illinois.

Fast, Julius. *Body Language*. New York: M. Evans and Co., 1970.

Ginott, Haim G. *Between Parent and Child*. New York: Avon Books, 1965.

Glasser, William. *Reality Therapy*. New York: Harper & Row, 1963.

Glasser, William. *Schools Without Failure*. New York: Harper & Row, 1969.

Glasser, William. *The Identity Society*. New York: Harper & Row, 1972.

Harris, Thomas. *I'm O.K.—You're O.K.* New York: Harper & Row, 1967.

Howard, Jane. *Please Touch—A Guided Tour of the Human Potential Movement*. New York: McGraw-Hill, 1970.

Laing, R.D. *The Politics of Experience*. New York: Ballantine Books, 1968.

Morris, Desmond. *Intimate Behavior*. New York: Random House, Inc., 1972.

Morris, Desmond. *The Naked Ape*. New York: Dell Publishing Co., 1967.

Nierenberg, Gerald I. and Calero, Henry H. *How to Read a Person Like a Book*. New York: Hawthorn Books, Inc., 1971.

O'Neill, Nena and O'Neill, George. *Open Marriage*. New York: M. Evans and Company, Inc., 1972.

Perls, Frederick S. *In and Out of the Garbage Pail*. Lafayette, Calif.: Real People Press, 1969.

Powell, John, S.J. *Why am i afraid to tell you who i am?* Chicago: Peacock Books, 1969.

Prather, Hugh. *Notes to Myself*. Lafayette, Calif.: Real People Press, 1970.

Reuben, David. *Everything You Always Wanted to Know About Sex And Were Afraid to Ask*. New York: McKay, 1969.

Schutz, William C. *Joy: Expanding Human Awareness*. New York: Grove Press, 1967.

Stevens, John O. *Awareness: exploring, experimenting, experiencing*. Lafayette, Calif.: Real People Press, 1971.

Toffler, Alvin. *Future Shock*. New York: Random House, 1970.

Walters, Barbara. *How to Talk With Practically Anybody About Practically Anything*. New York: Doubleday and Co., Inc., 1970.

Wheelis, Allen. *The Desert*. New York: Basic Books, Inc., 1970.

ABOUT THE AUTHORS

Leonard M. Zunin, M.D. is a practicing psychiatrist in West Los Angeles and a nationally known lecturer, educator and author. He has served as a consultant to numerous organizations including the State Department-Agency for International Development, Puerto Rican Crime Commission and the Center for Prisoner of War Studies. He was founder and director of Operation, Second Life—a program for women whose husbands were killed in Viet Nam, and co-director of the National Institute of Mental Health Study on LSD and Alcoholism.

From 1969 to 1971 he was the director of the Institute for Reality Therapy.

Natalie Zunin Harnage is a medical assistant and former dental assistant. She resides with her children and her husband, Tom, in Santa Monica, California.

6 for success from BALLANTINE BOOKS Help yourself.